THE NATIONAL
TRAILS SYSTEM
AN ILLUSTRATED HISTORY

*Cover photo: Summertime wildflower display south
of Donner Pass, California, along the Pacific Crest NST.
Photo by Kate Hoch courtesy PCTA.*

THE NATIONAL TRAILS SYSTEM

AN ILLUSTRATED HISTORY

HISTORY

STEVE ELKINTON

Vertel Publishing

Charleston, SC

First Edition

Printed in South Korea

ISBN-13: 9781641120197

ISBN-10: 1641120193

TABLE OF CONTENTS

Tables

WHERE TRAILS LEAD: OUR HERITAGE

STEWART UDALL, 2007 [1]

Eighty years ago, when I was a boy growing up on a ranch near St. Johns, Arizona, trails formed the contours of my world. I'd take a trail to get to a neighbor's house or follow one along the river if I were looking for stray cattle. Trails were the most practical way of getting around in those days. But they were also irresistible to me. I'd walk a trail just to see where it led.

As we near the 40th anniversary of the National Trails System Act, I look out on a footpath that leads past my house into the mountains and think about the age-old pull of America's trails — the

Stewart Udall hiking along the Potomac Heritage Trail, Washington, DC, 1968. Photo courtesy National Archives II, College Park, Maryland.

ones that led through the Cumberland Gap and over the Continental Divide, across the Rockies and the Sierra Nevada.

One of the greatest overland migrations in history followed a trail. During the mid-1800s nearly 400,000 emigrants walked or rode over the Platte River Road, the dusty thoroughfare formed by the convergence of the Oregon, California, and Mormon Trails. The first drafts of American history are recorded in the diaries of the people who followed frontier

---

1. "Where Trails Lead: Our Heritage," *Albuquerque Journal* (Albuquerque, NM), December 31, 2007, accessed June 5, 2018, https://archive.org/stream/nationaltrailssy00elki/ nationaltrailssy00elki_djvu.txt.

trails. They also can be read in the crude inscriptions and epitaphs scrawled on rocks and grave markers along the way.

Much of that history would have passed into oblivion, ploughed under or paved over, were it not for the National Trails legislation signed into law by President Lyndon Johnson in 1968. The idea behind the National Trails System Act was to ensure the survival of our historic corridors. Those of us who endorsed the legislation wanted to make it possible for Americans to share some of the adventure, the toil, and even a bit of the danger experienced by our forebears — the native people, explorers, and pioneers who first laid eyes on the American scene.

Today, the National Trails System encompasses more than 40,000 miles of trails. They extend from Maine's Mount Katahdin, where the Appalachian National Scenic Trail begins, to Nome, Alaska, where the Iditarod Trail ends. Wisconsin's Ice Age Trail traces the southern terminus of the last continental glacier to push down over North America. The Trail of Tears National Historic Trail follows the route taken by some 16,000 Cherokee when they were driven from their ancestral home in southern Appalachia in 1838 and forcibly relocated in Oklahoma's Indian Territory.

The longest trails celebrate the American outdoors. The 2,150-mile Appalachian Trail, started in the 1920s, was the first. It was followed by the slightly longer Pacific Crest National Scenic Trail from Canada to Mexico, and more recently by the Continental Divide National Scenic Trail that winds more than 3,000 miles from the crown of Glacier National Park in northern Montana to the aptly named Hatchet Mountains in the southwestern tip of New Mexico. Traveling on foot or horseback down any one of those trails provides an intense exposure to a world that would otherwise be accessible only in history books and atlases.

Unfortunately, the National Trails System Act did not include a budget for completing all of the trails or preserving their historic environs. Instead, the trail system has relied heavily on the contributions and hard work of volunteers. By the year 2000, volunteers had put in more than a half-million hours building, maintaining and protecting the trails.

Over the years Congress has appropriated some funds to help complete work on the trails. But there is so much more to do to fill all of gaps, including a 45-mile stretch of the Continental Divide Trail in New

Mexico that would allow hikers to walk the same terrain that the Spanish explorer Coronado passed over in 1540.

The future of our trail system will continue to depend on the generosity of private land owners as well as the continuing efforts of volunteers. Supporting our national trails is more than an exercise in nostalgia. Think of how much richer a child's knowledge of history might be after a few days spent along the Lewis and Clark National Historic Trail. Imagine how a student's grasp of our constitutional liberties might benefit from a drive along the Selma to Montgomery National Historic Trail, where civil right marchers braved billy clubs and tear gas in 1965 to campaign for voting rights for African American citizens.

As I sit in my home in Santa Fe, I think of the significance of one of our most storied frontier trails. In 1846, Col. Stephen Watts Kearny led his Army of the West down the Santa Fe Trail to claim New Mexico territory and later California for the United States. The annexation of those lands marked the triumph of Manifest Destiny, the idea held by many at the time that America was destined by divine providence to expand its dominion from the Atlantic to the Pacific.

A national trail is indeed a portal to the past. But it is also an inroad to our national character. It tells us how we got where we are. Our trails are both irresistible and indispensable. And while I may not be hiking the Continental Divide Trail from Canada to Mexico any time soon, I am doing everything I can to help with the monumental task of completing it.

It is up to all of us who care so deeply for the future of this great country to join in this uniquely American undertaking of building, maintaining, and protecting these unique treasures. I hope you will join me, for the sake of the generations to come.

ACKNOWLEDGMENTS

I write this chronicle as an inside observer. I was privileged to serve as program leader for the National Trails System with the National Park Service (NPS) for 25 years from 1989 to 2014. This was life-changing for me. As the development of the National Trail System unfolded, it proved to be a rich drama featuring colorful characters, political intrigue, changing tastes and fashions, sad defeats, and unexpected victories. For many of those years, I also served as chairperson of the Federal Interagency Council on Trails.

This 50th anniversary chronicle uses some of the text and photos from my booklet, *The National Trails System – A Grand Experiment*, published by NPS in 2008 to commemorate the System's 40th anniversary. This new version (first called *A Grand Experiment – the National Trails System at 50* and now re-issued under the current title) includes sources unavailable in 2008 and describes events that occurred between 2008 and 2018. Most of the new sources are taken from the NPS 40th Anniversary National Trails System Oral History Project in 2007–8 and additional documents in the National Trails System Administrative History Archives (NTSAHA) located in the NPS Washington Office.

I wish to thank all of those who participated in the NPS 2007–8 Oral History Project as well as Rita Hennessy and Bob Ratcliffe at NPS who made the NTSAHA archival materials available; Christopher Douwes and Aaron Mahr for filling in missing details; Art and Marge Miller and Frank Norris who provided essential editing; Bart Smith, Daniel Carmin, Bryan Petrtyl, Dan Jackson, Tyler Ray, Stuart Macdonald, Luke Kloberdanz, Brandon Hayes, Dawn Merritt, Laura Stark, Cindy Chance, and many others for providing excellent photos; and the very helpful librarians at the Library of Congress, the Department of the Interior Library, and the National Archives II in College Park, Maryland. I am also deeply indebted to Ben Harris who assembled the maps.

This book is dedicated to a host of memorable, outsized characters who helped shape the National Trails System. Many are now deceased — but all have inspired me in this work, both as a federal employee and as a retired volunteer. These people include George Cardinet, Marianne Fowler, Emily Gregor, Susan "Butch" Henley, Louise Marshall, David and Bernice Paige, Ethel Palmer, Leo Rasmussen, David Richie, Bill Spitzer, Bill and Jeanne Watson, and Gary Werner. I especially dedicate this book to my strongest mentors and fellow NPS trail program colleagues, Tom Gilbert and David Gaines, who were the first to educate me about the intricate, complex, and balanced authorities of the National Trails System Act.

INTRODUCTION

The establishment of a nationwide system of trails will be an accomplishment worthy of a place beside other conservation programs . . . . The fundamental objective of a nationwide system of trails is to provide simple, inexpensive recreation opportunities for all people by having an abundance of trails for walking, cycling, and horseback riding near home, as well as providing some major historic and scenic interstate trails of national significance. (Stewart Udall, 1967) [2]

The National Trails System Act of 1968 has given millions of people opportunities to experience our nation's past while enjoying its remarkable natural beauty. Set in motion by various federal and state agencies, supportive members of Congress, and a handful of citizen volunteers, the Act identifies and preserves trails of outstanding scenic, historic, and recreational value across America.

These trails offer benefits that improve health, boost energy, and lift the spirits of people from all walks of life. They allow public access to landscapes that reflect the Nation's rich cultural and natural diversity. In addition, they can be a catalyst for significant economic investment and spending in communities of all sizes. Ultimately, as a conservation and recreation effort, national trails embody the visions and struggles of a far-flung network of individuals and groups dedicated to preserving these remarkable routes for the enjoyment of future generations.

---

2. Stewart Udall, in testimony, 1967, in GPO, *Hearing Before the Subcommittee on National Parks and Recreation . . . on HR 4865 and Related Bills to Establish a Nationwide System of Trails*, March 6-7, 1967, Serial No. 09-4, p. 23.

The original National Trails System Act of 1968 established three types of trails: national scenic trails (NSTs), national recreation trails (NRTs), and connecting-and-side trails. National historic trails (NHTs) were added in 1978. And the railbanking authority — the basis of the nation's rails-to-trails movement — was added in 1983.

Hikers and horseback riders enjoy the superb vistas and wilderness experiences available along the national scenic trails. History buffs appreciate following the routes traversed in the past by indigenous peoples, explorers, pioneers, and even civil rights marchers. Many of these pathways are marked and mapped as national historic trails. Both types of trails provide excellent opportunities to experience the natural and cultural heritage of the United States.

NSTs are intended to "provide for maximum outdoor recreation potential and for the conservation and enjoyment of the nationally significant scenic, historic, natural, or cultural qualities of the areas through which such trails may pass." [3] Therefore, the routes of NSTs are usually planned and constructed to be continuous and are primarily recreational.

Meanwhile, NHTs attempt to follow as closely as possible original prehistoric or historic travel routes of national significance. Their intent

Looking south along the Appalachian NST at the Delaware Water Gap National Recreation Area, New Jersey and Pennsylvania, spring, 2018. NPS photo courtesy Delaware Water Gap staff.

is to identify and protect the historic route and its remnant resources

---

3. National Trails System Act, 16 U.S.C. 1242 (a)(2).

and artifacts. Public use of the NHTs is envisioned in the Act to primarily occur through historic interpretation and appreciation rather than
by use of a continuous recreational pathway. Due to land use changes
and subsequent development, NHTs and their associated sites are often
fragmented and located on both public and private properties, usually
linked together by an auto tour route. [4]

According to the National Trails System Act, both of these types of congressionally established trails are usually established in a four-step process:

1. a law requesting a feasibility study,
2. a feasibility study by a federal agency to recommend (or
    not) establishment of the trail as part of the Trails System,
3. another law establishing the trail under the authorities of
    the Trails Act, and
4. a comprehensive plan conducted according to the plan-
    ning requirements of the Act.

The average time
span to accomplish all
four of these steps has
been about 13 years —
so these trails are neither
created nor planned in a
casual manner.

National recreation
trails (NRTs) are shorter
trails that are recognized
through secretarial action
rather than by congressional lawmaking. Some are

Register Cliffs, Wyoming, where overland
pioneers on several trails carved their
signatures. NPS photo by Lee Kreutzer.

in metropolitan areas; some are on federal or state lands; some accommodate different types of uses (and some only one); some are short; and
some are long. Today, there are about 1,350 officially recognized NRTs
scattered across every state and several territories. Secretarial designation
is much easier than congressional action (and in the U.S. Forest Service,

---

4. *Ibid.* subsection (a)(3).

designation authority has been delegated to regional foresters). Although NRTs have played a key role in bringing trails to many communities, their purpose and roles usually differ from NSTs and NHTs. Most NRTs are local in nature (such as the Des Moines River Trail System in Iowa), while others are regional (the longest being the Seaway Trail in New York and Pennsylvania). Few are more than 100 miles in length.

Railbanking enables abandoned railway corridors to be preserved intact and used as recreational trail corridors until needed, perhaps at some future time, for rail use again. For such corridors to be protected, a viable nonprofit organization or unit of government must come forward to finance and manage the trail. [5] With the help of the Rails-to-Trails Conservancy — today the largest trail organization in the U.S.

A National Recreation Trail, with NRT logo, in Oregon. Photo by Mike Bullington courtesy American Trails.

— more than 20,000 miles of former rail corridor have been converted to trail use.The Appalachian and the Pacific Crest NSTs were the first two long-distance trails to receive national trail designation in 1968. Today, the National Trails System — those trails established under the authority of the National Trails System Act — has grown to 11 NSTs, 19 NHTs, seven connecting-or-side trails, almost 1,350 NRTs, and 4,000 miles of rail-banked trails all authorized by the Act.

The NSTs and NHTs alone total more than 54,000 miles in combined lengths and are administered by either the Department of the Interior (through the National Park Service or the Bureau of Land Management) or the Department of Agriculture (though the U.S. Forest Service).

---

5. Search the web under "Rail-banking," especially on *Rails-to-Trails Conservancy* website.

The National Trails System is an experiment in democratic principles. Crafted alongside other significant environmental and social legislation of the 1960s, this movement reflects deep American impulses, such as love of outdoor recreation and scenery, devotion to iconic trail experiences (such as hiking the Appalachian Trail or retracing the ruts of overland wagons along the Oregon or Mormon Pioneer Trail), volunteerism, and reverence for the struggles that Native Americans, early explorers, and pioneers endured. Many of these trails embody a yearning for freedom and liberty. In operation, it is a balanced system that seeks to honor private property rights while still securing public access to outstanding portions of the American landscape.

This experiment was not a sure bet. Early cost estimates were low by magnitudes. And no one could predict how many trails would be enough to make an actual system. Yet somehow, in the 50 years since passage of the Trails Act in 1968, this disparate collection of trails coalesced into a coherent system touching every state and offering a wide range of recreational and cultural experiences. This experiment is a story of American democracy at work.

The Monterey Bay Coastal Recreation Trail was built on the former Southern Pacific rail line through Monterey, California. Photo by Stuart Macdonald.

GLOSSARY OF ABBREVIATIONS

ADT	American Discovery Trail
AFB	American Farm Bureau
AGO	America's Great Outdoors
AHS	American Hiking Society
AIA	American Institute of Architects
AMC	Appalachian Mountain Club
ARRA	American Recovery and Reinvestment Act
AT	Appalachian Trail
ATC	Appalachian Trail Conference (later Appalachian Trail Conservancy)
ATPO	Appalachian Trail Project Office
BIA	Bureau of Indian Affairs
BLM	Bureau of Land Management
BOR	Bureau of Outdoor Recreation
CCS	Challenge Cost-Share
CLP	Collaborative Landscape Planning
CTTP	Connect Trails to Parks
DAR	Daughters of the American Revolution
DOI	U.S. Department of the Interior
DWGNRA	Delaware Water Gap National Recreation Area
EIS	Environmental Impact Statement
EO	Executive Order
EPA	Environmental Protection Agency
FHWA	Federal Highway Administration
FLPMA	Federal Land Policy and Management Act
FS	U.S. Forest Service
FTA	Florida Trail Association
FTDS	Federal Trails Data Standards
GIS	Geographic Information System

GPO	Government Printing Office
HCRS	Heritage Conservation Recreation Service
ISTEA	Intermodal Surface Transportation Act of 1991
ITDS	Interagency Trail Data Standards
IWL	Izaak Walton League
MOU	Memorandum of Understanding
NEPA	National Environmental Policy Act
NHT	National Historic Trail
NLCS	National Landscape Conservation System
NPS	National Park Service
NRT	National Recreation Trail
NST	National Scenic Trail
NTD	National Trails Day
NTS	National Trails System
NTSA	National Trails System Act of 1968, as amended
NTSAHA	National Trails System Administrative History Archive
NTTP	National Trails Training Partnership
OCTA	Oregon-California Trails Association
OMB	U.S. Office of Management and Budget
ORRRC	Outdoor Recreation Resources Review Commission
P.L.	Public Law
PATC	Potomac Appalachian Trail Club
PCTA	Pacific Crest Trail Association
PCTC	Pacific Crest Trail Conference
PNTS	Partnership for the National Trails System
REI	Recreation Equipment, Inc.
RTC	Rails-to-Trails Conservancy
RTCA	NPS's River and Trails Conservation Assistance program
RTP	Recreational Trails Program
SAFETEA-LU	Safe, Accountable, Flexible, Efficient Transportation Equity Act – A Legacy for Users Act of 2005
STB	U.S. Surface Transportation Board
TE	Transportation Enhancements
TEA-21	Transportation Equity Act for the 21st Century
TTEC	A Trail to Every Classroom
USDA	U.S. Department of Agriculture
USF&WS	U.S. Fish & Wildlife Service
YMCA	Young Men's Christian Association

CHAPTER 1
FORERUNNERS 1906–1963

The dynamic interplay of linear and area conservation cannot be underestimated. Ideally, the only permanent sign of man in wilderness is the trail that marks his travels. . . . In a real sense, "trail country" is another term for wilderness. As important as is the highway in determining circulation and development patterns of the city, the trail forms the outdoorsman's relationship to the back country. (Frederick Eissler, 1966) [1]

During the early 20th Century, American citizens actively sought to protect and preserve sites and landscapes dear to them — and the United States Congress responded by passing various laws that protected and preserved both natural and historic resources. One early preservation law, the Antiquities Act of 1906, authorized the president to set aside "historic landmarks, historic and prehistoric structures, and other objects of historic or scientific interest that are situated upon" federal lands. As a result, treasured sites such as Devils Tower, Casa Grande, and the Grand Canyon came under federal protection as national monuments.

The 1906 DAR Santa Fe Trail marker at Elm Creek Crossing in Lyon County, Kansas. 2008 photo courtesy Pat Traffas, OCTA.

1. Frederick Eissler, "The National Trails System Proposal," *Sierra Club Bulletin*, June 1966, Vol. 51., No. 6, pp. 16–7.

Two federal agencies, the Forest Service and National Park Service — established as federal agencies in 1905 and 1916 respectively — gradually developed expertise in natural and historic landscape stewardship. Meanwhile, private groups founded in the 19th Century — such as the Appalachian Mountain Club (1876) and the Sierra Club (1892) — expanded their efforts to rescue resources from burgeoning industrial growth while providing superlative recreational experiences for their members. This rising interest in resource stewardship also included memorializing historic routes.

In 1906, members of the Daughters of the American Revolution (DAR) set out to mark the Santa Fe Trail in Kansas using stone monuments to mark the old trail route. Eventually, this concept sparked the idea for the National Old Trails Road, a cross-country highway that highlighted important pioneer routes throughout the United States. In 1911, the DAR created a committee to establish the Old Trails Road as a national memorial highway, choosing to erect trail monuments along its historic routes. The most notable of these markers remains the "Madonnas of the Trail," featuring a sculpture of a hardy pioneer

The Madonna of the Trail in Council Grove, Kansas, erected in 1928. 1997 photo courtesy Pat Traffas, OCTA.

mother by August Leimbach exhibiting the grace and determination necessary for survival on the westbound overland trails. The DAR installed 12 of the Madonnas along the National Road in 1927 and 1928. [2]

Ezra Meeker, as a child, had gone west in a covered wagon with his family in 1852. In his retirement, after serving as founder and mayor of Puyallup, Washington, as well as founder of the Washington State Historical Society, Meeker wanted to commemorate the overland trails — especially the Oregon Trail. In 1906, he began to retrace the Oregon Trail from west to east in a reconstructed covered wagon pulled by oxen.

---

2. "Madonna of the Trail," *Wikipedia*, last modified May 18, 2018, https://en.wikipedia.org/wiki/Madonna_of_the_Trail.

He had granite trail markers erected along the way, each marker funded and produced by local supporters. After completing his family's earlier trek route to Iowa, Meeker took his wagon farther east to New York City and Washington, DC. There he met with President Theodore Roosevelt and encouraged Congress to pass a bill authorizing $50,000 for marking the Oregon Trail. Although the bill failed to pass, Meeker remained undaunted.

In 1910, Meeker began a second journey across the Oregon Trail, this time meeting with local historians and searching for lost sections of the trail. By the end of this trip, 150 trail monuments had been erected. In 1915, he drove the length of the Oregon Trail in a Pathfinder touring car with a hooped wagon

Ezra Meeker at the Harding Stone in Emigrant Springs State Park, Oregon, 1926. Photo courtesy Roger Blair.

cover mounted on top. The next year, he met with President Woodrow Wilson to discuss the idea of a national trail highway. Meeker traveled sections of the Oregon Trail for the last time in 1924 by airplane. He died in 1928, a few days shy of his 98th birthday. His contributions to trail preservation and awareness inspired others to give increased recognition to historic routes throughout the nation. [3]

Similarly, the centennial of the Lewis and Clark Expedition in the years 1903–6 inspired Olin D. Wheeler to retrace that expedition's routes across the West and publish a two-volume work, *The Trail of Lewis and Clark*, chronicling his travels and the conditions along the routes at that time. Also, the first complete verbatim edition of Lewis and Clark's journals were published in seven volumes by Reuben Gold Thwaites in 1904 and 1905. [4]

3. "Ezra Meeker," Wikipedia, last modified May 31, 2018, https://en.wikipedia.org/wiki/Ezra_Meeker.
4. "Olin Dunbar Wheeler," Wikipedia, last modified April 15, 2018, https://en.wikipedia.org/wiki/Olin_Dunbar_Wheeler; "Reuben Gold Thwaites," Wikipedia, last modified September 3, 2017, https://en.wikipedia.org/wiki/Reuben_Gold_Thwaites.

And it was during these early years of the 20th Century that recreational trails emerged as a distinct type of outdoor experience. America's first long-distance hiking trail — Vermont's Long Trail — was conceived by James Taylor and completed for end-to-end use in 1910. (In fact, New England's first foot trails had been built in the early 1800s in the White Mountains. They were formalized and organized by the Appalachian Mountain Club, founded in 1876 "to explore the mountains of the Northeast and adjacent regions for both scientific and artistic purposes, and in general to cultivate an interest in geographic studies.") [5]

In 1921, Benton MacKaye — a forester, planner, and visionary from eastern Massachusetts — conceived of a multistate trail following the crest of the eastern mountains from Maine to Georgia. (He had first published the idea of a long-distance Appalachian mountain range trail in 1916.) His idea of an eastern mountain-chain trail evoking wilderness values appeared in the seminal article "An Appalachian Trail: A Project in Regional Planning" in the October 1921, issue of the *Journal of the American Institute of Architects*. In this article, he laid out a vision for a multistate backwoods highland footpath intended to welcome hikers, help preserve a portion of the mountain wilderness, and provide an antidote to the nation's growing industrialization. [6]

MacKaye summarized the purpose of the Appalachian Trail with these words:

Its ultimate purpose is to conserve, use, and enjoy the mountain hinterland . . . . The Trail (or system of trails) is a means for making the land accessible. The Appalachian Trail is to this Appalachian region what the Pacific Railway was to the Far West — a means of 'opening up' the country. But a very different kind of 'opening up.' Instead of a railway, we want a trailway. [7]

MacKaye clearly intended a trail that combined recreation and the conservation of wilderness values. One key piece of this visionary, multipurpose "trailway" included the construction, maintenance, and protection of the trail largely by the work of dedicated volunteers. After

---

5. Dyan Zaslowsky and T.H. Watkins, *These American Lands: Parks, Wilderness, and the Public Lands,* (New York: H. Holt, 1986), p. 313.
6. Brian B. King, "Trail Years: A History of the Appalachian Trail Conference," *Appalachian Trailway News,* July 2000, pp. 3–7.
7. *Ibid.*

four years of promotion and route layout, MacKaye's idea took wing with the founding of the Appalachian Trail Conference (ATC) in 1925. This interstate organization has coordinated the trail's routing, development, and protection ever since.

MacKaye's vision has inspired modern readers:

The most daring and radical aspect of MacKaye's 1921 proposal . . . is not its unprecedented 2,000-mile length, but rather his call for citizens from the smoggy cities to come to the healthy, clean air of the mountains during their vacations to build the trail by working together in community camps. . . . . What seems very remarkable is that MacKaye, who knew Stephen Mather and worked with Gifford Pinchot, proposed this citizen-led project just five years after the formation of the National Park Service and 15 years after the establishment of the U.S. Forest Service and U.S. Fish & Wildlife Service. In this era of establishing federal professional agencies to manage the national parks, forests, and wildlife refuges led by Pinchot and Mather, he proposed a radically different approach that relies on the dedication and persistence of ordinary citizens organized through scores of inter-organizational and interagency partnerships to preserve, develop, and manage these new national trail resources . [8]

MacKaye's dream of the trail serving as a wilderness escape was soon modified by Myron Avery, a Harvard Law School graduate and avid outdoorsman. Shortly after MacKaye helped organize the Appalachian Trail Conference in 1925, Avery was hired as its chairman. His view of the trail as a user-friendly footpath for all hikers dif-

Myron Avery, center, with Albert Jackman and Frank Schairer, at the summit of Mt. Katahdin, Maine, August, 1933. Photo courtesy ATC.

fered fundamentally from MacKaye's wilderness escape approach. These differences created tension between the two men and within the ATC,

---

8. Gary Werner, "The National Trails System – A Culture of Citizen Stewardship," *Pathways Across America*, Autumn/Winter 2013–2014, p. 13.

culminating in the 1930s in bitter arguments over the proposed Skyline Drive in the newly-established Shenandoah National Park in Virginia — and how it might displace the trail. Curiously, this dynamic tension between idealistic vision and pragmatic action has helped make the Appalachian Trail the success it is today. [9]

A wilderness trail is only enjoyable if the trail corridor is adequately protected from intrusions. Recognizing this, Avery and the ATC forged some of the first trail protection and operations agreements between a private organization and federal government agencies. In 1938, the ATC signed agreements with the National Park Service and the Forest Service to create a protective buffer zone along parts of the Appalachian Trail. These agreements defined a two-mile-wide strip surrounding the pathway to protect the trail from disruptive development and industrialization, with a 200-foot-wide corridor where timbering was to be minimized. The buffer zone would therefore help evoke a wilderness setting wherever possible. [10]

Long-distance recreational trails also developed in the West. In 1926, Catherine Montgomery, a schoolteacher in Bellingham, Washington, envisioned a mountain hiking trail from Canada to Mexico linking the peaks of the Cascade and Sierra Mountain ranges. Inspired by both the Appalachian Trail and Ms. Montgomery's vision, Clinton C. Clarke — a consummate Boy Scout, Harvard graduate, and successful oilman — organized the Pacific Crest Trail Conference (PCTC) in 1932. He intended the PCTC to plan and develop a rugged backcountry trail along the Sierra and Cascade

Clinton Clarke, founder of the Pacific Crest Trail Conference. Photo courtesy PCTA.

mountain slopes, connecting several already well-known high-elevation trails such as Oregon's Skyline Trail and the John Muir Trail in California. He enlisted PCTC members, Boy Scouts, the Young Men's

---

9. Brian B. King, "Trail Years: A History of the Appalachian Trail Conference," *Appalachian Trailway News*, July 2000, p. 7.
10. "Appalachian Trailway Agreement," *Appalachian Trailway News*, Vol. 1, No. 1, January 1939.

Christian Association (YMCA), and even young San Francisco photographer Ansel Adams in this challenging effort. During the summers of 1935 to 1938, Clarke organized YMCA-PCTC relay hikes that featured 40 teams of young hikers between the ages of 14 and 18.

These relay hikes were directed by Warren Rogers, who guided the teams to scout an optimal route for the connecting trail. They carried a logbook from Campo, California, on the Mexican border, north to the Canadian border. Rogers, who later worked extensively with Clarke on developing the Pacific Crest Trail, followed him as PCTC executive secretary, working tirelessly to organize support for the trail even after Clarke's death in 1957. [11]

Meanwhile, other groups became organized around public land issues. In 1935, Bob Marshall, Benton MacKaye, Bernard Frank, Harvey Broome, and others organized the Wilderness Society, asserting that wilderness values were essential to the American character. Its mission focused on the preservation and protection of undisturbed public land areas of "untrammeled" wild beauty. Joining Marshall and MacKaye on the first Wilderness Society board were conservation luminaries such as Aldo Leopold, Olaus and Mardy Murie, and Howard Zahniser. [12]

The establishment of the Wilderness Society responded to two national trends that threatened wilderness areas: urban growth (as towns and cities grew to accommodate burgeoning industry and housing needs) and timbering (which removed irreplaceable remnant virgin forests). Bob Marshall intended the Wilderness Society to help provide strong protection

Four Wilderness Society founders, left to right: Bernard Frank, Harvey Broome, Bob Marshall and Benton MacKaye. Photo courtesy The Wilderness Society.

11. "History," Pacific Crest Trail Association, accessed June 11, 2018, https://www.pcta.org/about-us/history/.
12. Douglas Scott, 2001, "A Wilderness Forever," Campaign for America's Wilderness.

measures to counteract these damaging developments. The Society was instrumental in the eventual passage of the Wilderness Act of 1964.

Various people and organizations helped raise public awareness about different types of trails for recreational, historic, and conservation purposes. In February 1945, the first federal trail bill was introduced by Representative Daniel Hoch (D-PA). Hoch was a friend of MacKaye's, an ATC board member, and longtime leader of Pennsylvania's Blue Mountain Eagle Climbing Club. His legislation proposed an amendment to the Federal Highway Act of 1944 to establish a national system of wilderness foot trails administered by the Forest Service. The "Hoch Bill" named the Appalachian Trail as the first path for designation in the system and recommended a trails system of approximately 10,000 miles — with development and maintenance of these trails intended to help preserve the wilderness values of the trail corridors. Although a House hearing was held, Hoch's bill never became law. [13]

Another thread in the tapestry underlying the future National Trails System was the 1922 establishment of the Izaak Walton League (IWL). Named after the 17th Century British author of *The Compleat Angler*, the IWL's purpose was to preserve the landscape for future generations of American fishermen. Today, IWL actively participates in conservation and public education about respecting natural resources and the environment. The IWL played a key role in shaping mid-20th Century federal government conservation and recreation policies. Joe

Joe Penfold, Executive Director IWLA, c. 1971.
Photo courtesy IWLA.

Penfold, the IWL conservation director in the 1950s, is credited with the idea for the Outdoor Recreation Resources Review Commission. This federally appointed commission, established in 1958 and chaired by Laurence S. Rockefeller, paved the way for much of the United States' environmental,

13. Donald Dale Jackson, "The Long Way 'Round: The National Scenic Trails System and How It Grew. And How It Didn't," *Wilderness Magazine*, Summer, 1988, pp. 19–20; Doug Scott, Keynote Address, Second National Conference on National Scenic and National Historic Trails, November 14, 1991.

recreational, and conservation legislation for the next 40 years — including the national system of trails. [14]

Philanthropy by wealthy donors was yet another influence, and one that was especially instrumental in the land conservation movement. Many charitable and family foundations promoted social welfare and physical fitness. And certain donors feared that if the natural environment and the heritage of the outdoors did not become priorities, then these factors in American life would be lost forever. Wealthy families such as the Rockefellers and the Harrimans acquired significant parts of the American landscape in hopes of preserving their beauty for future generations to enjoy. Most of these lands were donated to public agencies. Such gifts included Harriman State Park in New York, much of Great Smoky Mountains National Park in North Carolina and Tennessee, and the Rockefeller family donations that became Acadia National Park in Maine.

These philanthropic activities influenced federal government conservation policy in the late 1950s and certainly influenced — along with the Izaak Walton League — the authorization by Congress of the Outdoor Recreation Resources Review Commission, or ORRRC. This

The many volumes of the ORRRC Report. Photo by author.

group was chaired by Laurence Rockefeller, and its main charge was to examine the recreation trends of the United States and to inventory the recreational opportunities available to all Americans. The commission based its examination on three fundamental inquiries:

- What are the recreation needs of the United States in 1960, 1975, and 2000?
- What are the nation's recreation sources available to fill those needs?
- What policies and procedures should be recommended to ensure that these present and future needs are met?

---

14. See Izaak Walton League of America, www.iwla.org/index.php?id=9; Edward C. Crafts, June 21, 1962, "Birth of a Bureau," remarks made at the fortieth annual convention and conservation congress at the Izaak Walton League of America, Portland, OR.

The Commission's findings resulted in the January 1962 report *Outdoor Recreation for America*. This summary of extensive research and public surveys outlined the many types of outdoor recreation interests then pursued by Americans based on age and socioeconomic factors. It predicted a substantive increase in recreation over the next few decades — especially walking for pleasure. To better serve the public and its recreational needs, the ORRRC report recommended the creation of a federal agency responsible for coordinating, implementing, and developing outdoor recreation resources throughout the United States. [15]

One observer noted the long-term effects of the ORRRC report:

May, 1962, l to r: Edward C. Crafts, Director, BOR; Governor Gaylord Nelson, D-WI; and Secretary Stewart Udall. Photo courtesy National Archives II, College Park, Maryland.

I think the [National] *Trails* [System] *Act has been part of that larger picture of all those things that came out of the ORRRC report in the late 1950s. Have you ever looked at that stuff? My God,* [it was a] *huge effort that goes back half a century now. And the Wilderness Act, the Land and Water Conservation Fund Act, Trails, Rivers — all those things flowed out of that effort. I think that is a legacy that is not going to go away.* [16]

Based on the ORRRC findings, President John F. Kennedy called for the creation of an agency to coordinate outdoor recreation resources. In April 1962, Secretary of the Interior Stewart Udall established the Bureau of Outdoor Recreation (BOR) by secretarial order. In a message to Congress earlier that year, President Kennedy stated that this new bureau would "serve as the focal point within the Federal Government

15. Laurence S. Rockefeller, Chairman, 1962, *Outdoor Recreation for America: A Report to the President and Congress by the Outdoor Recreation Resources Review Commission*, Washington, DC.
16. Cleve Pinnix, 2007, NPS Oral History interview, NTS 40th Anniversary Oral History Project, p. 20.

for the many activities related to outdoor recreation." BOR was the first conservation agency established at the federal level since the 1930s. [17]

Directed by Edward C. Crafts, former assistant chief of the Forest Service, BOR coordinated and supported the provision of increased recreational opportunities and facilities throughout the United States. However, BOR was not a land management agency. Although President Kennedy — one of the new bureau's primary supporters — was tragically assassinated in November 1963, the new administration under President Lyndon B. Johnson continued to support the mission of this fledgling agency and its essential role of coordinating interagency efforts.

One key legislative initiative growing directly from ORRRC recommendations was a trust fund called the Land and Water Conservation Fund (LWCF), which was first funded from federal land sales and later augmented with revenues from offshore oil and gas drilling. It was created by law in late 1964 and administered by the newly created BOR.

Drying Up Wild Life

Meanwhile, celebrated cartoonist and conservationist Jay N. "Ding" Darling proposed in 1961 that the Missouri River be part of "a national outdoor recreation and natural resources ribbon along the historic trail

Ding Darling's 1937 cartoon, *Drying Up the Wildlife*, is typical of his scorn for development and his deep appreciation for wild things. Image from the University of Iowa Special Collections Department courtesy of the Jay N. "Ding" Darling Wildlife Society.

of Lewis and Clark." His idea is still considered the forerunner of the future Lewis and Clark National Historic Trail. [18]

---

17. U.S. Department of the Interior press releases, April 2, 1962, "Udall Establishes Bureau of Outdoor Recreation in Interior Department"; Edward C. Crafts, May 30, 1962 remarks, "Birth of a Bureau." Both in NTSAHA.
18. Wallace G. Lewis, 2002, "Following in Their Footsteps: Creating the Lewis and Clark National Historic Trail," *Columbia, the Magazine of Northwest History*, Vol. 16, No. 2.

One early BOR project was a study of the Lewis and Clark trail corridor. Brian O'Neill (who later in his career served as noted superintendent of the Golden Gate National Recreation Area in California) had just been hired into BOR. His very first assignment . . .

. . . was a study of the Lewis and Clark Trail. And it was just a fabulous opportunity for me, because the report that evolved out of that was called "Lewis and Clark Trail: Proposal for Development." It was the whole study to determine whether this wonderful route of exploration should be recognized in some way as an important part of Americans' history and included in some measure within the National Park System. At that time, the concept of a national system of trails had not really reached its pinnacle (that led later to the establishment of the National Trails System Act). This was a precursor really of that. So I had the opportunity to do a lot of the legwork on this study. We went around and had hearings across the country. We got input from all of the key agencies along the route of the Lewis and Clark Trail. We ended up preparing this document that was a forerunner of the legislation that ultimately established the Lewis and Clark National Historic Trail and the whole commission concept that was set out to implement that. [19]

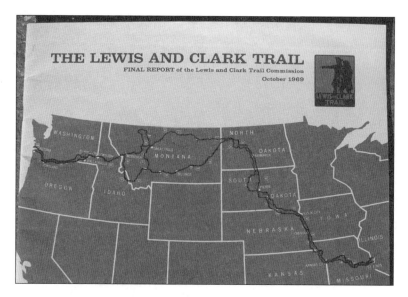

Cover of the 1969 close-out report by the Lewis and Clark Trail Commission.

19. *Brian O'Neill, 2007, NPS Oral History interview, NTS 40*[th] Anniversary Oral History Project, p. 3.

BENTON MACKAYE

Benton MacKaye in the 1920s.
Photo courtesy ATC.

BENTON MACKAYE, born in 1879 in Stamford, Connecticut, was the sixth child of actor and inventor Steele MacKaye. From the age of nine, MacKaye began living at the family retreat in rural Shirley Center, Massachusetts, and wandering the countryside. His father was often away on the call of the theatre life. He lost an older brother at age 10 and his father at 15. About then Benton began an intensive countryside exploration, compiling a detailed nature journal. Later, while living in Washington, DC, he gained access to experts and expertise at the Smithsonian Institution. In short, he became a self-taught naturalist.

At age 18 he had his first taste of actual wilderness—bicycling from Boston with college friends to Tremont Mountain in New Hampshire and then hiking into the backcountry. In 1905, after graduating from Harvard University as its first graduate forester, he joined the newly established U.S. Forest Service under Gifford Pinchot. MacKaye later recalled a meeting of the Society of American Foresters at Pinchot's home in "about 1912" to which he read a new paper by his friend Allen Chamberlain of the Appalachian Mountain Club. "*[It]* was, I think, the first dissertation on long-distance footways," he wrote.

MacKaye became an outspoken pioneer in several fields including regional planning and fighting urban sprawl. As a fledgling forester, his research into the runoff resulting from deforestation in the White Mountains led to the creation of the White Mountains National Forest. Back living in Washington, DC, in 1915 he married Jessie Hardy "Betty" Stubbs and became an active socialist. Gradually, MacKaye's focus shifted from science, woodlot management, and other aspects of silviculture, to the humanities — the effect of resource management on humans. He became a pioneer in the field of regional planning, having as contemporaries a wide range of reformer colleagues such as Stewart Chase, Arthur Carhardt, Aldo Leopold, Clarence Stein, Bob Marshall, Lewis Mumford, and Howard Zahniser. MacKaye's wife, Betty, was a committed suffragist and pacifist who went into a deep depression after women succeeded in their decades-long campaign to get the vote — and she took her own life in early 1921 by drowning in New York City's East River.

Upon MacKaye's wife's death, several of his friends persuaded him to devote himself to a big project to get past his grief — and he developed the concept of the Appalachian Trail as a chain of worker vacation communities linked by a footpath helping protect the eastern mountain chain. His friend Charles Harris Whitaker, editor of the *Journal of the American Institute of Architects* and a proponent of English "garden cities," invited him to publish it in that publication. Then he spent the next four years publicizing the idea, culminating in the founding of the Appalachian Trail Conference in 1925.

MacKaye went on to many other adventures — working on Tennessee Valley Authority projects in the 1930s, helping found the Wilderness Society in 1935 (for him growing directly out of road-building threats to the Appalachian Trail), coining the term "geotechnics" to offer a way of balancing human needs with those of nature, and helping organize the 1954 hike by Supreme Court Justice William O.

Douglas that preserved the Chesapeake & Ohio Canal in Maryland. Despite such a wide-ranging and restless career, MacKaye will always be known as the founder of the Appalachian Trail and the idea of long-distance, multi-state trails. After his death, a scenic side trail at the southern end of the Appalachian NST in Georgia and North Carolina was named in his honor. [20]

20. Larry Anderson, *Benton MacKaye: Conservationist, Planner, and Creator of the Appalachian Trail* (Baltimore and London: Johns Hopkins Press, 2002), 452; Benton MacKaye profile in ATC, 2000, *Appalachian Trailway News, Special 75th Anniversary Issue*, 5; "Benton MacKaye," Wikipedia, last modified January 7, 2018, https://en.wikipedia.org/wiki/Benton_MacKaye.

CHAPTER 2
FOUNDATION STONES
1964–1966

As Congress finally stirs itself into action to preserve what little is left of this nation's great misspent heritage of natural beauty, it is only just that special recognition be given to those valiant citizens who have for many years been carrying on this national task from their private resources. (Gaylord Nelson, 1965) [1]

In the Johnson White House, Lady Bird Johnson, an avid outdoorswoman and wildflower enthusiast, embarked on efforts that complemented the goals of the new Bureau of Outdoor Recreation. A *Washington Post* staff writer verified Lady Bird's love of the outdoors in a 1967 article: "She reacts to our national parks and forests with genuine pleasure and has said, 'How wonderful it is to be able to get so completely out in the wilderness away from towns and cities' . . . . Blazing new paths . . . . being fascinated by exotic new plants, her pleasure is an inspiration for all women." [2]

Her pleasure in the outdoors was shared with her husband, President Lyndon Johnson. Often upon returning to Washington, DC, from Texas or campaign trips, they would take time to sit on the Potomac River shoreline at twilight and admire the skyline of the Nation's Capital. Therefore, the large billboards and scrubby landscapes proliferating around the nation's highways and tourist attractions offended her. Early in the Johnson

1. Gaylord Nelson, September 16, 1965, in *Hearing Before the [Senate] Subcommittee on Parks and Recreation . . . on S. 622 . . .*, p. 6, in NTSAHA.
2. "Eager Mrs. Johnson Feels Free as a Bird Outdoors," *The Washington Post, Times Herald*, April 16, 1967, H12. Accessed online through ProQuest Historical Newspapers.

administration, she began a highway cleanup campaign that would lead to the Highway Beautification Act of 1965. She raised both public and private funds to clean up the landscape and plant flowers and trees along roadsides and in parks, beginning in the National Capital Region and then around the entire country. She believed that beauty could improve the mental health of society.

The concept of beautifying America was a lofty goal for 1960s America. It was an era of social and political ferment as the Civil Rights movement reached a fevered pitch and the War in Vietnam grew in scope. However, there was also deepening public concern about America's natural environment, launched by Rachel Carson's seminal *Silent Spring* in 1962. This era saw significant federal legislation that focused on the environment and outdoor recreation, including the

Lady Bird Johnson assists 4Hers to plant a tree on the National Mall, 1966. Photo in USIA Files 306 PSC, National Archives II, College Park, MD.

Outdoor Recreation Act of 1963, the Wilderness Act of 1964, and the Land and Water Conservation Act of 1965.

In 1964, Senator Gaylord Nelson (D-WI), former Wisconsin governor and longtime friend to environmental and conservation concerns, introduced two trail bills in the U.S. Senate. The first bill, with strong support from the Appalachian Trail Conference (ATC), proposed federal recognition and protection for the Appalachian Trail. It came about after Nelson was entreated at a cocktail party by ATC's Cecil Cullander, who described how besieged the trail was by development. Nelson realized immediately that this was a virtuous cause and thought, "Well, hell, I'll introduce a bill to preserve the trail. We designed a bill that authorized the federal government to pick up, by easement or acquisition, private lands along the trail." [3]

Nelson's bill launched three concepts which have influenced the national trails ever since: MacKaye's term "trailway" (now meaning the full corridor of the trail to protect views and adjacent resources), the concept of willing seller land acquisition, and funding trail corridor protection from the newly established Land and Water Conservation Fund. The second bill proposed a national system of hiking trails on lands of the Department of the Interior and Agriculture. Neither bill went far in Congress, but Senator Nelson persevered. [4]

Gaylord Nelson portrait, c. 1960.
Photo courtesy University of
Wisconsin Archives ID: 2018s00332.

President Johnson's "Beautification Message" in 1965 accomplished what previous legislation failed to do for trails. In his *Special Message to Congress on Conservation and Restoration of Natural Beauty*, delivered following the White House Conference on Natural Beauty, Johnson articulated his administration's view of environmental and conservation concerns, touching on cleaning up pollution, protecting rivers, cleaning up water sources, and preserving natural landscapes. Of trails, he said:

The forgotten outdoorsmen of today are those who like to walk, hike, ride horseback, or bicycle. For them we must have trails as well as highways . . . . I am requesting, therefore, that the Secretary of the Interior work with his colleagues in the federal government and with state and local leaders and recommend to me a cooperative program to encourage a national system of trails, building up the more than [one] hundred thousand miles of trails in our National Forest and Parks . . . . In the backcountry we need to copy the great Appalachian Trail in all parts of America, and to make full use of rights of way and other public paths.

3. Donald Dale Jackson, "The Long Way 'Round: The National Scenic Trails System and How It Grew. And How It Didn't," *Wilderness* Magazine, Summer, 1988, p. 20.
4. Stanley A. Murray, September 16, 1965, testimony in *Hearing Before the [Senate] Subcommittee on Parks and Recreation . . . on S. 622*, GPO: Wash., DC, pp. 25–7 and U.S. Senate, 1965, Senate reports on S 622 and S 2590.

In his message he also promised an administration bill to protect wild and scenic rivers. [5]

This excerpt from the "Beautification Message" summarizes a few key ideas about national trails that have resonated throughout the history of the National Trails System as it has developed since that time: the emphasis on non-motorized recreation, cooperation between citizens and government agencies, interagency coordination, the use of existing trails on federal and public lands, the health benefits of trails (especially in urban areas), and the inspiring model of the Appalachian Trail.

President Johnson's message sparked a seminal study — the first major federally sponsored nationwide study solely about trails. *Trails for America*, released by the Department of the Interior in 1966, became the final block in the foundation for the National Trails System Act. The study was completed quickly in nine months by BOR staff and their colleagues in the NPS, BLM, and Forest Service. Daniel M. Ogden, Jr., BOR's Assistant Director for Planning and Research, chaired the study team. Each participating agency polled their field offices to come up with ideas for trails that could be featured in this nationwide survey. Such information helped fill in gaps, enabling the Department of the Interior to recommend comprehensive legislation based on factual conditions and popular needs. [6]

One of the *Trails for America* team members has noted:

. . . the initial nationwide trail study was limited in scope. It was looking at what were the more obvious long trails. They weren't intended . . . to be but a context for national historic trails, national scenic trails, and national recreation trails. And it identified what would be a core group of initial ones. So it tried to be inclusive in terms of looking at what would represent different segments of the country — looking at the concepts of the Pacific Crest Trail and the Continental Divide Trail and the Appalachian Trail — and then looking at the key east-west links like the Lewis and Clark Trail. The North Country Trail was part of it, too. It was intended to show what the trail system would look like — like the interstate highway system . . . What you ideally want over time is to have a linkage of trails across the country. We've never put this in the

---

5. President Lyndon B. Johnson, February 8, 1965, *Special Message to Congress on Conservation and Restoration of Natural Beauty* in NTSAHA.
6. Lawrence N. Stevens, BOR Acting Director, April 2, 1965, in memo to Directors of NPS and BLM, in NTSAHA.

interstate highway jargon, but the idea would be to have interlinking trail experiences. The thing would connect to the regional trails. [7]

Trails for America focused on the recreational opportunities that trails provide to the public. It found that trails could be inexpensive and available to all — and can be located in metropolitan, suburban, and rural environments. The study recommended three types of trails for further development: national scenic trails that would capture the nation's unique beauty for future generations, park and forest trails to highlight existing trails

Cover of *Trails for America*, 1966. Source: NTSAHA.

within national forests and parks, and metropolitan trail systems. *Trails for America* stated that the most urgent need for trails was in or near urban areas. This finding reflected the suffering that cities such as Detroit and Los Angeles had recently experienced during devastating urban riots. It also evoked medical studies that indicated that outdoor recreation could relieve mental stress. The report went on to say that trail systems should be included as an integral part of broader outdoor recreation planning and general urban planning to offset some of the health hazards endemic to metropolitan life. The report also proposed the first national interstate trails — the Appalachian, Pacific Crest, Potomac Heritage, and Continental Divide National Scenic Trails — and recommended many others for further study, including the Lewis and Clark, Oregon, North

---

7. Brian O'Neill, 2007, NPS Oral History interview, NTS 40th Anniversary Oral History Project, p. 17.

Country, Natchez Trace, and Santa Fe Trails. In short, *Trails for America* laid a firm foundation for the National Trails System Act. [8]

Immediately following publication of *Trails for America*, Interior Secretary Stewart Udall submitted to Congress draft legislation to establish a "Nationwide System of Trails," using many of the concepts detailed in the booklet. His cover letter noted, "A nationwide system of trails will open to all an opportunity to develop an intimacy with the wealth and splendor with America's outdoor world for a few hours at a time, or on one-day jaunts, overnight treks, or expeditions lasting a week or more."

The draft legislation outlined several types of trails:

- national scenic trails;
- federal park, forest, and other recreation trails;
- state park, forest, and other recreation trails; and
- metropolitan area trails.

Regarding the Appalachian Trail, estimated costs were $4.7 million for land acquisition, $2 million for development, and $250,000 annually for operations. Also, specifically for the Appalachian Trail, the draft bill established federal authorities to select and mark the route, appoint an advisory council, buy land, transfer land, offer cooperative agreements, and develop and administer the trail. One key phrase that has proven critical to the sound management of federally established trails in the future was: ". . . and other uses that will not substantially interfere with the **nature and purposes** of the Appalachian Trail may be permitted or authorized . . . " (emphasis by author).

Also, nine additional trail routes were to be studied for possible future inclusion in the trails system. Many passages from this original Interior bill found their way verbatim into the final language of the National Trails System Act in 1968. [9]

An article in the *Washington Post* claimed that the bill held nationwide appeal and stated: "These paths are part of our historic as well as our

---

8. U.S. Department of the Interior, Bureau of Outdoor Recreation, December 1966, *Trails for America;* Daniel M. Ogden, Jr., September 2008, "Development of the National Trails System Act," *Pacific Crest Trail Communicator*, Vol. 20, No. 4, pp. 14-15.
9. U.S. Department of the Interior, March 31, 1966, cover letter, draft legislation, and press release, in NTSAHA.

scenic heritage. They will doubtless be highly prized by future generations as well as our own." [10]

However, the 89th Congress came to an end in late 1966 with no action taken on any of the trail bills. Interior Secretary Udall vowed to send to the next Congress an ambitious set of environmental and recreation bills establishing the Redwoods National Park, a comprehensive trails system, and a system of protected wild and scenic rivers. [11]

BIGGER LANDSCAPES

[Until the mid-1960s,] *preservation of place was more about a singular site or maybe a few sites in close proximity that told an important aspect of the Civil War, the Revolutionary War, or the First World War, and those were important. Or people that were instrumental in creating important chapters of the American experience, and there you then told the broader story of that person's contribution. But [our work at BOR] . . . began to be of a much broader landscape scale where you began to look at how sites really interlocked to represent a heritage.*

That is where the National Wilderness system concept had its origin, and the national system of trails. It was a very exciting period to work in. I think what was unique about the Bureau of Outdoor Recreation was that it was set up to be a change agent. The Udall administration had the principal responsibility for studying new areas being considered for addition to the American Federal land management effort — regardless of whether it was BLM, the Fish and Wildlife Service, mainly the Park Service, the Forest Service, and the Bureau of Land Management. Yes, BOR staff were people who were not vested in the sort of singular perspective of a given agency. Park Service people tend to be Park Service-centric. They see the Park Service as the management solution to every study. The Forest Service, the same, and BLM — so I love the people. But the Bureau of Outdoor Recreation tended to hire people that could get out of the agency-centric box.

Well, it was an interesting period. One, it was one of the most important eras in terms of major legislation that was passed about conserving the American

---

10. "National Trails," *Washington Post*, April 8, 1966, p. A6. Accessed through ProQuest Newspapers: *Washington Post*.
11. "Udall to Press 4 Outdoor Trails," November 18, 1966, *New York Times*, 27, courtesy ProQuest Historic Newspapers, in NTSAHA.

landscape or conserving American history. It was really a dynamic period with Stu [Stewart] Udall as the [Interior] Secretary and John Kennedy as the President. It went out into the Nixon administration as well. It was a period of recognizing the importance of a more holistic approach to deal with the challenges of landscape conservation. So when you think about that whole period, it was about the national wild and scenic river system — that whole concept to preserve segments of our American rivers in a protected status to represent the composite value of that important part of our landscape.

Now, stepping back and looking in that period, I said, "My goodness, that was quite an era. We will never replicate that in total." I think that the demise of the Bureau of Outdoor Recreation when Jim Watt became Secretary of the Interior was a tragic loss, because there needed to be an agency that didn't have a vested interest in who managed this [or that], one that was very open and objective looking at what should be the best approach to stewarding a place or a series of places, and what should the governance structure look like. It is really hard to ask an agency to manage its land not to find themselves as the magic answer to everything. So, I realized what a golden period that was and what a mass of important legislation that occurred during a relatively few number of years between 1968 and 1972. It was just an amazing set of authorities that came into being. [12]

A large landscape typical of western U.S. trails: the peaks of the Cascade Mountains along the Pacific Crest NST in Oregon. Photo by Kristi Kose courtesy PCTA.

12. Brian O'Neill, 2007, NPS Oral History interview, NTS 40th Anniversary Oral History Project, pp. 5–7.

CHAPTER 3
ORIGINAL ACT 1967-1968

This is one of the most attractive proposals which has been developed in recent years during the great resurgence of interest in natural outdoor recreation throughout the nation. Foot and horse trails offer the best opportunities for large numbers of people to escape the pressure of mechanized urban life and to enjoy the finest kind of healthful outdoor recreation in unspoiled natural environments. (Grant Conway, 1967) [1]

As the 90th Congress convened in January 1967, President Lyndon Johnson issued a special message to Congress, "Protecting Our Natural Heritage." It was impelled by a recent period of polluted air over greater New York City when an estimated 80 people died. Although this message mainly addressed air quality, it also touched on several subjects, including highway safety, resource and energy development, safe drinking water, new national parks (specifically Redwoods, North Cascades, Potomac Valley, and Apostle Islands), new wilderness areas, and scenic rivers and trails.

I again urge the Congress to establish a nationwide system of Trails. We should begin with authorization on the Appalachian Trail from Maine to Georgia. The system should include similar status for the Pacific Crest and Continental Divide Trails from the Canadian border almost to Mexico, and for the Potomac Heritage Trail along that great river from Tidewater to its source. Our proposal will call for expansion of

---

1. Grant Conway, for the National Parks Association, *Hearing Before the Subcommittee on National Parks and Recreation . . . on HR 4865 and Related Bills to Establish a Nationwide System of Trails*, held March 6–7, 1967, Washington, DC: GPO, p. 90.

metropolitan, State, and Federal trails where our people can hike and bicycle and ride horseback near the cities in which they increasingly live. [2]

A few days later, the Interior Department resubmitted for the new 90th Congress a bill titled "Nationwide System of Trails Act" to both the House and Senate. It was largely the same bill as submitted the year before, with additional cost and manpower figures attached. Several members of Congress immediately championed it, especially Senators Gaylord Nelson (D-WI) and Henry "Scoop" Jackson (D-WA). [3]

George Cardinet, longtime trails activist in California, recalled 25 years later some of the circumstances surrounding the passage of the Trails Act:

The 1967-8 struggle to pass [the trails bill] *brought high spirits to the trails community which had never been unified before. Key leaders were Gunnar Peterson, of Chicago's Open Lands Project; Les Holmes, first executive director of the Appalachian Trail Conference; Kay Smith, a Virginia horsewoman; and Charley Vogel, later a California member of the Pacific Crest Trail Advisory Council. California's* [former] *Governor* [Earl] *Warren was also a strong advocate of the Act. The struggle required educating both Congress and the federal land managing agencies about the values of trails.* [4]

Personal connections to trails and treasured landscapes by high-level officials helped create support for this bill. The U.S. House of Representatives Subcommittee on National Parks and Recreation chaired by Roy A. Taylor (D-NC) considered the bill. During two days of hearings held March 6–7, 1967, Representative Taylor admitted that he favored the bill, for he had grown up in the mountains of North Carolina where trails were an important part of his life.

At the House hearings, the subcommittee members heard from 28 witnesses and received 52 letters. Most were highly supportive, including one from Chairman Wayne Aspinall (D-CO). The few opponents were

---

2. Lyndon B. Johnson, January 30, 1967, *Special Message to the Congress: Protecting Our Natural Heritage*, courtesy the American Presidency Project, in NTSAHA.
3. Charles F. Luce, February 1, 1967, letter with attachments to Hubert Humphrey, President of the U.S. Senate, and *Congressional Record*, February 3, 1967, S 1426, both in NTSAHA.
4. George Cardinet in NPS and OCTA, 1993, *Connection – '93: The Third National Conference on National Scenic and National Historic Trails, Proceedings*, p. 45, in NTSAHA.

more skeptical than fully against the idea of a federally assisted national system of trails. As the hearings progressed, various House members recommended additional trails for future study. Some sympathized with wilderness interests, while others sought urban recreational opportunities. The numerous and complex topics addressed in the hearing reflected the incredible multifaceted undertaking they were tackling, including land protection, funding, maintenance, crime potential, liability, motorized trail uses, trail width, easements, magnitudes of use, shelters, fencing, and pathway relocation. [5]

The Senate Subcommittee then held hearings ten days later, March 15–16, 1967, where no outright opposition was evident. During the two full days of the Senate hearing several participants (including three senators) testified or submitted letters of support, with only a handful expressing skepticism or suggesting major revisions. As Subcommittee Chairman Scoop Jackson (D-WA) was not present, Senator Frank Moss (D-UT) opened the hearing (advocating inclusion of the Mormon Trail) and Senator Gaylord Nelson presided over most of the sessions. The Senate hearing panels discussed many issues, too, such as advisory councils, state and local interests, water trails, international connections, use of eminent domain (especially on the proposed east-west historic trails), costs and funding, fire danger, corridor width, number of users, trespassing and littering, youth corps, effects on timbering, flexibility, and local control. [6]

These hearings endure as some of the major foundation stones of the National Trails System — perhaps the single best source of Congressional intent. Concepts that arose in the hearings and that have shaped the National Trails System ever since include the importance of volunteers, the balance of public benefits and private property rights, the possibility of including routes of history, and the diversity of trail opportunities found throughout the nation. By embarking on a system that was nationwide in extent, a wide range of senators and representatives could support the bills under consideration, creating the necessary bipartisan support for passage. Legislators' support of the Trails System Act was particularly useful when they became personally involved by advocating the addition

5. GPO, 1967, *Hearing Before the* [House] *Subcommittee on National Parks and Recreation . . . on HR 4865 and Related Bills to Establish a Nationwide System of Trails*, March 6–7, 1967, Serial No. 90-4.
6. GPO, 1967, *Hearings Before the* [Senate] *Committee on Interior and Insular Affairs . . . on S. 827, A Bill to Establish a Nationwide System of Trails and for Other Purposes*, March 15–16, 1967.

of a particular trail. For example, Representative Joe R. Pool (R-TX) suggested adding the Chisholm Trail to those listed for study and potential inclusion. [7]

A month after the House and Senate hearings, Interior Secretary Udall submitted a "supplemental statement" to explain why eminent domain should be included as a National Trails System land protection authority, even as a last resort. Without such authority, individual landowners could easily thwart establishment of a continuous (but narrow) trail corridor. His letter was accompanied by an Interior Department solicitor's letter referring to existing U.S. Code authorities for acquisition of private land and showing various Congressional restrictions for a variety of national park areas and programs. [8]

Initial votes on different versions of the trails system bills passed the Senate on July 1 and the House of Representatives on July 16, 1968 (378 to 18). In the course of these discussions and votes, Chairman Aspinall remarked on the House floor:

Mr. Speaker, I view H.R. 4865 as an experiment — a pilot program. If, under this bill, we succeed in developing a meaningful start toward a balanced recreation program for the American people, this will truly be landmark legislation. It calls for every ounce of cooperation by all concerned if it is to do the job we seek to accomplish without substantial Federal expenditures. . . . Conversely, if the establishment of the Appalachian National Scenic Trail results in the deterioration of cooperation and an expensive land acquisition and development program, then the future of other national scenic trails will be very uncertain. [9]

A conference committee of five senators and five representatives met on September 9–10, 1968, to iron out final wording, largely following the

---

7. Two participants in these hearings were to play leading roles later. One skeptical member of the House Committee on Interior and Insular Affairs, James A. McClure (R-ID), was later elected to the Senate in 1972, where he chaired the Committee on Energy and Natural Resources from 1981 to 1987 and was largely responsible for the NTSA Section 10(c) funding restrictions for federal land acquisition. A letter from the American Farm Bureau Federation (AFB) was signed by Craig L. Thomas, AFB Assistant Legislative Director, who was elected to the House of Representatives in 1989 (R-WY) and the Senate in 1995 (R-WY, succeeding Dick Cheney). He played key roles in trails legislation from 2000 until his death in 2007.

8. Stewart L. Udall, April 13, 1967, *Supplemental Statement by Secretary of the Interior Stewart L. Udall on Condemnation in Reference to S. 827 and S. 1092, Bills to Establish a Nationwide System of Trails and a Nationwide System of Scenic Rivers, Before the Senate Interior and Insular Affairs Committee, 4-13-67,* copy in NTSAHA.

9. Wayne N. Aspinall, July 16, 1968, in *Congressional Record,* p. H 6696, in NTSAHA.

House subcommittee's outline. Of note, the category of "Park, Forest, and Other Recreation Trails" was consolidated into "National Recreation Trails." The conference committee recommended that only the Appalachian and Pacific Crest Trails be established as the first two national scenic trails — the others that had been proposed earlier for establishment (the Continental Divide and Potomac Heritage Trails) had too many controversies still needing to be settled. The final bill language limited federal government land acquisition by eminent domain to 25 acres per mile on average. Funds for land acquisition for the two new NSTs were limited to $5.5 million. [10]

After these deliberations and other delays, and exactly two years after the release of *Trails for America*, both houses passed the National Trails System Act (in the Senate by unanimous consent). President Lyndon B. Johnson signed

Signing ceremony for the National Trails System Act at the White House, October 2, 1968. Photo courtesy the LBJ Library, Austin, Texas.

it into law on October 2, 1968, in the East Room of the White House. In the same ceremony, the Wild & Scenic Rivers Act of 1968 was also signed.

The 1968 Trails Act designated three types of trails: national recreation trails (NRTs), national scenic trails (NSTs), and connecting-and-side trails. The act established the Appalachian and Pacific Crest Trails as the first two NSTs, creating a geographic and administrative balance — one paralleling the East Coast, the other paralleling the West Coast; one administered by the National Park Service and other by the Forest Service. Such interagency balance and collaboration has been a hallmark of the National Trails System ever since.

10. U.S. House of Representatives, September 12, 1968, 90th Congress, Second Session, *Conference Report: Nationwide System of Trails*, Report 1891.

The Act also requested that 14 additional routes be studied for possible inclusion later as potential NSTs in the System: Continental Divide, Potomac Heritage, Old Cattle Trails of the Southwest (including the Chisholm Trail), Lewis and Clark, Natchez Trace, North Country, Kittanning, Oregon, Santa Fe, Long, Mormon, Gold Rush, Mormon Battalion, and El Camino Real (in Florida) Trails.

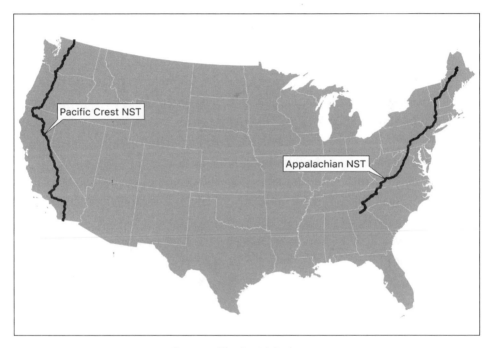

Trails Created by the Original Act, 1968

The Act, as passed into law in 1968 as Public Law 90-543, provided a solid skeleton on which many later amendments were added. Its authorities included:

- Procedures for recognizing national recreation trails (Section 4),
- Advisory councils for the first two NSTs (Section 5a3),
- Requirements for future feasibility studies (Section 5b),
- Establishment of connecting and side trails (Section 6),
- Administrative functions for NSTs, including selection of right-of-way, mapping, facility development, use regulations, marking, cooperative agreements, land

acquisition (including limited eminent domain as
a last resort), and land exchanges (Section 7),

- Encouraging other federal agencies, states, and local
jurisdictions to foster trails and trail systems (Section 8),

- Reserving trail rights-of-way, especially on
an interagency basis (Section 9), and

- Appropriation of funds to acquire lands
for the first two NSTs (Section 10).

BOR did its best to be ready. Even before the Trails Act was passed,
it geared up delegations of authority, solicitors' opinions, and information
sheets to its regions so that it could help implement the bill as soon as it
should become law. [11]

Remarkably, at that time there were no national trail organizations. All
of the citizen advocacy to establish this national system of trails was carried
out by individuals or organizations with other agendas, such as the Sierra
Club. While champions of the trails system saw their goals being framed at
the national level, they were not yet organized at a national scale.

The year 1968 was
remarkable in many
respects, culminating in
a contentious presidential
election marking a trou-
bled climax to the turmoil
of the 1960s. Seldom in
the United States had
there been such a conver-
gence of social unrest in
one single year: the assas-
sinations of civil rights
leader Martin Luther
King, Jr. and presidential

A soldier stands guard at 7th and N Streets, NW, in
Washington, DC, during the riots that followed the
assassination of Martin Luther King, Jr., in April,
1968. Photo by Warren K. Leffler courtesy Library
of Congress Prints and Photographs Division.

candidate Robert Kennedy; escalation of the unpopular Vietnam War;
urban riots; worldwide student unrest; draft resistance; the debut of *60*

---

11. William R. Wolph to BOR Director Crafts, August 2, 1968, *Memorandum on Delegation of Authority to BOR on Trails*, in NTSAHA.

Minutes as TV investigative journalism; and the election of the first black woman, Representative Shirley Chisholm, to the U.S. Congress. The National Trails System was born in the midst of these troubled times — perhaps launched with the hope that it could bring balm and inspiration to future generations.

That whole era in which the concept for the National Trails System Act was laid out in the study, and then of the fairly quick turnaround in terms of being able to move from the study to the legislation. It was . . . carefully orchestrated. Yes, it had — in the history of legislation — it had fewer bumps than practically anything. Yes, there was enough homework done. There was enough excitement about the concepts of long-distance scenic trails and long-distance historic trails to tell the story of America, it was a pretty compelling sort of mood there that helped advance the legislation quickly and got it through. [12]

STEWART UDALL (1920–2010)

STEWART LEE UDALL served for four years as an Air Force gunner over Europe during World War II before returning to Arizona where he'd grown up and obtained a law degree (and helped racially integrate the university's cafeteria in the process). He and his brother, Morris ("Mo"), both became lawyers, and eventually both ran for Congress — Stewart in 1954 and Mo in 1961 succeeding his brother.

President John F. Kennedy appointed Stewart Udall as Secretary of the Interior in 1961, and he served in this position for eight years under both Kennedy and Johnson. Both administrations sought an active expansion of public lands and comprehensive environmental and conservation programs. By 1969, Udall and his agencies had overseen the creation of four national parks, six national monuments, eight national seashores and lakeshores, nine national recreation areas, 20 national historic sites, and 50 national wildlife refuges. Whole new systems were created — Wilderness Areas, National Trails, and Wild & Scenic Rivers — and new conservation protection came into being

---

12. Brian O'Neill, 2007, NPS Oral History interview, NTS 40th Anniversary Oral History Project, p. 8.

under federal law helping rare and endangered species, historic sites and resources, land and water conservation, and solid waste disposal. He helped implement the recommendations of the ORRRC by setting up the Bureau of Outdoor Recreation and the Land and Water Conservation Fund. He prepared the way for the Clean Air and Clean Water Acts that followed soon after. And he helped set in motion the National Endowment for the Arts and the National Endowment for the Humanities. On the side, he penned the influential environmental manifesto *The Quiet Crisis* in 1963. He also had the foresight to make aerial mapping and satellite imagery a key function to serve all Interior agencies. This is a remarkable and unmatched eight-year record.

Secretary Udall speaking, 1966.
Photo courtesy National Archives II,
College Park, Maryland.

After his years at the Department of the Interior, Udall became a policy writer about energy issues (promoting solar energy in the 1970s) and an environmental advocate, moving back to Arizona in 1979. He published a variety of books and papers, including *America's Natural Treasures: National Nature Monuments and Seashores* (1971), *To the Inland Empire: Coronado and Our Spanish Legacy* (1987), *The Quiet Crisis and the Next Generation* (1988), *Beyond the Mythic West* (as a coauthor in 1990), *The Myths of August: A Personal Exploration of Our Tragic Cold War Affairs with the Atom* (1998), and *The Forgotten Founders: Rethinking the History of the Old West* (2002). Along the way, he won a number of prizes that recognized his legacy. These included the Wilderness Society's Ansel Adams Award, the United Nations's Gold Medal for Lifetime Achievement, and Common Cause's Public Service Achievement Award. After his death, the headquarters building of the United States Department of the Interior in Washington, DC, was named for him. [13]

Today this plaque honors Stewart L. Udall at the entrance of the Department of the Interior Building in Washington, D.C. Photo by author.

13. "Stewart Udall," *Wikipedia*, last modified June 4, 2018, https://en.wikipedia.org/wiki/Stewart_Udall.

CHAPTER 4
GETTING STARTED 1968–1976

Establishing a system of trails is not easy. Administratively, it involves Federal, State, and private areas, as well as a number of different Federal agencies. The authors of the legislation are to be commended in this undertaking. (Spencer Smith, 1967) [1]

B efore the end of the Johnson administration in early 1969, the Bureau of Outdoor Recreation (BOR) quickly moved to make the newly passed National Trails System Act (NTSA) operational. Delegations of authority from the departmental level to agencies were proposed, and letters were crafted for Secretary Udall to send to all state governors. In one of these, he wrote:

The Act, a copy of which is enclosed, encourages states to assume the leadership role in operating, developing, and maintaining portions of the National Scenic Trails (Appalachian and Pacific Crest) and also to acquire lands for utilization as segments of these trails. . . . The legislation offers your State the opportunity to assume a lead role in this challenging trails program. [2]

After the presidential election of 1968, the nation shifted. Republican Richard Nixon followed Democrat Lyndon Johnson. Issues important in the 1960s faded as new priorities rose. However, the nation continued in the throes of deep social turmoil with campus and urban riots, the appearance of the "counterculture," increasing drug use, growing worries about

---

1. Spencer M. Smith, 1967, for the Citizens Committee on Natural Resources, GPO, *Hearings Before the [Senate] Committee on Interior and Insular Affairs . . . on S. 827, A Bill to Establish a Nationwide System of Trails and for Other Purposes,* March 15 and 16, 1967, p. 151, in NTSAHA.
2. Stewart Udall to Alabama Governor Albert P. Brewer, November 15, 1968, in NTSAHA.

pollution and environmental degradation, and the increasingly hated Vietnam War. It was a time of turmoil and distrust.

The BOR parceled out among its regional offices the 14 trail feasibility studies requested in the newly-passed NTSA. Staff members were busily put to work developing a standard format and criteria for national scenic trails (NSTs) so that there would be consistency among these studies. In May 1969, Walter Hickel, the new Secretary of the Interior, and Clifford Hardin, recently appointed Secretary of Agriculture, established an Interagency Trails Task Force to help coordinate trails work and policy among the different fed-

President Richard M. Nixon, 1972. Photo courtesy National Archives II, College Park, Maryland.

eral agencies with trail responsibilities. For the next 11 years, A. Heaton Underhill, BOR Deputy Director, chaired this new interagency task force.

In the agreement setting up the Trails Task Force, the secretaries charged it to develop:

- Procedures for the studies of routes identified in Section 5 of the National Trails System Act as well as studies of other trails to determine feasibility for including them in the Trails System,
- Uniform markers for the National Trails System, including standards for their installation and maintenance along trails,
- Criteria and standards for selection of trail location,
- Regulations governing use, protection, management, development, and administration of national trails,
- Uniform regulations for governing conduct on and along trails,
- Procedures for identification and designation of national recreation trails (NRTs), and
- Recommendations to the respective secretaries as needed.

Criteria for additional trails, guidelines for trails studies, trail markers, and interagency coordination were the first issues addressed by the task force. In September 1969, Under Secretary of the Interior Russell E. Train issued the first federal government policy statements about the National Trails System as Interior Secretarial Order 2924. It delegated Interior's responsibilities for administering the Appalachian Trail to the National Park Service but assigned feasibility studies to BOR. [3]

In this era of turmoil and change, Americans wanted trails for many purposes, including enjoying the beauty of nature and retracing the footsteps of their ancestors. While conducting the first 14 trail studies, BOR staff and their interagency counterparts soon realized that establishing continuous hiking trails — like the Appalachian and Pacific Crest NSTs — along the nation's historic routes would be all but impossible. In many places, development (such as railroads, highways, pipelines, housing, and urbanization) along or across these routes ruined or compromised their historic qualities.

As the studies proceeded, members of Congress urged various agencies involved with the new trails system to carry out their favored sections of the Act. Senator Gaylord Nelson, who had been the Act's primary champion, wrote an article explaining the trails system to the public. "Hiking trails provide the entire American family with perhaps the most economical, most varied form of outdoor recreation. So this new law gives us a much needed opportunity to preserve and more widely enjoy many significant parts of our country's natural heritage." [4]

His colleague, Senator "Scoop" Jackson (D-WA), wrote to Interior Secretary Hickel in early 1970 to encourage trails along utility rights-of-way and roadways, since many of them served urban areas. [5]

In an effort to coordinate agency efforts with the public's wishes, a National Trails Symposium was called for June 2–4, 1971, in Washington, DC, to listen to and encourage citizen support for trails. Some 350 people attended. Hickel's successor as Secretary of the Interior, Rogers C. B. Morton, chaired the major plenary sessions. The Symposium's themes included the status of the 14 feasibility studies ("meaningful progress"

3. *Federal Register*, September 12, 1969, Vol. 34, No. 175, p. 14337 in NTSAHA.
4. Gaylord Nelson, 1969, "Trails Across America," *National Wildlife*, Vol. 4, June-July 1969, pp. 21–27, in NTSAHA.
5. Henry M. Jackson, March 25, 1970, letter to Walter J. Hickel, in NTSAHA.

was reported by BOR staff), the status of the two NSTs (including coordination, public information, environmental impacts, liability, effects on adjacent land uses, anticipated costs and public use, land costs and acquisition), and a general discussion about national recreation trails (NRTs) which were considered a "primary purpose" of the National Trails System — in fact, they appeared to have been largely ignored thus far. To rectify this last complaint, the Symposium opened with a ribbon-cutting ceremony recognizing the first 27 NRTs at Fort Dupont along the Fort Circle Hiker/Biker Trail that links many of Washington, DC's Civil War sites. [6]

Another complaint was voiced by citizen activist George Cardinet from California. Speaking on behalf of the private sector side of trails, he noted that the Trails Act's primary purpose was "to establish trails in or reasonably accessible to urban areas." Yet the Act's appropriated funds were all devoted to its secondary purpose of protecting the more remote NSTs. He also noted that just recognizing existing trails as NRTs was "rubber stamping that which is accomplished"

Interior Secretary Rogers C.B. Morton at his confirmation hearings, 1971. Photo courtesy National Archives II.

instead of funding and supporting the creation of new trails in urban areas. In his enthusiasm, Cardinet went on to suggest:

Every Federal dollar allocated, loaned or expended for any function — flood control, highways, urban renewal and development, utilities, conservation, recreation, etc. — that possesses a trail potential, should before disbursement, elicit a positive commitment for trail provision within such function or project. [7]

The first National Trails Symposium was such a success that the Openlands Project of Chicago was contracted to organize another national trails symposium two years later. Held June 14–17, 1973, in

6. *Proceedings, National Symposium on Trails*, Washington, DC, June 2–6, 1971, in NTSAHA.
7. George Cardinet, 1971, *Proceedings, National Symposium on Trails*, Washington, DC, June 2–6, 1971, pp. 19–20, in NTSAHA.

Colorado Springs, Colorado, and hosted by the newly created National Trails Council, this second symposium attracted 200 people and touched on many important topics:

- The increasing interest in historic trails. It was announced by BOR that the Oregon Trail study which was then being written would "be selected as the Pilot Study for the study of other [historic] trails" to follow.
- A report on the first 39 NRTs recognized so far.
- Emphasis on trail-making at state and local levels, especially trails for special uses and disabled persons.
- Status of trail user groups and management agency issues. These included overwhelming problems with meeting demands of increased trail use and an expanding need for trail construction and development.
- An international perspective offered by the Ramblers' Association of Great Britain about the ancient British system of walking routes and efforts to preserve them. [8]

These national trails symposia proved vital to maintaining interagency cooperation and contacts with interested citizens and organizations. From 1973 on, National Trails Symposia have been held more or less every two years in locations across the nation. However, since the mid-1980s, these symposia have only tangentially addressed NST and NHT issues. They have focused mostly on local trails and recreation facilities. (One result was that NST and NHT advocates, as we shall see, started their own nationwide conferences in 1988.)

As the 1970s progressed, the efforts of the Interagency Trails Task Force increased. In 1974, responding to congressional discussion and actions, it issued draft guidelines and criteria for the three existing types of trails under the original Trails Act (NSTs, NRTs, and connecting-and-side trails) and guidelines and criteria for the potential category of national historic trails (NHTs). The components and questions in response to these issues included various observations:

---

8. *Proceedings: The Second National Symposium on Trails,* Colorado Springs, CO, June 14–17, 1973, 181+ pp., in NTSAHA.

- The language of the original Trails Act was confusing for it specifically created a "National Trails System" but supported a more generic "national system of trails;"
- Because NRTs were community-based and self-nominated, they were a key category within the trails system but had received the least amount of attention;
- NSTs and NRTs needed clearer justification as parts of a system of extensive long trails. When were they merited? (Inquiries at this time supported the need for a clearer outline of the significance of these trails that made them notably different from nonfederally designated trails.); and,
- Since portions of the historic trails had been obliterated by development, obtaining continuous rights-of-way to preserve them would be nearly impossible and somewhat meaningless. Discussions covered developing sections of historic trails to commemorate their importance in national history while marking the gaps in each route with markers as appropriate. [9]

The Task Force's discussions showed that inconsistency in terminology and meanings continued as a chronic issue, that there was confusion about how to justify the national trails, and that the proposed national historic trail category remained a desired but questionable addition.

During the mid 1970s, while the first 24 feasibility studies were underway, several other federal governmental actions helped shape public and agency support for the National Trails System:

- May 13, 1971 – Executive Order 11593, *Protection and Enhancement of the Cultural Environment*, furthered the National Environmental Policy Act of 1969 by enlarging environmental compliance to include cultural, historical, and archeological factors.

---

9. Agreement between the USDA and U.S. DOI for the development and operation of the National Trails System, Federal Interagency Council on Trails, 1969–2000 file, and Federal Regional Working Groups on Trails Criteria, March 1974, NTSAHA.

- October 17, 1976 – P.L. 94-527 requested eight additional trail feasibility studies for the Bartram, Dominquez-Escalante, Florida, Indian Nations, Nez-Perce, Pacific Northwest, Desert, and Daniel Boone Trails. This law continued to expand the scope of the National Trails System and heightened the need to understand and define future historic trail routes. In preparing for this legislative action, the first-ever oversight hearings were held to review the progress being made to implement the original National Trails Act of 1968 (See Chapter 7 below).

- October 21, 1976 – P.L. 94-579, the *Federal Land Policy and Management Act*, formed the first "organic act" for the Bureau of Land Management and defined BLM's multiple use land management policy. By its authorities, BLM became a consolidated agency on an equal footing with the National Park Service and the Forest Service.

THE ENVIRONMENTAL LEGACY OF THE 1960S

Passage of the National Trails System Act was part of a sequence of conservation and environmental legislation actions that occurred throughout the 1960s and early 1970s. Some of those acts — especially as they have impacted national trails — are sketched out below:

OUTDOOR RECREATION ACT OF 1963

Signed into law by President Kennedy, P.L. 88-29 was the first fruit of ORRRC. For the first time at the federal level it fostered comprehensive interstate programs promoting outdoor recreation. This act soon led to coordination, assistance to states, management of the Land and Water Conservation Fund (see below), and special programs. Within three years under this authority, BOR conducted a nationwide inventory of recreation needs and resources, compiled a comprehensive nationwide outdoor recreation plan, offered technical assistance as requested, sponsored research, reviewed surplus public lands to be used for recreational purposes, supported the Lewis and Clark Trail Commission, assessed possible wild river designations, conducted a study of scenic roads and parkways, and reviewed recreation components in federal housing grant applications. [10]

WILDERNESS ACT OF 1964

Successfully promoted by the Wilderness Society, this act was the first at the federal level to define and protect wilderness areas. The original designations in 1964 totaled 9.1 million acres — mostly in national forests. Since then, more than 100 million acres of additional wilderness areas in 44 states and Puerto Rico (almost 5 % of the United States acreage) are administered by the same agencies responsible for the National Trails System: BLM, NPS, FS, and USF&WS. Criteria for such areas include minimal human impact (no motorized activities), opportunities for unconfined recreation, a unit size of at least 5,000 acres, and preeminent historic, educational, and/or scientific values. [11]

LAND AND WATER CONSERVATION FUND ACT OF 1965

This creative approach to park funding also grew directly out of ORRRC recommendations. Available funds were to be split between federal agencies and states. For states to participate, they had to periodically complete statewide comprehensive outdoor recreation plans. Grant-assisted areas were to remain open to the public for recreation

10. See John F. Kennedy, 1963, "Remarks Upon Signing the Outdoor Recreation Bill" on The American Presidency website; W.W. Dreskell, 1966, "Bureau of Outdoor Recreation, P.L. 88-29; Land and Water Conservation Fund Act of 1965, P.L. 88-578."
11. "Wilderness Act," *Wikipedia*, last modified June 8, 2018, https://en.wikipedia.org/wiki/Wilderness_Act.

purposes in perpetuity (or be replaced with lands of equal recreational value). At first funded with revenues from the sales of surplus federal property, motorboat fuel taxes, and federal recreation area revenues, the revenue base was expanded in 1968 to fees from outer continental shelf mining leases. Capped at $900 million per year in 1977, annual appropriations have usually been a fraction of that figure. In 1978, the Urban Park and Recreation Recovery Program was added to emphasize urban projects. In 1989, the program was authorized for another 25 years. By 2006 on the state side, the LWCF had funded 40,000 projects in all 50 states totaling $3.6 billion. On the federal side, a similar amount has aided the protection of many federal land units such as national parks, forests, and wildlife refuges. All the funding to protect the Appalachian NST and help the Collaborative Landscape Program has come from this fund. LWCF 's 50-year authorization expired in 2015 but was extended to 2018. [12]

HISTORIC PRESERVATION ACT OF 1966

Fulfilling decades of effort to preserve and protect the nation's archeological and historic legacy through law — starting with the Antiquities Act of 1906, and continuing with the Historic Sites Act of 1935, and the founding of the National Trust for Historic Preservation in 1949 — this became the nation's most far-reaching preservation legislation. In 1966, Lady Bird Johnson coordinated a booklet, *With Heritage So Rich*, which brought into focus what would soon be lost without comprehensive attention. The resulting act set up a National Advisory Council on Historic Preservation, a network of state historic preservation officers, the National Register of Historic Places, and the Section 106 review process affecting all potentially eligible federally owned or funded properties. These authorities have been especially helpful in protecting sites and segments of National Historic Trails. [13]

12. See NPS website entry for "Land and Water Conservation Fund."
13. "National Historic Preservation Act of 1966," *Wikipedia*, last modified February 14, 2018, https://en.wikipedia.org/wiki/National_Historic_Preservation_Act_of_1966.

WILD & SCENIC RIVERS ACTS OF 1968

Both the National Trails System Act and the Wild and Scenic Rivers Act were signed into law on October 2, 1968, at the same ceremony. Both systems were envisioned in the ORRRC, both concepts blend principles of conservation and recreation, both bills were largely crafted by U.S. Department of the Interior staff, and many legislators had interests in both programs, especially Senator Gaylord Nelson. To be eligible for designation as a wild and scenic river — either at the federal or state level — river segments must have "outstandingly remarkable values," and these can be a combination of scenic, recreational, geologic, natural, historic, or cultural factors. In the original act, eight river segments were designated. By 2011, 203 additional river segments had been added, bringing total protected river segments to 13,000 miles. The same four federal agencies that administer national trails and wilderness areas (BLM, FS, NPS, and USF&WS) also operate and protect the federally designated wild and scenic rivers. State-nominated rivers (approved by the Secretary of the Interior) and Partnership Wild and Scenic Rivers must also meet the same eligibility standards as those created by Congress. [14]

NATIONAL ENVIRONMENTAL POLICY ACT

This landmark legislation was actually passed a few months before Earth Day, 1970. It required all federal government actions to be subject to environmental assessments and, if needed, environmental impact statements (EISs). These actions included construction projects, permits, and even projects receiving federal funding, such as highway projects carried out by the states. Difficult issues were to be resolved by the newly created President's Council on Environmental Quality. Soon after "NEPA" was passed, President Richard Nixon established the Environmental Protection Agency (EPA) by executive order to help carry it out. Sometime later, Congress authorized the EPA by law. NEPA has been used as a model for environmental protection in more than

---

14. "National Wild and Scenic Rivers System," *Wikipedia*, last modified April 9, 2018, https://en.wikipedia.org/wiki/National_Wild_and_Scenic_Rivers_System.

100 countries. All of the planning and construction projects associated with the NSTs and NHTs have been subject to NEPA requirements. [15]

EARTH DAY

April 22, 1970, became the first Earth Day. It is now celebrated worldwide annually on that day. Its origins during the depths of the Vietnam War reflected public dismay at the nation's deteriorating environment highlighted by Rachel Carson's *Silent Spring* in 1962, a major oil spill off Santa Barbara, and the burning of the Cuyahoga River in Ohio, both in 1969. Senator Gaylord Nelson, key architect of both the National Trails System

Gaylord Nelson speaking at an Earth Day Rally, April, 1970. Photo courtesy University of Wisconsin Archives, ID: 2018s00331.

and Wild and Scenic Rivers Acts, proposed a day for environmental teach-ins. Grassroots offices nationwide helped bring out an estimated 20 million people that first Earth Day, many in thousands of college, university, and school events. In New York City, both Fifth Avenue and Central Park were made available for Earth Day events. Afterward, Nelson and some colleagues founded Earth Day USA to make this an annual event. It later went international, and today the Earth Day Network coordinates events in 193 countries. Through mobilized popular support, 1970's Earth Day strongly paved the way for the Clean Air Act of 1970, the Clean Water Act of 1972, and the Endangered Species Act of 1973. [16]

---

15. See Wikipedia site for "Environmental Protection Act."
16. "Earth Day," *Wikipedia*, last modified June 11, 2018, https://en.wikipedia.org/wiki/Earth_Day; "Gaylord Nelson and Earth Day."

CHAPTER 5

IMAGINING HISTORIC TRAILS 1971–1975

How to handle preservation of historic routes and have recreational use is a major problem. Historic routes do not necessarily make good recreation trails. Many of the historic routes, or at least parts of them, were developed by the pioneers who were not primarily interested in scenery, but a quick and safe route to their destination. Today these routes pass through cornfields and villages, and are frequently covered over with reservoirs, railroads, or highways since these routes also followed the easiest terrain. The Oregon Trail has many of these problems and is one of the best-known routes. Therefore it will be the first of the historic routes to be studied in detail. (Stuart P. Davey, 1971) [1]

Popular support to commemorate historic routes was not new. Its roots went back to Ezra Meeker, the DAR, and the Lewis and Clark Tourway Association. Even *Trails for America* reflected strong popular interest in historic trails. Yet the operational concept of historic trails was a difficult one, and the Interagency Trails Task Force continued to wrestle with this and other issues presented by the secretaries throughout much of the 1970s. At this time, there was only one citizen-based historic trail organization, and it was devoted to the Lewis and Clark story. Task Force members felt that such trails must be both nationally significant and viable as recreation corridors for inclusion in the National Trails System. While the first 14 feasibility studies were being conducted by BOR during this decade, no additional

---

1. Stuart P. Davey, June 3, 1971, "The National Scenic Trail Study Program, Status and Problems," *Proceedings, National Symposium on Trails*, Washington, DC, 16, June 2–4, 1971, in NTSAHA.

trails were established by the NTSA. Supporters of the trails system knew it needed to grow but were still trying to figure out how.

As the BOR study teams examined the historic routes recommended for study in the original National Trails System Act, they generally recommended against their establishment as National Scenic Trails because the recreational values of these routes were low and the associated landscape settings often highly disturbed. However, because some of these routes — such as the Oregon and Santa Fe Trails — were very popular with scholars, the public, and local communities, a recommendation for "no federal action" to protect these routes was unpalatable to trail supporters. These routes and the stories they embodied were too important to the nation to be cast aside. It became clear to the Interagency Trails Task Force that an additional type of trail designation would be needed in the National Trails System to fit the particular issues and circumstances of these historic routes. [2]

The BOR eventually completed and produced the 14 feasibility studies requested in the original Trails Act. Early in that process, most of the potential historic trails were assessed according to their suitability as hiking trails, modeled on the Appalachian and Pacific Crest NSTs. Therefore, BOR recommended against several worthy historic routes, such as the Santa Fe Trail, by suggesting "no further action" for them. However, its staff soon realized that a new category of "national historic trail" was needed to accommodate

Tourists enjoy a modern-day wagon train near Chimney Rock, Nebraska, in 2007 along the Oregon, California, and Pony Express NHTs. Photo courtesy NPS.

the increasing public interest in these routes, and first proposed amendment language appeared as early as 1973. This idea was quickly reinforced by bill S. 3316 introduced by Senator Frank Moss (D-UT) in April 1974. [3]

2. "America's Trails," 1976, *Outdoor Recreation Action*, a BOR publication, Report No. 42, Winter, 1976, pp. 3–4, in NTSAHA.
3. James G. Watt, Director BOR, memo to Legislative Counsel, Office of the [Interior] Secretary, December 4, 1973, and S. 3316, April 5, 1975, *A Bill to Establish National Historic Trails as a New Category of Trails within the National Trails System*, both in NTSAHA.

Almost two years later, after the BOR polled the regional office staff who were conducting the feasibility studies, the concept of NHTs became more and more refined as a variety of field conditions were examined and partner organizations consulted.

A historic trail is different [from an NST corridor], *however, . . . unless the route* [strictly] *follows its historic location it loses its capacity to provide recreationists with "the intangible elements of historic feeling and association." We therefore feel that the designation of a national historic trail should apply to the specific route along its historic alignment rather than to a corridor. Appropriate segments of the actual historic route should be established as public trails, and continuous travelways should be established where appropriate along the approximate routes of national historic trails.* [4]

Later that year, the chief of the BOR Division of Resource Area Studies that oversaw all 14 feasibility studies stated:

We view the historic trail and travelway concept as an opportunity to commemorate the historic significance of such things as the Oregon Trail without consideration of making a footpath from Leavenworth, Kansas, to the west coast. We're thinking in terms of both segments of the trail that can be through areas that still have remnants of the trail or where there is the opportunity for historic interpretations. These should be historic trails and they should be footpaths. The historic significance of the area should be acquired and protected and interpreted. The roadways adjacent to the trail would be travelways and would be designated as such. [5]

The evolving concept of national historic trails took place at the same time that the National Park Service and the Forest Service struggled to figure out how to protect the newly established long multi-state NSTs that they had recently been assigned. Because much of the Pacific Crest NST's pathway already fell across federally controlled lands, it was the Appalachian NST that became the laboratory where federal agencies learned how to protect "long, skinny corridors" devoted to recreation.

Despite the progress made through 1975 in recognizing the value of and trying to define the special attributes of national historic trails, it would

---

4. Richard L. Winters, Assistant Regional Director, BOR Northwest Region, memo to Director, BOR, March 12, 1975, in NTSAHA.
5. Robert L. Eastman, November 1975, BOR Division of Resource Area Studies, "The National Trails System," *Proceedings of the Third National Trails Symposium, 1975,* 201–2, in NTSAHA.

be another three years before this type of trail was officially added to the NTSA. The final push to recognize these trails is found in Chapter 7.

Mormon handcart re-enactors in 2005 at Tom Sun Ranch, near Martin's Cove, Wyoming, along the Mormon Pioneer NHT. BLM photo courtesy NPS, Salt Lake City, Utah.

ORIGINS OF HISTORIC TRAIL PRESERVATION GROUPS

Ezra Meeker with his wagon and oxen at the Pan Pacific Exposition in 1915. Photo courtesy University of Washington Libraries, Special Collections, #UW 63738.

EZRA MEEKER, after several cross-country trips promoting preservation of the Oregon Trail, founded the Oregon Trail Memorial Association in 1922. In 1926, it became the American Pioneer Trails Association and moved to New York City (housed with the newly formed National Highways Association), funded in part by the sale of commemorative coins. Following Meeker, its next president was Howard R. Driggs (1873–1963), a Mormon writer and historian who moved from Utah to New York City in the mid-1920s to obtain his PhD. He and his family stayed in the New York area where he wrote many books as an English teacher and two about westering trails: *Ox-Team Days on the Oregon Trail* (with Ezra Meeker) and *The Old West Speaks Out*. Other similar groups included Walter Meacham's Old Oregon Trail Association, started in 1922 in Baker, Oregon. (It was later known as Old Oregon Trail, Inc.) All of these groups faded away by the early 1960s. [6]

THE LEWIS AND CLARK TRAIL HERITAGE FOUNDATION (1969)

In 1964, the U.S. Congress established the Lewis and Clark Trail Commission. Over its chartered five-year lifespan, it sought to identify the complex routes followed by these intrepid explorers in the early 19th Century. It was also chartered to advance public awareness about the expedition's importance and encourage contemporary recreational and educational activities along the route. It even originated the "pointing fingers" route marker logo now found on trail markers. As the Commission came to an end, many of its members regrouped and founded the Lewis and Clark Trail Heritage Foundation in 1969. The Foundation has published *We Proceeded On* since 1974, played a key role in advocating for the Lewis and Clark NHT in the late 1970s, and laid a strong foundation for commemorating the bicentennial of the Lewis and Clark Expedition in 2003 to 2006. Today, the Foundation organizes annual membership meetings, offers grants and

6. "Ezra Meeker," *Wikipedia*, last modified May 31, 2018, https://en.wikipedia.org/wiki/Ezra_Meeker; "Howard R. Driggs," *Wikipedia*, last modified March 20, 2018, https://en.wikipedia.org/wiki/Howard_R._Driggs and personal communication with Roger Blair, OCTA historian, January, 2019.

scholarships, promotes Lewis and Clark-related education services, and supports 28 local and regional chapters. By 2012, membership held steady at about 1,200 members. [7]

OREGON-CALIFORNIA TRAILS ASSOCIATION (1982)

The Oregon-California Trails Association was founded in 1982 by publisher Gregory Franzwa when he called together a circle of friends and activists interested in preserving the trails of the American West. They organized themselves into a board of directors, started publishing *The Overland Journal*, and convened annual conventions that have been held ever since. OCTA is the direct heir to the earlier historic trails associations described above. Today, OCTA is the largest historic trail organization in the U.S., membership once peaked above 5,000, but now is somewhat lower. Nevertheless, it carries out a number of essential functions serving several overland trails, including marking and signing trail corridors, issuing publications, supporting 11 regional or state chapters, promoting a speakers bureau, offering a book and map store, and coordinating trail preservation training programs. OCTA pioneered the field of historic trail corridor preservation and has worked effectively with public land agencies to minimize the visual impacts of oil and gas drilling along the western historic trail routes. [8]

SANTA FE TRAIL ASSOCIATION (1986)

The Santa Fe Trail Association was founded just before the Santa Fe NHT was officially added to the National Trails System. Its origins go back to a trail center operated by the Fort Larned Historical Society in Kansas. Starting in 1980, a biennial rendezvous of Santa Fe Trail enthusiasts held in Fort Larned brought together scholars, landowners, and others interested in this trail. Joy Poole in Trinidad, Colorado, with funding support from the Colorado Endowment for the

---

7. "Our History," *Lewis and Clark Trail Heritage Foundation*, accessed June 12, 2018, http://www. lewisandclark.org/about/foundation_history.php.
8. Early history essay, "OCTA Beginnings" and current programs on OCTA's website.

Humanities, the Trinidad Historical Society, the American Association for University Women, the Ballantine Family Charitable Fund, and the Colorado Historical Society, strove to organize a trail symposium in Trinidad in 1986. Meanwhile, she incorporated the Santa Fe Trail Council in 1985 to help get the trail establishment bill passed through Congress. The 1986 the Santa Fe Trail Symposium drew 230 participants, several times the number anticipated. Decisions made at the Council's first business meeting included remaining an independent organization (rather than joining forces with another similar group, such as OCTA), publishing a quarterly newsletter (known as *Wagon Tracks*), holding biennial symposia, and organizing a board of directors and local chapters. The Council's first funds were raised at a book raffle following the business meeting. A year later, it changed from a council to an association. Within a few years, membership exceeded 500 people — and reached 1,000 by 1991. [9]

In subsequent years, as more NHTs were added to the National Trails System, citizen-based nonprofit groups have been organized to support each one. All of these groups currently are members of the Partnership for the National Trails System.

---

9. Marc Simmons, 2006, "SFTA – The Early Years" and Jackson, Hal, 2006, "SFTA – The Mature Years" essays on SFTA website under "History."

Panorama of the Oregon NHT at Three Island Crossing on the Snake River near Glenns Ferry, Idaho, 2016. NPS photo by Bryan Petrytl.

On Oct. 2, 1968, Secretary Udall and President Johnson examine a map of the proposed National Trails System at the White House signing ceremony. Photo courtesy LBJ Library, Austin, Texas.

Gaylord Nelson's article from *Wilderness* magazine, 1969.
Courtesy U.S. Department of the Interior Library.

The founders of the American Hiking Society gather in Florida to plan a hike across
the U.S. that became HikeANation. Left to right: Jim Kern; Tom Deans, President
of the Appalachian Mountain Club; Bill Kemsley, founding editor and publisher
of *Backpacker*; Paul Pritchard, president of the Appalachian Trail Conference;
Louise Marshall, editor of *Signpost* and board member of Washington Trails
Association (WTA); and Nancy Miller, Kern's assistant. Photo courtesy Jim Kern.

Joyce Badgely Smith, dressed as "Fanny," closed the Menucha Conference in 1991 with a dramatic monologue based on her great-grandmother's Oregon Trail journals. NPS photo courtesy PNTS.

A Volunteer Vacation group works along the Kekekabic Trail in Minnesota's Boundary Waters Canoe Area. Photo courtesy Matthew Davis, NCTA.

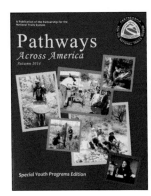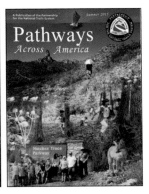

Colorful covers of recent issues of *Pathways Across America*. In NTSAHA."

Sample NST and NHT trail marker logos pre-1995. Photo by author.

Left: Sample of NHT and NST logos revised by Paul Singer and Associates, photo by author.
Right: *Federal Register* Notice from March 28, 2000, alerting the public that various
National Trails System trail marker logos are protected as official federal insignia.

The Federal Interagency Council on Trails meeting at FHWA offices, Washington, DC, fall 2008. Photo courtesy the author.

In September, 2006, the St. Charles Men – Corps of Discovery re-enactors return after three years on the rivers to their homes in St. Charles, Missouri. Photo by author.

Left to right: Jeff Jarvis, BLM; Jim Hughes, BLM Deputy Director,, BLM, Gary Werner, PNTS; Lynn Scarlett, Assistant Secretary of the Interior; Deb Salt, BLM; and Greg Miller, AHS; help celebrate the official launching of the BLM policy package, February, 2006, at the U.S. Department of the Interior, Washington, DC. Photo courtesy BLM.

Celebrating the 40th anniversary of the National Trails System at the National Trail Symposium in Little Rock, Arkansas, November, 2008. Left to right: Gary Werner, PNTS; Marianne Fowler, RTC; Christopher Douwes, FHWA; Nathan Caldwell, USF&WS; Steve Elkinton, NPS; and Terry Eastin, Mississippi River Trail. Photo courtesy American Trails.

At the 2009 PNTS conference in Missoula, Montana, the first group of Trail Apprentices made a strong impression. Photo courtesy PNTS.

This group enjoyed the Ice Age Trail Summer Saunters program, near Lodi, Wisconsin, in 2009. Photo by Eric Sherman courtesy Ice Age Trail Alliance.

The National Pony Express Association commemorates the 150th anniversary of the Pony Express by the U.S. Senate in Washington, DC, April, 2010. NPS photo by Chuck Milliken.

Lewis and Clark NHT enthusiasts lead the Trail Fest parade in Damascus, Virginia, coincident to the PNTS Conference in 2011. Photo by author.

In March, 2015, thousands of people crossed the Edmund Pettus Bridge in Selma, Alabama, to commemorate the 50th anniversary of the Selma Movement for universal voting rights. Photo copyright Bart Smith, used with permission.

AT Volunteers
Along the Appalachian NST in southern Virginia, members of the Mt. Rogers Trail Club wrestle rocks at The Scales. Photo by Cheryl Heydrich courtesy ATC.

Aerial view showing the Werowocomoco archeological site along the York River in Virginia along the Captain John Smith Chesapeake NHT. Photo courtesy PNTS

Kalani DeSouza, Waimakaloni Iona, and others celebrate the Ala Kahaki NHT, April, 2009. Photo by author.

THE TRAILS

By date, as added to the National Trails System

1968 – APPALACHIAN NST

Hikers savor reaching the top of Mount Katahdin in Maine, the northern end of the Appalachian NST. Photo copyright Bart Smith, used with permission.

The Appalachian NST is a 2,190-mile, 250,000-acre greenway extending from Maine to Georgia. Based on the inspiring vision of Benton MacKaye in the 1920s, this trail was first completed in 1938, although through-hikers along the entire route were uncommon until the 1960s. One key leader, Myron Avery, a federal government admiralty lawyer and chairman of the ATC from 1930 to 1952, was able to attract and organize many people to work on the AT cause. The ATC, founded in 1925, is known today as the Appalachian Trail Conservancy. It works to maintain and protect the trail and educate people involved with the trail. Its volunteers work in every season to maintain trail tread, stonework, blazes, and signs. The trail is administered by NPS in close coordination with the USDA Forest Service.

1968 – PACIFIC CREST NST

The Pacific Crest NST emblem in the Cottonwood Valley,
Cleveland National Forest, California.
Photo by Chris Sanderson, courtesy PCTA.

The Pacific Crest NST features both dramatic elevation changes and long, relaxing sections just at timberline along the Sierra and Cascade Mountains of the American West. It connects the hot and arid Mojave Desert to the High Sierras, the dramatic volcanic Cascade peaks of the Northwest to the forests of Canada. Organized by Californian Clinton C. Clarke in the 1930s, this trail runs 2,650 miles between the Mexican and Canadian borders through California, Oregon, and Washington. In the Sequoia-Kings Canyon National Parks the trail runs along the western slopes of 14,494-foot Mount Whitney. This trail links together 25 national forests, six NPS units, and numerous state parks. It is administered by the Forest Service in close partnership with the Pacific Crest Trail Association. It offers unparalleled mountain landscapes, canyons, lakes, and fascinating wildlife.

1978 — OREGON NHT

Along the Oregon NHT at Scotts Bluff, Nebraska, at sunset.
Photo copyright Bart Smith, used with permission.

Hundreds of thousands of emigrants followed this 1,200-mile route in the 1840s and 1850s, leaving the United States for the fabled Oregon Territory in search of wealth and fresh opportunities. Families and individuals traveled in covered wagon trains that crossed the Great Plains and snaked through rough mountain terrain. This overland route crossed the Rocky Mountains at South Pass in what is now western Wyoming, an area first explored by European fur traders in the early 1800s. In 1836, a missionary party headed by Marcus and Narcissa Whitman proved that it could be accomplished by wagon — and the flood of westward expansion began. The Oregon NHT today stretches over 2,000 miles of routes between Independence, Missouri, and Oregon City, Oregon and is administered by NPS in close partnership with the Oregon-California Trails Association. This was the first national historic trail added to the National Trails System — and many of the underlying concepts for NHTs were articulated in this trail's feasibility study.

1978 – MORMON PIONEER NHT

Handcart re-enactors at the Sun Ranch in Wyoming along the Mormon
Pioneer NHT. Photo copyright Bart Smith, used with permission.

Considered one of the most highly organized expeditions in U.S. history,
the Mormon migration symbolizes courage and hope. It memorializes the
exodus of the Mormons from Nauvoo, Illinois, west to the Great Salt Lake
basin in 1846–7. In the mid-1840s, on the banks of the Mississippi River
at Nauvoo, the Mormon Church established its temple and community.
However, nearby residents became enraged at the Mormons' presence, and
an angry mob murdered Mormon leader Joseph Smith. When Brigham
Young was elected their new leader and they faced increasing persecu-
tion, most of the Mormon population embarked upon a highly organized
migration west. Upon reaching their destination near the Great Salt Lake
and setting up an independent community, church members traveled east
again to guide other converts to their new refuge. In the 1970s, when it
was announced that the federal government would be conducting studies
on potential national trails, floods of letters were sent to the BOR proposing
a Mormon Trail. Congressman Frank Moss from Iowa gave the measure
his full support and frequently contacted BOR officials about this matter.
Today, this trail is administered by NPS with assistance from the Mormon
Trails Association and the Iowa Mormon Trails Association.

1978 – CONTINENTAL DIVIDE NST

A late spring snow high in the Rocky Mountains along the Continental Divide NST.
Photo copyright Bart Smith, used with permission.

This challenging trail more than fulfills hikers' dreams of journeying along North America's mountain backbone. Extending from Canada to Mexico, the CDT crosses many ecosystems from tundra to desert. It hosts a rich variety of wildlife and links together hundreds of natural, cultural, and historical assets. Considered one of the great long-distance trails of the world — together with the Pacific Crest and Appalachian NSTs, one of hiking's "Triple Crown" — it is the most remote of the NSTs. In the mid-1970s, Baltimore lawyer and Appalachian Trail through-hiker Jim Wolf hiked part of this route and became so enamored with it that he published a guidebook and advocated for its establishment as an NST. In 1976, the BOR completed the feasibility study and noted that the scenic quality of the trail was superlative. Today, the trail is administered by the Forest Service in partnership with both the Continental Divide Trail Coalition and the Continental Divide Trail Society. Both groups catalyze public awareness and volunteer enthusiasm for the Trail in the five states it crosses.

1978 – LEWIS AND CLARK NHT

A scenic overview of the Columbia River Gorge where the
Lewis and Clark Expedition finally came within
sight of Pacific tidewater. NPS photo.

Americans have always loved Meriwether Lewis and William Clark, the first European-Americans to explore much of the newly acquired Louisiana Purchase and the Pacific Northwest. Their journals documenting scientific observations, exploration, commerce, and conflict have inspired generations of readers. The trail traces their journey from the western edge of U.S. territories in 1803 (now Wood River, Illinois) to the Pacific Coast at the mouth of the Columbia River and back, largely afloat on the Missouri and Columbia Rivers.

President Jefferson charged them with learning about the Native American nations that they would encounter, the plant and animal life along the route, and the nature of the land for future settlement. They left as an organized military expedition, taking two years to reach the Pacific Ocean, returning once the mountain snows melted in less than nine months. The bicentennial of the Lewis and Clark Expedition in 2003 to 2006 proved to be the single largest and most publicized event in the entire saga of the National Trails System. Today, the trail is administered by NPS with the support and assistance of several devoted organizations.

1978 – IDITAROD NHT

Mushers show off their teams in Anchorage before the big race, March, 2013.
Photo by author.

It is fitting that Alaska's premier dogsled trail—the Iditarod—was among the first NHTs established by law. Each year, parts of this Alaskan route host the Iditarod Dogsled Race in late winter for 11 days over 1,100 miles. The mushers race their teams across the harsh Alaskan wilderness against time and the elements. In many places, dog sledding still serves as the most effective method of transportation carrying people, goods, and supplies across frozen terrain. Senator Ernest Gruening (D-AK) participated in the discussions leading to the 1968 Trails Act. He wondered if trails like the Iditarod could be included in this new national system of trails. This trail has deep prehistoric routes, for it is believed that people have been negotiating trails across "The Great Land" for approximately 15,000 years. For centuries, this trail served as a trade route for the native Ingalik and Tanaina peoples. This NHT is administered by BLM with the help of the Iditarod National Historic Trail Alliance. Many trail sections are maintained by dedicated trail volunteers.

1980 – NORTH COUNTRY NST

One of the few overnight shelters along the North Country NST.
Photo copyright Bart Smith, used with permission.

Winding through seven states, the North Country NST presents hikers with myriad natural and cultural treasures. Linking unspoiled scenic landscapes and historic sites, this trail wanders across the Great Lakes states from the Adirondack Mountains in New York to the Missouri River in North Dakota. The trail was conceived in the 1960s during the Nationwide Trails Study and was included in the 1966 *Trails for America* report as a proposed NST. When completed, it will be the longest continuous scenic trail at over 4,200 miles in length. The trail is administered by NPS, while the ongoing tasks of blazing and maintaining the trail are taken up largely by the North Country Trail Association and regional affiliates such as the Finger Lakes Trail Conference (New York) and the Buckeye Trail Association (Ohio). NCTA's mission is to develop, maintain, preserve, and promote the trail through a wide network of volunteers, chapters, partner organizations, and government agencies.

1980 – OVERMOUNTAIN VICTORY NHT

Re-enactors line up to demonstrate firearms along the
Overmountain Victory NHT, NPS photo.

Tracing 330 miles of American Revolutionary War history, the Overmountain Victory National Historic Trail crosses parts of Virginia, Tennessee, North Carolina, and South Carolina. When first established, it was not well known—yet its story is key to American history. Noted by Thomas Jefferson as a major turning point of the Revolutionary War, this trail commemorates the journey of the Overmountain Men, a group of 2,000 backwoods patriots, who sought to defeat British loyalists during the Southern Campaign in 1780. That September, men gathered at various points along the route, such as Abingdon, Virginia, and Sycamore Shoals, Tennessee, and rode hundreds of miles in 14 days, finally catching up with the British at Kings Mountain, South Carolina. There, they defeated Major Patrick Ferguson and his loyalist followers, killing or capturing every one. This skirmish helped turn the tide against the British during the Revolutionary War. The trail was added to the National Trails System during its bicentennial year in 1980. Today, it is administered by NPS with the help of many partners, including the Overmountain Victory Trail Association.

1980 — ICE AGE NST

A haunting wooded scene along the Ice Age NST. Photo
copyright Bart Smith, used with permission.

The Ice Age NST leads visitors and hikers through a set of glacial land-scapes — moraines, eskers, kettle holes, kames, and outwash plains. Administered by NPS in a "triad" relationship with the Ice Age Trail Alliance and the Wisconsin Department of Natural Resources, it will eventually wind 1,000 miles across Wisconsin, witness to the most south-ern extent of North American continental glaciation 10,000 years ago. Trail segments offer many charming opportunities for walking and snow-shoeing — for both day trips and longer hikes. The trail also touches many towns along the way, each offering local character. The Alliance offers nonprofit support, coordinates volunteers, and provides maps and educational opportunities while the Wisconsin DNR leads efforts to pro-tect land corridors needed to complete the trail.

1983 – POTOMAC HERITAGE NST

Along the Chesapeake and Ohio Canal towpath (part of the Potomac Heritage NST) when dogwoods are in bloom. Photo copyright Bart Smith, used with permission.

The Potomac Heritage NST snakes through five physiographic provinces among the lush and historic landscapes of Virginia, Maryland, the District of Columbia, and Pennsylvania. The trail was originally proposed by President Lyndon Johnson in 1965, documented in *Trails for America* in 1966, and added to the National Trails System in 1983. Today, this trail is a network of locally-managed trails, including the 184-mile towpath of the Chesapeake and Ohio Canal National Historical Park, the Mount Vernon Trail, other trails in northern Virginia and Maryland, and the Great Allegheny Passage connecting Cumberland, Maryland, to Pittsburgh, Pennsylvania. Administered by NPS, this trail network traces places and events at the heart of the nation's evolution. Bridging two major watersheds, this trail's segments guide visitors through a rich combination of natural areas, historic sites, and vibrant cities and towns.

1983 – NATCHEZ TRACE NST

The sunken roadbed of the old Natchez Trace NST. Photo
copyright Bart Smith, used with permission.

This trail, although established as an NST, evokes deep history and pre-history. In addition to navigating beautiful landscapes, the Natchez Trace reveals many haunting layers of the past. Initially footpaths of the Choctaw and Creek Indians, this chain of trails was used by Spanish explorer Hernando de Soto, frontier European immigrant farmers, and even Meriwether Lewis as he traveled from New Orleans to Washington, DC. In 1809, Lewis died — either from foul play or suicide — at Grinders Stand near the northern end of the trace. Connecting Natchez, on the Mississippi River, to Nashville, on the Cumberland River, about half of the remnant trace lies within the boundaries of the Natchez Trace Parkway. Of the 694 miles of the original trace, 65 miles in four segments are now open to the public for recreation and retracement. Along these segments, visitors will find Native-American burial mounds, a restored Chickasaw village, Civil War battlefields, and the remains of U.S. Army posts. The trail is administered and managed by NPS as part of the Parkway.

1983 – FLORIDA NST

Gary Werner and Jim Schmid enjoy a stop along the Florida
NST near White Springs, Florida. Photo by author.

The Florida NST pays homage to the unique and varied subtropical beauty of Florida. This 1,400-mile trail follows backcountry alignments across the Florida Panhandle from the Gulf Islands National Seashore down the length of central Florida to Big Cypress National Preserve. Along the way, it passes through three national forests and circles Lake Okeechobee. The original concept of this trail was developed by realtor and AHS founder Jim Kern after a sojourn on the Appalachian Trail in the early 1960s. Wanting to create long-distance hiking trails in his home state, he founded the Florida Trail Association. In 1966, FTA volunteers began blazing this trail. Today, the FTA works vigorously in close partnership with the Forest Service in Florida to maintain and connect this trail to other trails throughout Florida.

1986 – NEZ PERCE (NEE-ME-POO) NHT

An Appaloosa rider explores the Montana grasslands along the Nez Perce (Nee-Me-Poo) NHT. Photo copyright Bart Smith, used with permission.

This trail memorializes the 1877 forced march of the Nez Perce people when they fled their homeland to escape the United States Army. Tensions over land rights between white settlers and the Nez Perce nation were growing in the 1870s. When violence erupted, many Nez Perce attempted to flee to Canada in hopes of living in peace again. Their circuitous journey from eastern Oregon through Idaho and Montana — during which they fought and generally outwitted the pursuing Army forces — ended at the Bear Paw Mountains in Montana. Cold and decimated, they were forced to surrender there. Today, visitors to the Nez Perce NHT can reflect on this tragedy that befell the native people while taking in a variety of impressive landscapes. The trail connects 38 sites managed by NPS as the Nez Perce National Historical Park. The trail, however, is administered by the Forest Service in partnership with the Nez Perce Trail Foundation.

1987 – SANTA FE NHT

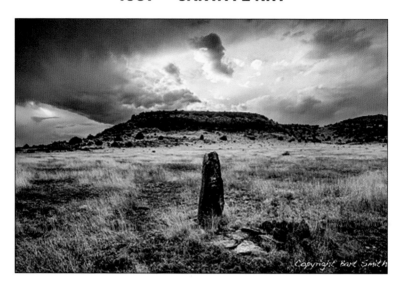

This desolate section of the Santa Fe NHT was captured by photographer Bart Smith. Copyrighted and used with his permission.

Representing a blending of cultures and communities, the Santa Fe NHT holds a mythical place in America's collective memory. This route has long been a trail of popular interest and folklore. In 1821, it first opened as a trade route between the western edge of the United States and newly independent Mexico. It quickly became an international commercial highway and military road for decades mixing cultures: Spanish, *mestizo*, Anglo, Cheyenne, Arapaho, Kiowa, Comanche, Osage, Kansas, Ute, and Jicarilla Apache. At the conclusion of the Mexican-American War in 1848, the trail connected the United States and their newly acquired southwestern territories. Throughout its history, the trail hosted freight wagons, stage coaches, emigrants, traders, and fur traders. NPS, as trail administrator, and the Santa Fe Trail Association work together to maintain the trail, promoting and preserving its physical landscape and historical legacy.

1987 – TRAIL OF TEARS NHT

Members of the Trail of Tears Association dedicate a new sign along the
Trail of Tears NHT. NPS photo.

This trail also commemorates Indian removal. It was added to the National Trails System in 1987 at the 150th anniversary of the Cherokee Removal and retraces the routes used by the U.S. Army to forcibly remove the Cherokee and other native peoples from their homelands in Tennessee, North Carolina, Georgia, and Alabama to Indian Territory in present-day Oklahoma. Nearly one-fifth of the Cherokee nation died in the holding forts and during the journey. In 2009, 2,845 miles of additional routes were added (after an appropriate feasibility study) to tell the fuller story of this complex and tragic chapter of American history. Today, the trail consists of an interstate skein of routes — some overland and a few by river routes — representing the many different ways that the evacuation took place. The trail is administered by NPS in close cooperation with the Trail of Tears Association. Both parties, and many other partners along the way, are devoted to the protection, preservation, development, and interpretation of the trail. At many sites, visitors learn of the effects of the U.S. Government's Indian Removal policy on native peoples, including the Cherokee, the Chickasaw, Choctaw, Muskogee Creek, and Seminole tribes.

1990 – JUAN BAUTISTA DE ANZA NHT

The route of the Juan Bautista de Anza NHT near Tumacocari National Historical Park in southern Arizona. Photo copyright Bart Smith, used with permission.

This trail follows the 1775–6 journey of a Spanish frontier governor who guided a military guard, several church fathers, and 200 settlers and their stock from Sonora, Mexico, to colonize the Golden Gate for Spain. Throughout the journey, this plucky expedition suffered rough weather, lack of water, and even an earthquake. Remarkably, only one person perished. This expedition established the Presidio of what is today's San Francisco, California, along with the missions at San Francisco de Asis (Mission Dolores) and Santa Clara de Asis. The trail was strongly promoted by George Cardinet, a longtime equestrian trail enthusiast in California. He founded the nonprofit group Amigos de Anza that is dedicated to the preservation and protection of the trail. Twice — in 1976 and again in 1996 — riders reenacted the journey from Mexico to California, riding horses and wearing appropriate period outfits. The trail was added to the National Trails System in 1990 and is administered by NPS.

1992 – CALIFORNIA NHT

Lightning strikes along the California NHT at City of Rocks National Reserve
in southern Idaho. Photo copyright Bart Smith, used with permission.

The California NHT traces many of the routes that gold seekers (known then as "49ers") followed to California between 1849 and 1852. After the discovery of gold in late 1848 at Sutter's Mill, a flood of 250,000 novice prospectors and settlers headed west to California from many points in the East. The trail starts in a variety of places along the western shore of the Missouri River and merges onto the earlier Oregon and Mormon Pioneer routes in Nebraska's Platte River Valley. On the far side of the Continental Divide at South Pass, the trail braids as the 49ers raced west on the best routes they could find. There are over a dozen ending points in the California goldfields. All these routes total more than 5,600 miles in combined lengths. The trail is administered by NPS, and much hard work is carried out by volunteers to mark, map, and maintain the historic and auto tour routes. The Oregon-California Trails Association is integral to this trail's survival.

1992 – PONY EXPRESS NHT

Getting ready for the annual Pony Express re-ride at the Patee House Hotel in St. Joseph, Missouri. Photo copyright Bart Smith, used with permission.

The Pony Express NHT follows the route ridden by young men on horseback who delivered the nation's mail on the eve of the Civil War. A legendary aspect of the Old West, the Pony Express mail delivery service linked St. Joseph, Missouri, to San Francisco, California. It operated only 19 months, from April 1860 to November 1861. Yet, despite its short life, the Pony Express delivered 34,000 pieces of mail. Messages that once took six weeks to reach their destination could be delivered in 10 days via these tenacious riders. Once the Civil War began, a string of telegraph wires soon rendered the Pony Express obsolete by cutting transcontinental delivery time to an instant. In present times, the National Pony Express Association keeps the memory and mystique of the storied riders alive by protecting and preserving the trail and also organizing an annual re-ride between St. Joseph and Sacramento — eastbound one year and westbound the next. This 24-hour-a-day nonstop ride lasts for ten days. The trail is administered by NPS.

1996 – SELMA TO MONTGOMERY NHT

Walking Classroom staff and participants arrive in Montgomery, Alabama on March 25, 2015, commemorating the 50th anniversary of the Selma to Montgomery March. Photo courtesy of Joel Cadoff, NPS Incident Command Team.

This trail commemorates the voting rights struggle in central Alabama in the mid-1960s, a struggle that galvanized the Nation. On Sunday, March 7, 1965 the marchers – trained in non-violence and wishing to carry the coffin of a recently slain civil rights advocate to the State Capitol in Montgomery – started out from Selma across the Edmund Pettus Bridge. On the far side they were attacked by state troopers wielding tear gas and clubs. The procession turned back, bloodied, but not defeated. Eyewitness TV news of the attack captured worldwide attention. Outraged by the severe violence used against peaceful protestors, thousands came to join the cause. Assisted by a court order, a subsequent march began on March 21, now under the protection of state and federal law enforcement. The five-day march along Highway 80 ended at the State Capitol where Dr. Martin Luther King, Jr., movingly addressed the huge crowd. Two months later, the Voting Rights Act of 1965 was passed and signed into law. This route has also been designated an All-American Road by the U.S. Secretary of Transportation. The Trail is administered by the NPS.

2000 – EL CAMINO REAL DE TIERRA ADENTRO NHT

A replica caretta like those used along El Camino Real de Tierra Adentro NHT.
Photo copyright Bart Smith, used with permission.

This route is one of North America's oldest and longest colonial roads. It served as the route of settlers, priests, and traders coming north from Mexico City to the edge of the Spanish Empire hard against the Rocky Mountains. Over time, it became a blending of Native-American, Colonial Mexican, and American cultures. Trade and travel that took place on this trail shaped America's Southwest, encouraging economic stability and permeating cultural barriers. This route began as a chain of Native-American trails that was linked together by the Spanish in 1598, connecting the capital of Mexico to northern provincial outposts and towns. After Mexican independence in 1821, it became an extension south for traders on the Santa Fe Trail. In the 1840s, American troops followed it to invade Mexico in the Mexican-American War. Administered jointly by NPS and BLM, the trail is supported by El Camino Real Trail Association (CARTA), which works closely with El Camino Real International Heritage Center near Socorro, New Mexico.

2000 – ALA KAHAKAI NHT

Hikers thread the smooth stone surface of the 600-year old
Ala Kahakai NHT in Hawaii. 2009 photo by author.

Featuring ancient cultural remains, this 175-mile footpath links numerous communities, prehistoric, and historic sites around the shoreline of the Big Island of Hawai'i. Cultural highlights include royal centers, *heiau* (temples), *loko 'ia* (fishponds), *ko'a* (fishing shrines), and *wahi pana* (sacred places). The rise of Hawai'ian king Kamehameha I and the death of renowned British sea captain James Cook took place along this trail. Its natural resources include coastal vegetation, tropical ecosystems, migratory birds, and several threatened and endangered endemic species of plants and animals. The trail's establishment was championed by Hawai'ian Senators Daniel Akaka and Daniel Inouye, and today it is administered by NPS. Two nonprofit groups, E Mau Na Ala Hele ("to perpetuate the trails") and the Ala Kahakai Trail Association, work together to make this trail a cherished route of Hawai'ian heritage.

2002 – OLD SPANISH NHT

The Old Spanish NHT runs alongside the Virgin River in this
desolate corner of northeast Arizona. NPS photo.

Some of the most remote and barren landscapes of North America are crossed by the Old Spanish NHT. This route followed a succession of Native-American footpaths to form several mule-train trading paths between Santa Fe and Los Angeles in the period between Mexican Independence and the Mexican American War (1821–1848). Slowly moving mule train caravans carried wool and woolen goods west in trade for horses. It was not a settlers' route and was too rough for wheeled wagons — yet it enhanced trade across the country. In addition, parts of the trail saw Indian slave trade fueled by raids that took place in neighboring regions. The aftermath of this slave trade was felt in native communities for many years after the trail fell into disuse. American explorers, such as John C. Fremont, used parts of it. NPS and BLM share administrative responsibilities and work cooperatively with the Old Spanish Trail Association to protect and interpret the trail.

2004 – EL CAMINO REAL DE LOS TEJAS NHT

These swales along El Camino de los Tejas NHT northeast of Austin, Texas,
show how many years of use wore into the landscape. NPS photo.

Measuring more than 2,500 miles in Texas and Louisiana, this braided trail carried missionaries, soldiers, and settlers who established presidios, missions, and settlements throughout Texas, right up to the edge of French influence in the early 18th Century. This network of routes commemorates the Spanish Royal Road that tied Mexico City to the northeast edge on the Spanish frontier in present-day Louisiana. The road impacted many peoples and cultures and served as an agent for cultural diffusion, biological exchange, and communication for many years. According to NPS, "use of El Camino Real de los Tejas fostered a mix of Spanish and Mexican traditions, laws, and traditions with those of the United States, resulting in a rich legacy reflected in the people, natural and built landscapes, places names, languages, music, and arts of Texas and Louisiana today." The trail is administered by NPS and is supported by El Camino Real de los Tejas National Historic Trail Association.

2006 – CAPTAIN JOHN SMITH CHESAPEAKE NHT

Paddlers surround a copy of Capt. John Smith's shallop near Port Deposit, Maryland, along the Captain John Smith Chesapeake NHT, 2009. NPS photo by Lucia Degen.

First explored in 1608 by Jamestown settler John Smith, this all-water route winds around the edges of the Chesapeake Bay and up many of its tributaries to the first rapids. Captain John Smith was a controversial leader who helped establish the first successful British colony on American soil at Jamestown in 1607. The trail combines three different explorations by Smith and his crew in a 28-foot shallop (a type of sail-rigged longboat) during the summer of 1608. Today, more than 60 government and private agencies are responsible for making this trail a reality. It provides an opportunity for strong conservation and environmental action since its founding members were associated with The Conservation Fund, the National Geographic Society, and the Chesapeake Bay Foundation. Visitors in sailboats, motorboats, and kayaks can retrace the 1608 expeditions. Interactive buoys help provide trail interpretation. The trail is administered by NPS with strong support by the Chesapeake Conservancy.

2008 – STAR-SPANGLED BANNER NHT

Uniformed re-enactors light cannon at Fort McHenry in Baltimore, Maryland, to illustrate climactic scenes from the Star-Spangled Banner NHT. NPS photo.

This trail consists largely of water trail routes in the Potomac, Patuxent, and Patapsco Rivers and features the site near Baltimore, Maryland, where the national anthem was written. Toward the end of the War of 1812, in the summer if 1814, British forces invaded the United States after a long series of provocations and trade disputes. British forces in the Chesapeake Bay overwhelmed the small American navy and marched into Washington, DC, where most of the public buildings were burned. President and Mrs. Madison barely escaped to Virginia with the important papers of government. The British retreated to their ships and sailed north to lay siege to Baltimore, a port famous for its anti-British privateers. After being rebuffed at the Battle of North Point, the British started a 25-hour bombardment of Fort McHenry, the fortified gateway to the city's harbor. The fort held firm, and its survival was symbolized by a huge American flag flown at dawn. American lawyer Francis Scott Key, on board a British prison ship negotiating freedom for a client, saw the flag from afar and was inspired to write the poem "The Defense of Fort McHenry." Set to music, it eventually became the national anthem in 1931. The trail is administered by NPS in close coordination with the Chesapeake Conservancy.

2009 — ARIZONA NST

A saguaro cactus forest is found along the Arizona NST.
Photo copyright Bart Smith, used with permission.

The 800-mile Arizona NST was explored and laid out by a teacher from Flagstaff, Dale Shewalter, in 1985. He aimed to create a primitive trail for hiking, horseback riders, mountain biking, and even cross-country skiing, showcasing the wide variety of mountain ranges and ecosystems in the backcountry of Arizona. The Arizona NST spans the entire state from its northern to southern borders, connects five mountain ranges, and crosses the Grand Canyon just east of Grand Canyon Village. Along the way, it traverses four national parks and four national forests. Construction of the trail was completed just before national designation was sought. This trail is administered by the Forest Service in close cooperation with the Arizona Trail Association.

2009 – NEW ENGLAND NST

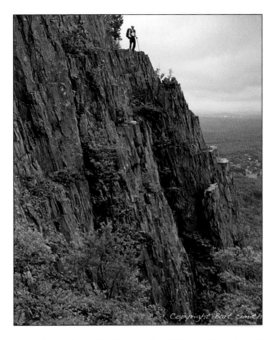

A craggy overlook above the Connecticut River valley along the New
England NST. Photo copyright Bart Smith, used with permission.

This trail combines three New England trails that date from the 1930s
— the Metacomet-Monadnock Trail, the Mettabessett Trail, and the
Metacomet Trail — into a 215-mile route linking together 41 communities
in Connecticut and Massachusetts. A new segment — the Menunkatuck
Trail — links these trails to the shore of Long Island Sound. The combined pathway explores iconic New England landscapes along both the
western and eastern ridges of the Connecticut River Valley, known there
as the Pioneer Valley. Its establishment as an NST and protection were
strongly supported by Representative John Olver (D-MA). Since designation, segments in Massachusetts have been relocated from private lands
to state-owned public lands. This trail is administered by NPS in close
cooperation with the Connecticut Forest and Park Association and the
Berkshire Chapter of the Appalachian Mountain Club.

2009 – WASHINGTON-ROCHAMBEAU REVOLUTIONARY ROUTE NHT

Revolutionary-period re-enactors in 2006 commemorate the 225th anniversary of the Battle of Yorktown in Virginia, climax of the Washington-Rochambeau Revolutionary Route NHT. NPS photo.

The "W3R" Trail commemorates the contribution that French armed forces made in helping Americans win the American War of Independence. Landing in July 1780, in Newport, Rhode Island, French General Rochambeau spent the winter there with his troops. The next summer, these forces, with artillery, moved across the Connecticut hills to join George Washington's forces at Philipsburg, New York. By this time, British General Cornwallis had brought his forces to the Yorktown Peninsula in Virginia. Sensing a strategic opportunity, Generals Washington and Rochambeau moved their forces south as quickly as possible, arriving in time to lay siege to the British and force a surrender, ending the war on the American mainland. The French then headed back north in July 1782, arriving in Boston in December where ships took them to the Caribbean. By then, all hostilities had ceased, and ships carried them back to France. Administered by NPS in close cooperation with W3R-U.S., this trail serves as an American Revolutionary War sequel to the Overmountain Victory NHT in the South.

2009 – PACIFIC NORTHWEST NST

A precarious stream crossing along the Pacific Northwest NST.
Photo copyright Bart Smith, used with permission.

The Pacific Northwest NST is a rugged backcountry hiking trail that connects three national parks, six national forests, and many wilderness areas
near the U.S. northwest border. It was first scouted out by Ron Strickland
in the early 1980s. The trail's feasibility study stated that the route was possible, but that it met no recreational need. Even so, the Pacific Northwest
Trail Association persisted, and the trail is now part of the National Trails
System and is largely built out, providing hikers from around the world
access to some of the most scenic and rugged landscapes in North America.
In addition, the PNTA has become a national leader in innovative youth
programs. The trail is administered by the Forest Service.

CHAPTER 6

BRINGING APPALACHIAN TRAIL PROTECTION TO LIFE

In . . . 7½ years the States, the U.S. Forest Service, and even our own hiking clubs have purchased land and obtained easements to protect the [Appalachian] Trail. But in those same 7½ years the National Park Service, which is the agency charged with primary responsibility for the trail, has acquired not 1 acre of land or obtained a single easement for protection of this trail. (Ed Garvey, 1976) [1]

President Nixon's appointee as Assistant Secretary of the Interior for Fish, Wildlife, and Parks, Nathaniel Reed, has stated:

. . . shortly after I became Assistant Secretary in May '71, I met rather mid-level staff members of the Park Service who came to brief me on the Park Service's responsibilities and actions under the National Trails Act. It became very apparent within minutes that it [the Trails System] *was the "brown chicken in the barn," that it was getting little attention and little financial support and little direction. That was understandable — if you understand the tremendous pressures on the Park Service in 1971. The Service was growing leaps and bounds. I cannot at this moment give you the names of the parks, the gateways, New York, Golden Gate in California, San Francisco, expansion. . . . George Hartzog, dynamic Director of the Park Service, considered that the highest priority that he had* [was Alaska land issues].

---

1. Ed Garvey in U.S. House of Representatives, 1976, *Oversight Hearings Before the Subcommittee on National Parks and Recreation . . . on the National Trails System Act of 1968*, etc., March 11–12, 1976, Washington, DC: GPO, Serial No. 94-50, p. 64, in NTSAHA.

[About 1972] . . . *I began to meet with regional proponents* [of trails] — *individuals who were deeply concerned about the loss of momentum in moving the Federal Government to acquire rights of way or fee simple areas needed to protect the National Trails System. They elevated my interest to the regional directors of the Park Service with a series of memoranda saying, "You are not complying with the Act."* . . . *I think I was unique in government, certainly in the Nixon administration. There was a constant stream of both representatives of the major and minor environmental organizations plus those activists who were really interested in the well-being of an individual park. They were always welcome to come in. So the Wilderness Act and the Trails Act.* . . . *It was a madhouse. There were people coming from every corner of the United States on Tuesdays, Wednesdays, and Thursdays.* . . . *First of all, the Park Service didn't know everything. Second of all, headquarters was resistant to trails.* [They were not] *spending money on trails because there were bigger fish to fry. And third, the NGOs, Wilderness Society, Wildlife Federation, Sierra Club and surely the National Parks and Conservation Association* [considered trails] *nowhere near as important then as they are now under the current direction. They had individuals who literally lived within those parks, and so they knew where the visitors should go by vehicle and where and what parts of the parks "should be left quiet and never touched" (that marvelous language of the Wilderness Act). So out of that came more and more people from the individual trails who would come in and say we are really hung up on the Sierra Trail or we are hung up on the Rocky Mountain Trail or.* . . . *I began to get apoplectic, and I began to look at the budget and at the rate that the Park Service was applying its Land and Water Conservation Fund to acquire easements for full fee — you could forget the National Trails System.* [2]

Nathaniel Reed, no date. Photo courtesy National Archives II, College Park, Maryland.

Assistant Secretary Reed came under increasing pressure to protect the Appalachian Trail using the authorities of the National Trails System Act. In 1975, he was invited to give a major speech at the Appalachian

---

2. Nat Reed, 2007, NPS Oral History interview, NTS 40th Anniversary Oral History Project, pp. 2–3 and 4–6.

Trail Conference's 50th anniversary gathering in Boone, North Carolina. Years later, he remembered that:

. . . while serving as Assistant Secretary . . . I had agreed to speak to the Appalachian Trail Conference. . . . I arrived to find this speech that had been prepared by the Park Service which I refused to give. I sat on the floor with yellow pads and scratched out a memorable speech where I committed the Office of the Assistant Secretary and the National Park Service to seek far greater funding and to accelerate not only the Appalachian Trail, but the system of trails across the United States.

I had no authority to make this promise without having cleared it first with the Office of Management and Budget, but I did it. I'll never forget when I got back to Washington, the head of OMB called me (it might even have been Cap Weinberger or James Lind) and he said, "We read in The New York Times and in the Boston newspapers about your pledge including, you know Nathaniel, you really shouldn't be pledging X number of millions of dollars without clearing it. But, on the other hand, it was very funny. On the other hand, it's really time to get the trail business going. We are all sitting around here chewing up your ass — yet at the same time, we are all looking at each other and saying 'God, the [trails] act passed years ago, and what a good legacy it would be for President Ford. And we should put our imprimatur on it.'

So that next budget cycle was very important to the acceleration of the land acquisition policy that the Park Service then carried forward. I'm rather proud of that. I still meet people (this is really unbelievable) all these years later that will come up (and this has happened a dozen times) and say, "You know, that speech that you gave at the Appalachian Trail dinner, they stood up on chairs!" . . . I'm not kidding, the place went upsy. It must have been one hell of a fight speech, because people were standing on chairs, throwing glasses against the wall. They had waited so long, and there were so many pitfalls and deadfalls that had been put in their way. At last somebody said, "We're cutting out all the crap, we are going to achieve finalization . . . " [3]

But the National Park Service was resistant. From Reed's perspective: *The Park Service wasn't looking forward to getting into the middle of lengthy, thin trails with adjacent landowners for miles and miles and miles. Man, the Lewis and Clark route went through ranchland, crossed mountains and rivers. Oh my god, what*

---

3. *Ibid.*, pp. 7–8.

are you getting? It just sounds so easy, it sounds so good, it sounds like something that America should want to do. And then you sit down and begin to design where the trail is and how it should be protected, and it's a hornets' nest. . . . And it's multiple states, it's counties, it's, in some cases, cities, county, state, everybody had a different idea of how that adjacent property should be acquired in fee or in easement — what do we do? [4]

Development pressure was building, threatening the Appalachian Trail. One trail activist at that time recalled later:

I got to know about the Trail. One thing that was very clear at that time, the trail was getting eaten away by development. That's 30 years ago. But still, the proponents of the Appalachian Trail recognized at that time that if they didn't get this thing on the ground permanently, instead of by handshake permission or whatever, it would never be a continuous thing. So the PATC at that time was actively involved in buying land for the trail. Being a land lawyer, I got involved in their land acquisition activities. We bought scattered parcels. But it was just "a lick and a promise" as far as really protecting the trail. So the PATC, if you read the testimony, was very instrumental in promoting the 1978 amendments to the Trails Act that actually funded the AT. [5]

Under increasing pressure to get the National Park Service to demonstrably help protect the Appalachian Trail, the House Subcommittee on National Parks and Recreation was persuaded to hold hearings in 1976. One version of how these hearings occurred was recounted years later by one of the Subcommittee's staffers, Cleve Pinnix:

Highway construction disfiguring the Appalachian NST in the 1970s. Photo courtesy ATC.

And, apparently, the [House National Parks] *Subcommittee* [chaired by Roy Taylor (D-NC)] *had for some time gotten contacts from some of the organized trail*

---

4. *Ibid.*, p. 10.
5. Jim Snow, 2007, NPS Oral History interview, NTS 40th Anniversary Oral History Project, p. 3.

*users on the Appalachian Trail — and they were not very happy with the initial imple-
mentation of the 1968 Act. So my first exposure to the Act and the program was as
our subcommittee began to meet with interest groups to gather information. That led to
oversight hearings the subcommittee carried out . . . [on], March 11th and 12th, 1976,
when the subcommittee carried out two days of oversight hearings on the National Trails
System Act. That was a really interesting learning experience for me, because I had not
had any real understanding of the Act.*

*What we heard from people with the Appalachian Trail Conference and with some
of the member clubs is that they felt that the Department of the Interior — and the
National Park Service as the lead agency — had not done what they and Congress
had intended with the 1968 Act. They expected there would have been a program of
land acquisition on the Appalachian Trail to protect the trail corridor. In fact, the Park
Service had not started and done any land acquisition in that by then, about eight years
later. From the perspective of these trail users not much had happened. . . . There was
an expectation that the National Park Service was going to be acquiring private lands
along the right-of-way corridor for the Appalachian Trail. That was one of the moti-
vating features of the Act. While the Appalachian Trail ran through national park and
national forest lands, the trail corridor also went through a lot of private land as well.
Some of the original impetus for the '68 Act was to see that these trails could have protected landscapes in which people could be assured of a quality recreational experience.*

*I remember a meeting where the Park Service staff looked us straight in the face and
said, "Well, there was never any intention that there would be federal land acquisitions
under the original act." But everything we could find in the records indicated differently.
There was a fair amount of tension between the subcommittee members and the agency
folks, because, from our perspective, they were not carrying out the intent of Congress.
I think to be fair to the agency folks, the Administration had changed by then. I think
they were operating under probably more restrained policies about willingness of that
Administration to spend federal money on recreation and conservation lands. So I think
they were doing what bureaucrats have to do.*

*One of the things I got as I went back and looked at the '76 hearings is that some of
the same people who were critical of National Park Service were quite complimentary
to U.S. Forest Service at the same time. From their perspective, the Forest Service
had moved with more alacrity in implementing the Act and had done some significant*

land acquisitions to protect corridors on the Appalachian Trail. Elsewhere, they felt that basically the people in Agriculture took the Act more seriously than the people in Interior. It's their impression (and I can't say that I know all about that), but it was very interesting to hear that it seemed like within the Federal establishment perhaps some cabinet agencies were doing more than others in terms of implementing some of those acts.

So it appeared that Interior's way of trying to divert some of the Congressional pressure was to say, "Gee, we think we can maybe do something dramatic in freeing up some matching funds, encourage some of the states to acquire more, and expect that that's going to take care of people's concerns."

In fact, . . . there were some people in land acquisition for National Park Service that had early on been . . . saying, "Oh, you know, Congress never really intended us to do much of this." I think that was the line they were expected to use. Some of those same people came around and actually did some really terrific work, the really difficult job of getting a protective corridor established. In terms of controversy, the heart of a lot of that stuff in the '76 hearings was about the agency not having moved forward as much as people felt that it should. To its credit, that agency really responded. It was Dave Richie, but not in a vacuum. I think other people in the agency stepped up as well. And I think agency leadership also, over time, stepped up and got that done. [6]

During the Watergate years of 1973 to 1975, most federal government action came to a standstill. Then, as the air cleared, oversight hearings were held for the Trails System Act in 1976 to track progress on the now eight-year-old system in the face of various bills requesting additional trail studies. House Subcommittee Chairman Roy Taylor (D-NC) opened the hearings by stating, "Before we add studies to the act, we need to understand the progress of the

Cleve Pinnix as shown in the proceedings for the 4th National Trails Symposium Proceedings, 1977. In NTSAHA.

6. Cleve Pinnix, 2007, NPS Oral History interview, NTS 40th Anniversary Oral History Project, pp. 3–7, 18.

program so far." On the Sunday before the hearings, many of the sub-committee members enjoyed a hike together on the Appalachian Trail.

The hearing opened with Assistant Interior Secretary Nathaniel Reed giving his department's perspective on the status of the 14 trail studies. He continued:

I believe that there is good justification for designating a limited number of these long-distance trails. There certainly is a demand and need for trails. . . . Also, this Nation should be able to afford the assurance that our most scenic and historic routes will be preserved. But we also recognize that it takes a considerable time to get these trails established. It takes much effort on the part of many — and, in some instances, substantial funding.

Then he spelled out how the Appalachian Trail Project was being implemented. He introduced newly selected David Richie as NPS coordinator for the trail and emphasized how federal funds used for land acquisition were being leveraged in some interested states in ratios as high as four-to-one. [7]

These hearings went on to address many related issues: Forest Service and National Park Service trail activities, the vulnerability of the Appalachian Trail outside federal area boundaries, disappointment that the National Park Service had not yet acquired any land to protect the Appalachian Trail, the potential of converting abandoned rail lines to recreational trail use, the dogged commitment of volunteers, the recent death of Benton MacKaye at age 96, the proposed category of historic trails, adequate trail corridor width, the importance of the Land and Water Conservation Fund and other funding sources for trails, the effectiveness of advisory committees, motorized trail uses, and landowner liability. [8]

One immediate result of the 1976 hearings was the first amendment to the NTSA, signed into law October 17, 1976 (PL 94-527), requesting an additional eight trail feasibility studies — the Bartram, Daniel Boone, Desert, Dominguez-Escalante, Florida, Indian Nations, Nez Perce, and Pacific Northwest Trails. [9]

---

7. U.S. House of Representatives, 1976, *Oversight Hearings Before the Subcommittee on National Parks and Recreation . . . on the National Trails System Act of 1968,* etc., March 11–12, 1976, Washington, DC: GPO, Serial No. 94-50, p. 1 and pp. 4–9, in NTSAHA.
8. *Ibid,* entire document.
9. Public Law 94-527, 1976, An Act to amend the National Trails System, etc., in NTSAHA.

The hiring of David A. Richie at about this time was a fundamental change that influenced both the Appalachian Trail and the National Trails System for years to come. As Cleve Pinnix assessed it later:

And during the time when we were doing this oversight effort and Congress began to focus more attention, the Park Service (I think very wisely) made that full-time commitment for Dave [Richie]. I think Dave was a visionary. He was a person that understood that there was an opportunity here with the Trails System to have a type of area that really should be something different from a long, skinny National Park. So I think it was Richie who really began to forge the long-term relationship with the Appalachian Trail Conference. He thought for the first time seriously about actually sharing the management responsibility. That is a very scary change for people who think about the superintendent as God Almighty in a square national park. So the National Park Service went through a sea change during that time for a period of several years while Dave Richie had the job. My own view is that the Park Service would not have made the progress it has made in past years without Richie being in that place at that time. I think he was instrumental in that change. [10]

Despite the paralysis of the Watergate era, it was during these early years of the National Trails System that the groundwork was laid on several different fronts for what would become a remarkable set of amendments to the NTSA. Not only were authorities pertaining to NSTs strengthened, but the Trails System was enriched with a new type of trail — one for which there was no established model or completed trail — national historic trails (NHTs).

10. Cleve Pinnix, 2007, NPS Oral History interview, NTS 40th Anniversary Oral History Project, pp. 7–8, 18.

DAVE RICHIE

David Richie, NPS Project Manager for the
Appalachian Trail Project Office from 1974 to 1987.

DAVE RICHIE is not your traditional person. He is not your traditional superintendent. He had been superintendent of parks, but he was not your traditional "parkie" — he didn't think that way. Dave Richie's appointment to the Appalachian Trail came at the right time, because Dave was creative. He thought outside the box. Dave was responsible for the agreement between the National Park Service and the Appalachian Trail Conference that provides annual funds to the Appalachian Trail Conference to aid in the management and maintenance of the Trail. A lot of people were critical of that. They said it shouldn't be. But, in my opinion, that's the best way to manage the Trail. You do not want to put your traditional maintenance people and park rangers and so on out on this Trail.

. . . Dave was a pain in the butt. He would change his mind frequently. In fact, the last person that he talked to, he would change his mind. He would drive me crazy. But he was the right person and he was finally settled in on something. The other issue with Dave was [easements]. . . . Well, easements work in

some places. The National Park Service has had extremely poor experience with easements. When the Blue Ridge Parkway and the Colonial National Park were authorized, there were a lot of easements required. Easements need to be managed. The person that you acquire the easement from knows what the restrictions are. When they sell that land to someone else, they seem to forget about it. The next thing you know you've got a house built on your easement area. And you can't get it removed. It is too late, you can't get it removed.

Well, Dave Richie was an easement person. And we had what was called a "right-of-way" easement and a "protective" easement. A right-of-way easement was that area right adjacent to the trail, and a protective easement was a kind of an easement to protect the right-of-way easement. And on the protective easement we had no rights to enter that property. It strictly prohibits the landowner from doing certain things. But we would not buy the right for hikers on the protective easement. With the right-of-way easement we were buying the right to put the hiker there. I was able to develop a right-of-way easement that was so tight that my kids, their kids and their kids would not have any problem enforcing it. It was very simple. I said the only rights you are retaining are those that are specifically mentioned herein. Nothing else. But I will reserve you the right to pay taxes. As a result of that, we would pay 105% and 110% of fee value for the right-of-way easement, because we were obligating the landowner to pay taxes forever and really had no more rights than the walking public. So it was a while before Dave could see that this was not the way to go. [11]

11. Chuck Rinaldi, 2007, NPS Oral History interview, NTS 40th Anniversary Oral History Project, pp. 11–12.

CHAPTER 7
WRAPPING UP THE FIRST DECADE 1976–1979

Trails can become the backbone of a system of national recreational opportunity when we also plan for and we protect the unique historic, natural, and scenic features that the trails connect. Recreational trails must not be seen as marathon courses, but as a means of providing an opportunity for historic and natural protection of the highest order and the opportunity for the private citizen to gain a "sense of place" through being part of the Trail management program. (Paul Pritchard, 1976) [1]

C leve Pinnix, staff assistant to Chairman Taylor, recalled the impact of the 1976 hearings years later:

One of the things that we heard in the '76 hearings was an increasing interest in adding trails that were more about historic preservation — historic interpretation, I think, is really a better term for it. Where the initial act had contemplated national scenic trails, there was an increasing amount of interest in trails that could represent pathways to the Nation's history — such things as the Lewis and Clark Trail. It is a kind of premier example, but there were a number of others. In those oversight hearings we heard about that from a number of witnesses from the National Trust for Historic Preservation to the local historic groups — interest groups that had gotten the idea that here was a way to both commemorate history and foster some recreation opportunity as well. In some cases, the intention was not necessarily that you would have a physical trail on the ground for

---

1. Paul Pritchard, 1976, testimony in U.S. House of Representatives, *Oversight Hearings Before the Subcommittee on National Parks and Recreation . . . on the National Trails System Act of 1968*, etc., March 11–12, 1976, Washington, DC: GPO, Serial No. 94-50, p, 102 in NTSAHA.

102

a national historic trail, but you might have a marked route. Then, through that, you might do better interpretation of the historic events that made it significant. So we heard those kinds of things. My sense was that Chairman Taylor at the time felt that we had done some useful work by having the hearings, raising people's awareness, and getting the attention of the folks down in the Interior Department that they had work to do on the existing Act. So he wasn't interested in rushing into passing a bill necessarily. He felt like the oversight hearings themselves accomplished much of his purpose. [2]

In 1976, the birth of the American Hiking Society (AHS) — the first nationwide trails advocacy organization in the U.S. — highlighted the changes that were occurring from within private trail groups to build greater public awareness of and support for a balanced national trails system. Almost a decade after the NTSA became law, this band of hiking activists realized that in order to influence Congress, they should be organized on a national scale. Specifically, the founders of AHS sought to promote and protect hiking trail opportunities by working closely with federal land-managing agencies. [3]

Meanwhile, others were exploring new ways of building trails, namely the recycling of unused railroad corridors for recreational trails. The Citizens' Advisory Committee on Environmental Quality (which involved many of the same people who had served on the ORRRC effort almost 20 years before) conducted a systematic study of converting railroad beds to trails following passage of the Regional Rail Reorganization Act of 1973. Their 1974 report led directly to language in the 1976 Railroad Revitalization and Regulatory Reform Act that opened the

The Illinois Prairie Path, one of the first "rail-trails" in the U.S., a suburban interurban rail line converted to a recreational trail in the early 1960s. 1991 photo courtesy Openlands, Chicago, Illinois.

door to providing grants to states to preserve abandoned rail lines "for

---

2. Cleve Pinnix, 2007, NPS Oral History interview, NTS 40th Anniversary Oral History Project, p. 10.
3. The National Trails Council had been organized immediately after the 1971 symposium with the single mission of organizing more biennial meetings, not as an advocacy organization.

recreation and conservation uses." In a 1976 *Sports Illustrated* article, Robert Cantwell noted: "These smooth and gentle paths wandering through the mountains or along riverbanks may be the simplest, least expensive, and most practical recreational asset in the country." [4]

In 1976, the nation shifted party leadership again, moving away from the Watergate years under a failed Republican president to newcomer Democrat Jimmy Carter, former governor of Georgia. At the Department of the Interior, he appointed a Minnesotan named Bob Herbst to succeed Nat Reed as Assistant Secretary for Fish and Wildlife and Parks. Despite the change in political parties and philosophies, Herbst was just as eager to enhance protection of the Appalachian Trail as Reed had been. Two of his contemporaries tell the story:

President Jimmy Carter, no date. Photo courtesy National Archives II, College Park, Maryland.

"Cecil Andrus from Idaho became Secretary of the Interior under Carter. And Herbst was appointed as the lead policy person as Assistant Secretary. . . . Bob Herbst let us know early on that he was really committed to getting the Appalachian Trail on the map, that it was something that was personally important to him, and that he wanted to see that done." [5]

You know the [Appalachian] Trail is very fortunate in Carter having appointed Bob Herbst as Assistant Secretary at the time that he did . . . . He really gave the Appalachian Trail the direction from on top that was needed to make things happen. He really played a tremendous role. Dave Sherman worked for Bob Herbst. He was a special assistant. Dave Sherman was one of the people that Bob relied upon to keep him posted on the progress. . . . Dave actually took the maps and went out on the ground to make sure that we did do the protection that was needed and was expected. So he modified the acquisition areas here and there, because you don't always see everything from the maps. He

---

4. Robert Cantwell as quoted in Henry L. Diamond, 1976, "From Rails to Trails," *Outdoor Recreation Action*, Report No. 42, Winter, 1976, pp. 9–10, in NTSAHA.
5. Cleve Pinnix, 2007, NPS Oral History interview, NTS 40th Anniversary Oral History Project, p. 11.

actually went out on the ground and walked each parcel of land, and he added a number of acres to the Appalachian Trail program to perfect the protection program. [6]

In May of 1977, President Jimmy Carter delivered to Congress his "Environmental Message," addressing a wide variety of topics including pollution and human health, toxic chemicals, workplace hazards, air and water quality, solid waste and pest management, energy, urban revitalization, wetlands, sea coast barrier islands, mining, forest management, heritage preservation, additional wilderness areas, wild and scenic rivers, wildlife protection, and even global population controls. In a small section titled

Bob Herbst c. 1981.
Photo courtesy ATC.

"National Trails" he noted that nine years after passage of the National Trails System Act, only two trails — the Appalachian and the Pacific Crest NSTs — had been designated by Congress. He also noted that, in the meantime, other unprotected trails on public lands had become unusable. In an effort to broaden and restore the National Trails System, he promised to submit legislation to Congress to designate three new NSTs: the Continental Divide, the North Country, and the Potomac Heritage Trails. He also stated that in the near future he would present legislation establishing a category of national historic trails. [7]

A week after President Carter gave his Environmental Message, Assistant Secretary Bob Herbst spoke before the Appalachian Trail Conference in Shepherdstown, West Virginia. He pledged, "**We are ready and willing to use the authority to condemn land should there be no action on the part of the states to protect the area identified as that needed for the trail environment.**" (emphasis his) [8]

---

6. Chuck Rinaldi, 2007, NPS Oral History interview, NTS 40th Anniversary Oral History Project, p. 11.
7. President Jimmy Carter, May 23, 1977, *The Environmental Message to Congress,* text in NSTAHA courtesy The American Presidency Project.
8. Bob Herbst, May 28, 1977, "The Appalachian Trail – A Model for a National Trails System," *Remarks of the Hon. Robert L. Herbst . . . at the Appalachian Trail Conference, Shepherdstown, West Virginia,* in NTSAHA.

Later in 1977, the fourth National Trails Symposium was held in North Carolina. There, at a panel discussion about progress being made on the National Trails System, speakers asked why more hadn't been done to carry out the intent of the National Trails System Act — and they identified factors such as the complex and protracted feasibility study process, inadequate funds for trail corridor protection, inadequate incentives for recognizing more NRTs, the need to strengthen volunteer programs and citizen involvement, and lack of a system-wide plan. [9]

Creation of the category of national historic trails (NHTs) by an amendment to the NTSA in 1978 was the result of presidential action coupled with tireless work by many individuals, both inside the agencies and elsewhere. The drafting of amendment language, starting as far back as 1973, took official form in 1977 following the 1976 hearings. In a letter dated October 5, 1977, on behalf of Interior Secretary Andrus, Interior Undersecretary James Joseph officially transmitted draft legislation to Representative Morris Udall (D-AZ), Chairman of the House Interior Committee, requesting that the Oregon Trail be established as an NHT. The letter outlined the purpose of NHT designation as well as the rationale for historic trails as a category:

These trail routes, although important for their historic aspects, do not fit readily into the scenic trail mold. They are, however, significant routes which have played major roles in the history of our country. For that reason, and because certain segments of the routes can provide nationally significant interpretive/recreation opportunities and have high potential for enhancing the public's identification with the Nation's heritage, these routes merit Federal recognition. [10]

Bills were introduced by both Senators Orrin Hatch (R-UT) and the House committee chairman on behalf of the Secretary of the Interior defining the new category of national historic trails. Hearings were held May 1, 1978, by the Senate Subcommittee on Parks and Recreation to hear testimony on the category of historic trails and seven bills proposing to establish the Iditarod, Oregon, Lewis and Clark, and Mormon Pioneer

---

9. U.S. Department of the Interior and others, 1977, *Expanding America's Trail System, An Investment in Energy-wise Recreation, Fourth National Trails Symposium*, September 7–10, Lake Junaluska, NC, pp. 83–111.
10. Cecil D. Andrus, Interior Secretary, to Walter F. Mondale, President of the Senate, May 26, 1977, in NTSAHA.

NHTs. Some western senators were nervous about authorizing long, linear, park-like corridors across their states. Others insisted that the historic trails would consist mainly of marked routes and interpretive facilities. The historic trails need not be continuous, but would feature only remnant ruts and traces. For NSTs, Edward Garvey, author and Appalachian Trail activist, spoke as legislative representative for the new American Hiking Society and urged dismissal of the Forest Service's amendment to discontinue the use of eminent domain on the Pacific Crest NST. [11]

Subcommittee staffer Pinnix has provided an in-depth reminiscence about how the 1978 amendments occurred within the broader context of an omnibus bill filled with many other controversial issues:

The committee had a standing practice of doing what were called omnibus bills — they had for years — and there were generally a number of things that only Congress could do, but they were small-scale. If you wanted to have a boundary adjustment in a national park, that had to be established by Congress. Congress typically authorized money to be spent for land acquisitions or development purposes in a national park unit. They did that, and they capped the authorization. Well, time passes, things change, inflation comes along. So you might need to change those numbers. Those are kind of small scale things, but [they would be] necessary legislative enactments, which were often handled in omnibus bills where you would roll up small scale boundary changes and authorization increases. . . .

[Subcommittee chairman Phil] *Burton* [(D-CA)] *began to think that there was a way to get some big things done by having a bill that would take a lot of what members wanted done with small things and stitch them all together and put some big things in there with it. So, as we worked on other legislation —* Redwoods [National Park expansion] *and other things, he also began to look at the kind of workload the subcommittee had with these things. He decided that he was going to weld all those things into something much larger and much more extensive than anybody had ever seen. He was going to use that to carry through other changes in law that might be controversial in their own right. . . . But if you look at the enactments during that period, a number of changes to the Trails Act were done as part of omnibus bills. . . . Some of what we worked on at the time, if you look at the legislative history of this enormous bill that was called the "park barrel bill," in its final form*

---

11. U.S. Senate, 1978, Publication 95-126, *Hearing Before the Subcommittee for Parks and Recreation*, May 1, 1978.

it authorized something over a billion dollars in new Federal spending, which at the time, 30 years ago, was pretty unheard of.

In that bill you'll find that there are changes to the Trails Act. . . . So, some of the amendments to the National Trails System Act got rolled into this. In essence, these were some of the more agreed-upon provisions in the Act. I think this is where we added in the category of national historic trails. Leading up to this act, there were some separate hearings done on that. There were some members of Congress that had separate legisla-tion to do that, and all of that got rolled into this giant effort that Burton spearheaded to put things together.

If you are trying to trace the history of amendments to the Trails Act, you find that in some cases they're really pretty well buried. This big omnibus bill is a good example that actually in some ways it is pretty significant. It added this whole new category to the National Trails System. It added units to the national system and authorized studies. But you'd have to look inside this act to see it. One of the things you'd also find is that there's not as much legislative history for scholars these days because, unlike the way Congress operated before Burton — with pretty extensive hearings building a record and getting consensus — he was operating at a different level. He tended to say, "If some work has already been done on this in the past, if the committee has had hearings on this in the past, let's do something that's pretty cursory. And if we've got some agreement on members and the administration is agreeable, let's get it in there and get going. Let's not waste time on building a very extensive record for some things that are pretty well agreed upon . . . . ."

I think that we had separate legislation that went through in the 95th Congress, which would have probably gone through in 1978. That's where we got the $30 million appropriation authorization for the Appalachian Trail land acquisition over a three-year period. A $90 million land acquisition tag for a national park project in those days was enormous. It was one of the largest land acquisition costs authorized at that time for the National Park Service. . . . [12]

Two amendments to the National Trails System Act — both of which profoundly reshaped the National Trails System — were eventually

12. Cleve Pinnix, 2007, NPS Oral History interview, NTS 40th Anniversary Oral History Project, pp. 12–4.

passed in 1978. Both were based on the 1976 hearings when Appalachian Trail supporters strongly criticized the National Park Service for not adequately protecting the "AT." (P.L. 95-248 was also based on testimony given during Senate hearings held November 1, 1977.)

The first of these amendments, P.L. 95-248, was passed March 21, 1978, and authorized $30 million per year for three years to acquire land to protect the corridor of the Appalachian NST. It stated Congress's intent that land acquisition for that trail to be largely completed in three years. It also requested that the Secretaries of Agriculture and the Interior establish federal advisory councils for both the Appalachian and Pacific Crest NSTs. These councils would help to ensure that management of these national trails remained as uniform and publicly responsive as possible. In addition, the new law also expanded the use of eminent domain (when needed as a last resort) to an average of 125 acres per mile (from 25 acres per mile) and called for the preparation within two years of a comprehensive plan for the management, acquisition, development, and use of the Appalachian NST.

The second important set of amendments to the Trails Act that year, signed by President Carter on November 10, was part of a large omnibus bill, P.L. 95-625, called the National Parks and Recreational Lands Act of 1978. Among many other things (contained in 98 separate sections), this landmark act established the new category of national historic trails (NHTs) and added five new trails — the first in ten years — to the National Trails System: the Oregon, Mormon Pioneer, Lewis and Clark, and Iditarod NHTs, as well as the Continental Divide NST. Specific criteria were cited for evaluating historic trail routes under study and their significance was to be linked to the evaluation criteria of the Historic Sites Act of 1935.

One important feature of the authorizations for these new trails was the significant weakening of the original land acquisition authorities of the Trails Act by prohibiting federal agencies from spending funds to acquire lands for these new trails (with small exceptions). This restrictive language may have been a reaction, in part, to the sweeping land acquisition program authorized for the Appalachian NST earlier that year and the concerns of conservative western members of Congress that eminent domain and resources on that scale might someday target ranch lands in their states. This language restricting acquisition by federal agencies (known as the "Section 10(c) prohibitions") was applied to several later

NSTs and NHTs and had far-reaching effects in slowing the pace by which these trails were established on the ground. (These restrictions were eventually eliminated by amendments more than 30 years later in 2009.)

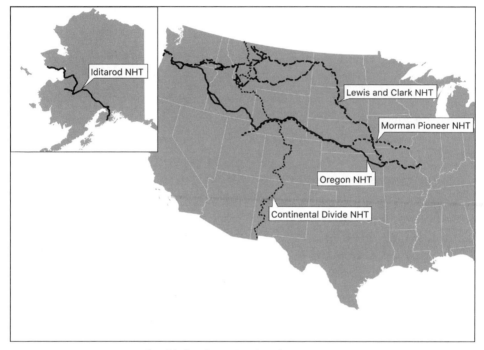

Trails Added to the National Trails System, 1978.

All of the new trails to be established in the 1978 amendments had been included among the 14 feasibility studies conducted by the Bureau of Outdoor Recreation. Table A below shows the trail studies conducted by BOR and NPS in the order they were completed. It also shows the order they were listed in the 1968 Act and indicates which studies led to trail designation.

In addition, Public Law 95-625 requested a feasibility study for the Overmountain Victory Trail and broadened the requirements for trail advisory councils to be established within one year of trail designation for all NSTs and NHTs. It also extended the requirement for a comprehensive plan to all the NSTs and NHTs established under the Trails Act.

After the addition of historic trails to the National Trails System, the direction of the system changed from an emphasis on long-distance backcountry hiking trails to a greater focus on historic trail preservation.

It should be noted that after the Natchez Trace, Potomac Heritage, and Florida NSTs were added in 1983, no more NSTs were added to the Trails System until 2009.

In fact, the [Appalachian] *Trail actually had a very low profile* [in the 1970s]. *The Appalachian Trail traverses many national forests and about, . . . six national park areas. Acquisition within those units continued, but outside those units actually literally nothing was being done. A couple of states did some acquisition, but not a great deal. So in 1977, I became the Director of Land Acquisition for the National Park Service. I became more directly involved in the Appalachian Trail and was participating in the development of the legislation, the amendatory legislation that was enacted in 1978. It was then that the Appalachian Trail really came to the forefront. I might add . . . that I think it is a blessing that acquisition did not take place between 1968 and 1978, because the original legislation was really inadequate. It talked about "eminent domain" being used to acquire land, 25 acres in a mile. This would give you a very narrow corridor. It would not have protected the environment. So we were fortunate, I think. Otherwise it would have been necessary to go back to previous landowners and acquire more land from them, and that is not a good scene. So in the legislation of 1978 the big change was that the "eminent domain" authority was increased to an average of 125 acres per mile. This really gave a lot of flexibility. . . . So your corridor might go from 200 feet wide to over a 1,000 feet wide, depending upon what the circumstances might be. So I was heavily involved in the initiation of the land acquisition program after the 1978 legislation.* [13]

And the additional appropriations for Appalachian Trail land acquisition by federal agencies helped continue the momentum established by Chuck Rinaldi, Dave Richie, and the ATC in protecting that trail from intrusions and unnecessary crossings. Meanwhile, the door opened with several significant and strongly-supported NHTs being established. Many more would be added over the coming decades.

---

13. Chuck Renaldi, 2007, NPS Oral History interview, NTS 40th Anniversary Oral History Project, pp. 2–3.

TABLE A
National Trails System Feasibility Studies 1968–1979

TRAIL NAME (in order listed in 1968)	COMPLETED	FOLLOW-UP ACTION
(1) Potomac Heritage	1973	Established as an NST in 1983
(13) Mormon Battalion	1974	
(3) Old Cattle Trails of the Southwest	1975	
(6) North Country	1975	Established as an NST in 1980
(7) Kittanning Path	1975	
(10) Long Trail	1975	
(9) Santa Fe	1976	Established as an NHT in 1987
(4) Lewis and Clark	1977	Established as an NHT in 1978
(8) Oregon	1977	Established as an NHT in 1978
(1) Continental Divide	1977	Established as an NST in 1978
(14) El Camino Real (Florida)	1977	
(12) Gold Rush Trails in Alaska	1977	Established as an NHT in 1978
(11) Mormon Pioneer	1978	Established as an NHT in 1978
(5) Natchez Trace	1979	Established as an NST in 1983

PHIL BURTON

Representative Phil Burton (center) speaking on Alcatraz Island,
California, in 1974. Photo courtesy Golden Gate NRA,
Park Archives, (image 35304-B 91-F2 #7.)

At the end of 1976, Roy Taylor retired. So the subcommittee was going to get a new chairman. The seniority on the subcommittee indicated that Chick Kazen from Texas was likely to be the next chairman. But what nobody expected was that Phil Burton — a member from San Francisco, California, who was the second ranking Democrat on the committee after Morris Udall — was appointed instead. Another person that was retiring at the end of 1976 was Jim Haley of Florida. He was the chairman of the full committee. So as people "handicapped the horses" in the fall of '76, the expectation was that Mo Udall would chair the full committee, and probably Chick Kazen would become the National Park Subcommittee chairman. Everyone expected Phil Burton to be majority leader and someday House Speaker. Then Jim Wright beat him as speaker. So Burton began to decide what was going to be next for him. This was really a man whose entire career train had just left the tracks. Burton's district was urban San Francisco. He was a labor lawyer by background, had done a lot of stuff on worker health and safety, with various strong union backing. He was one of the people that put the last nail in the coffin of the House Un-American Activities Committee when he came to Congress. He was a hell of a guy! (I wish I'd known more about it when I worked for the Committee. That would have explained some of the things [that happened later].*)*

In short, Burton wound up taking over the National Park Subcommittee, mostly from, I think, advice and encouragement from key senior Sierra Club people. Dr. Ed Wayburn and some others were longtime supporters and allies of Phil. They wanted to get some serious things done. A new administration was coming to town, too. Jimmy Carter had surprised everybody. So we went from a Republican administration to a Democratic administration, and there was a sense that maybe now was an opportunity to accomplish some really large-scale things in the conservation and national parks field.

He began to assemble his priorities. His one specific reason for taking on that subcommittee was to expand Redwoods National Park in northern California. He was from California. His constituency in the Sierra Club desperately wanted something to happen. . . . Burton came into the subcommittee knowing he had a couple of things that he wanted to do — Redwoods being the preeminent thing — but as he began to think about how he wanted to get a lot done, he began to operate in a way that people hadn't seen before. Amendments to the National Trails Act were swept into something that later people called the "park barrel bill." Phil

Burton was this incredible political animal. And in many cases, using some of the Trails System Act as leverage on the administration, he obtained other things.

[After the 1978 amendments were passed,] *He said, "You know, those amendments we did on the Trails Act, that's some of the best stuff that we got done during this whole time." And it just floored me, because I didn't know that Phil appreciated it in that way. It was very interesting to hear, as he looked back on his four years, that he really felt like the changes to the act, not just the AT, but the other things in the Act were something that he thought was really of lasting value for the people of the country and came to that conclusion on his own — not because somebody else told him so. I always found that fascinating. It is an interesting sort of take on that guy's own sense of what was good stuff.* [14]

---

14. Cleve Pinnix, 2007, NPS Oral History interview, NTS 40th Anniversary Oral History Project, pp. 10–1 and 18–9.

CHAPTER 8
BUILDING THE
SYSTEM 1978–1983

I would very much like to see reasonable scenic routes developed, but I favor the development of the historic trails and give them a higher priority than scenic routes. (Representative Joe Skubitz, 1967) [1]

After passage of the 1978 amendments, the National Trails System now contained seven interstate national trails. Public Law 95-925 added the category of national historic trails (NHTs), four new NHTs which together totaled over 9,500 miles in designated routes, and one new national scenic trail (NST) totaling almost 3,200 miles in length. To meet the new requirements for comprehensive management plans for each of these trails, the U.S. Department of Agriculture's Forest Service (FS) and the Department of the Interior's National Park Service (NPS) had to assemble teams to carry out these plans, while simultaneously gearing up jointly for a major land acquisition project to protect the Appalachian NST.

During this time, agency names and responsibilities changed. The Bureau of Outdoor Recreation (BOR) had almost completed the first 14 studies in 1978 when it was transformed as an agency into the Heritage Conservation Recreation Service (HCRS). But authority to conduct NST and NHT feasibility studies was then transferred to the National Park Service, not HCRS. [2]

---

1. Representative Joe Skubitz (R-KS), March 6, 1967, in GPO, *Hearing Before the Subcommittee on National Parks and Recreation . . . on HR 4865 and Related Bills to Establish a Nationwide System of Trails*, March 6–7, 1967, Serial No. 09-4, p. 43.
2. *Federal Register*, April 19, 1979, Vol. 44, No. 77, p. 23384.

From 1979 on, HCRS's major responsibility for the National Trails System was to provide the chairperson for the Interagency Trails Task Force and coordinate the designation of national recreation trails (NRTs) by the Secretary of the Interior. In May 1979, President Carter issued a second environmental message; it was as comprehensive as his first. This one included instructions that the USDA Forest Service seek to achieve "a goal of two national recreation trails in each National Forest System unit" while encouraging other federal land-managing agencies to do likewise. In addition, he urged the Secretary of the Interior to carry out a grassroots survey of trail needs nationwide and promised to establish the Natchez Trace, Potomac Heritage, and North Country Trails as NSTs. [3]

To help carry out the intent of President Carter's new Environmental Message, HCRS embarked immediately on an ambitious nationwide trail needs assessment. The idea was to glean grassroots input, aggregated by HCRS region. [4] By late fall 1979, the regional assessments were compiled, identifying many shortcomings in federal and state trail efforts such as the lack of a national trail plan, few state trail programs, low funding levels, numerous threats to existing trails, poorly organized trail groups, lots of red tape, lack of coordination, and a proliferation of user groups asking for a growing diversity of trail types. HCRS planners also asked for nominations for additional scenic and historic trails, and among these appeared, for the first time at a national level, trail concepts that would eventually become trail studies or established trails, including a Pacific Coastal Trail, a Hawaiian Coastal Trail, a north-to-south Arizona Trail, the Anza Trail, the Pony Express route, California Emigrant Trails, and the Applegate-Lassen Trail. [5]

A contemporary familiar with the HCRS assessment offered this observation about the state of America's trails in 1980:

Trails are an important recreational resource, a part of our national heritage. But because they rarely receive the attention they deserve, they are also a fragile resource

3. GPO, 1979, *Message from the President of the United States Transmitting a Review of His Administration's Programs for the Protection of the Environment*, House Document 96-174, p. 25, in NTSAHA.
4. Chris T. Delaporte, HCRS Director, September 21, 1979 memo to All State Liaison Officers, in NTSAHA.
5. HCRS Northwest Region, December 1979, *Trails System Planning, Phase I Report*, not paginated; Brian O'Neill for John D. Cherry, June 25, 1980, *National Trails Assessment, Pacific Southwest Region, Phase II*, both in NTSAHA.

— easily damaged and easily lost. Not only are trails often given low priority by government agencies and Congress, but most private trail groups are prevented by limited funds from adequately promoting trails and competing effectively with other interests. [6]

Following the 1976 hearings and the 1978 amendments, an effective land acquisition office for the Appalachian NST was finally established, called the Appalachian Trail Project Office (ATPO). Chuck Rinaldi, who set up this office and raised it to a high level of performance, later described this challenge:

I think that Nat's successor, Robert Herbst, was extremely instrumental. I think that from a trail standpoint it is very fortunate that he was selected as the Assistant Secretary at that time because of his interest in the Trail. . . . And even in his role as Assistant Secretary, he had assistance monitoring the progress being made and reporting back to him. . . . He became disenchanted with the Park Service's effort of acquiring land. I was the Director of Lands for the National Park Service. I had suffered a health problem, had a heart attack in 1972, and my doctor kept telling me that I should retire. And I said, "I'm not ready to retire." For some reason I went to the doctor in 1978, and he said, "You should retire." And for some reason I decided I was going to retire. My boss . . . knew, of course, that I am from the Harpers Ferry area in West Virginia. He figured I would be moving back to the area, so he said, "We're going to be opening offices up there. Why don't you just go up and head up the office? And, if it doesn't work out, you can retire." That sounded pretty good to me. So I did that. At that time we [ATPO] had three offices: one in New Hampshire, one in Allentown, Pennsylvania, and one in Martinsburg, West Virginia, to acquire land outside of the national park units. I headed the one in Martinsburg. And, as I said, Bob Herbst was disenchanted with the progress. Shortly after I arrived there, he asked me to take over the responsibility for the entire Trail. Along with that he gave me some flexibility to identify what my needs were to make this work. So I did an analysis, and came up with the number of positions I needed and where they should be, and I got what I asked for. It moved on from there, and we really made tremendous progress from that point on.

I am really proud of the fact that I was able to set up offices and a staff to implement and carry out this program. . . . During the time that I was in charge of the land

6. Craig Evans, 1980, "National Trails – the Unexplored Potential," *National Parks and Conservation Magazine*, October 1980, p. 7, in NTSAHA.

acquisition program, we acquired 1,790 parcels of land and nearly 80,000 acres of land, and we protected 523 miles of trail. I am really proud of that. I would say that when I left the protection program in 1987, the program was probably 85–90% complete. But I don't want to belittle the last 15%. The last ones are the toughest. [7]

Another perspective was provided years later by one of Rinaldi's colleagues, a solicitor at the U.S. Department of Agriculture:

What Rinaldi brought [to ATPO] *were tremendous bureaucratic skills. This is absolutely crucial. . . . When Rinaldi got that job, he got an agreement from the Director of the Park Service for something like 40 . . . positions that reported to him. And he would report only to the Director. In other words, the AT was set aside from everything else in the Park Service bureaucratically. They only reported to the Director, which basically meant that they were on their own. This is a big difference*

Ray Hunt (right) awards Chuck Rinaldi an honorary ATC Lifetime Membership in 1983 in appreciation for his work protecting the Appalachian NST. Photo courtesy ATC.

between the Forest Service and the Park Service, to the Park Service's credit. The Park Service defined this project as separate, they put the people in the separate office, and those people only reported to the top guy, that meant they could get the job done. . . . The reason why is that Rinaldi insisted on getting those slots assigned to him. The notion is this. As much as bureaucrats are maligned, the fact that you had someone with Rinaldi and Richie's organizational abilities in there and their ability to marshal the resources within a bureaucracy to get the job done, you know, there's no substitute for that. And I stand in awe of them. So, I'm just this young buck watching these guys operate and I'm thinking, "This is the way people get things done in government." I only realized later that that was how two extraordinary men got things done in government. But it was not typical. [8]

7. Chuck Rinaldi, 2007, NPS Oral History interview, NTS 40th Anniversary Oral History Project, pp. 3–4, 13.
8. Jim Snow, 2007, NPS Oral History interview, NTS 40th Anniversary Oral History Project, pp. 18–9.

Meanwhile, both the Senate and House during the 96th Congress (1979–1980) were busy proposing additional trails for study and establishment. Bills to study the Juan Bautista de Anza, Goodnight-Loving, General Crook, Beale Wagon Road, Illinois, Jedediah Smith, and Trail of Tears Trails were introduced, as were bills to establish the Santa Fe, Natchez Trace, Potomac Heritage, and Ice Age Trails. House subcommittee chair Phil Burton included a new NTSA section of definitions (including the elusive terms "high potential sites" and "high potential segments" in bill HR 8087) — and these terms survived debate and are now embedded in the Act. HR 8087 also proposed a trail volunteer support fund of $500,000 per year in small grants for five years. Other bills fostered visitor centers along historic trails (HR 8135). In fact, it took several years to get many of the HR 8087 provisions incorporated into the NTSA. The congressional actions that eventually passed into law as amendments to the NTSA are listed in Table B below. [9]

On the citizen side, one of the American Hiking Society's first public activities was organizing a coast-to-coast group hike in 1980 to promote the benefits of hiking nationwide during the year of the presidential election campaign. As a cosponsor, HCRS provided $10,000 for "HikaNation." The route east from San Francisco crossed 12 states to end at Washington, DC. A core group of 70-80

In March, 1981, four Hike-A-Nation hikers leave Bristol, Virginia. Photo courtesy "Hike A Nation 1981" website.

hikers was joined by many others from place to place. For example, in Oakland, California, 7,000 hikers joined to cross the Bay Bridge. The trek ended in Washington, DC, in the spring of 1981, with an extension to the Atlantic coast in Delaware. [10]

In late 1980, Ronald Reagan won the presidency, and once again, national leadership changed political parties and moved to conservative positions. In 1981, soon after the Reagan Administration assumed power, the president's newly appointed Secretary of the Interior, James Watt,

---

9. U.S. House of Representatives, Committee Report, 1980, *National Trails System Act Amendments of 1980* [to accompany H.R. 8087] in NTSAHA.
10. AHS and HCRS, June 1980, press packet for 1980 Transcontinental Hike Route, with related articles, in NTSAHA.

abolished HCRS as an agency by secretarial order. Its employees and program responsibilities were assigned to the National Park Service, and the Interagency Trails Task Force was disbanded.

The appearance of new trails in the 1978 amendments challenged the administering agencies assigned to operate them. As trails staffer Tom Gilbert recalls, NPS dealt with this issue in a typically bureaucratic way:

> . . . the Park Service in 1980–82 was just dealing with the first national trails to come online since the original act. There were four historic trails and one scenic trail authorized in the 1978 amendments. The Continental Divide (the one scenic trail) went to the Forest Service. The Iditarod went to BLM. The Park Service got three trails: Oregon, Mormon Pioneer, and Lewis and Clark. And they had a deadline of September 1982 to produce management plans and send them to Congress. They said, "What the heck do we do with these things?" Hardly anyone knew what a national historic trail was. . . . So there was a meeting of regional leadership at our Denver Service Center, and it was decided, "Okay, why doesn't each of us take one of them?" So each region took one trail to be responsible for. But, again, because there was no funding to give the Denver Service Center for planning (they are project-funded, not base-funded), the regional offices were really doing the bulk of the work through existing staff. And that's what I was brought out [to Omaha from Ann Arbor] to assist on in 1981.

> The Park Service had a continuing role — whether it was a park unit or not, whether we owned it or not — but there were issues then of other trails that were being authorized, and what region would they now be assigned to. It was capricious on those first three, each region just took one (pick the one you want). We [the NPS Midwest Region] ended up with Lewis and Clark. But then, when the plan was done, now we have work to do. If there is continuing work, who does it? Do we do it over the whole trail or just in our region? This raised a whole set of issues — I can't even remember them all now. . . . I argued strongly, and leadership in the region[al office] agreed that there needed to be one administrative point for the entire trail so that all partners and stakeholders knew where to go. The leadership of the NPS Rocky Mountain Region at that time disagreed. They wanted their portions (the North Dakota portion of the North Country Trail and their parts of the Lewis and Clark Trail and so forth). We said, "That's unworkable." It was quite an issue. And then it came up and spilled over as some more trails were being authorized. . . . "If one region does it, which region does it?" And I wrote several scenarios of criteria of the region that has the most mileage of the trail, the region that's most central to the trail,

the region that already has another trail that overlaps with the one being authorized. That was the case when the California Trail came along, because it overlies the Oregon Trail pretty much. And same with the Oregon and Mormon Pioneer Trails. I said, "The Seattle office has the Oregon Trail, Denver has the Mormon Pioneer. They ought to be administered by the same office since they overlap." [11]

The new tone in government and government-citizen relations became evident during the Sixth National Trails Symposium held in Davis, California, in the summer of 1981. In an opening letter to Symposium participants, Interior Secretary James Watt stated:

Secretary of the Interior James Watt, 1981, courtesy National Archives II, College Park, Maryland.

With this growth has come a demand for more trails and for better maintenance of existing trails. This demand comes, however, at a time when the Federal Government is under a clear mandate to cut spending significantly. It comes at a time when we are under mandate to return authority and responsibility to State and local jurisdictions and to the private sector. While the Department of the Interior will continue to be an enthusiastic partner in the national trails effort, it is clear that the Federal Government will not have the tax dollars to purchase the land and to construct the trails to meet the need. [12]

Meanwhile, a steady drumbeat of bills at the end of the Carter and beginning of the Reagan eras led to more National Trails System Act amendments. These either called for more trail feasibility studies or the establishment of new trails based on completed studies. Table B shows successful legislative actions on national trails between 1979 and 1984.

---

11. Tom Gilbert, 2007, NPS Oral History interview, NTS 40th Anniversary Oral History Project, pp. 5 and 19.
12. James G. Watt, *Sixth National Trails Symposium,* June 28–July 1, 1981, Davis, CA, workbook in NTSAHA.

TABLE B
Legislative Actions of the 96ᵗʰ and 98ᵗʰ Congresses

DATE	PUBLIC LAW	TRAIL ACTION
10/12/1979	96-87	Memorial to the late Representative Goodloe Byron in Maryland along the Appalachian NST
3/5/1980	96-199	Established the North Country NST
9/8/1980	96-344	Established the Overmountain Victory NHT
10/3/1980	96-370	Established the Ice Age NST (without a feasibility study)
3/28/1983	98-11	Established the Natchez Trace, Florida, and Potomac Heritage NSTs and requested studies for Juan Bautista de Anza, Trail of Tears, Illinois, Jedediah Smith, General Crook, and Beale Wagon Road Trails (plus other administrative authorities added or clarified, including a biennial interagency National Trails System Plan).
8/28/1984	98-504	Requested feasibility studies for the California and Pony Express Trails

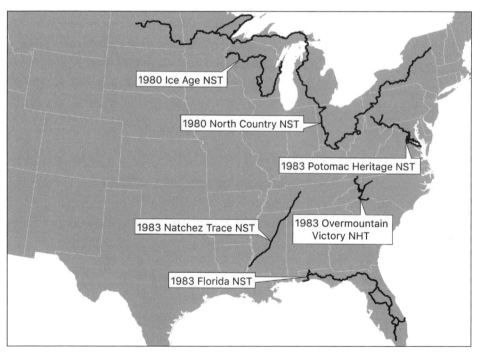

Trails Added 1980-1983.

Of these NTSA amendments, the most important was P.L. 98-11. Prior to its passage when first discussed on the floor of Congress, ranking House committee minority member Keith Sebelius (R-KS) commented: *In the preceding several years numerous trails have been and are added to the trails system. At the same time, the same Congress has weakened, and continues to weaken, the working provisions and tools of the trails act to the extent that the true workability of most of the trails system is greatly reduced. In the simplest words, we love to designate trails, while at the same time we seriously curtail their workability on the ground. . . . We are indeed deeply in the rut of creating "paper trails" — good stuff on paper, but fairly worthless on the ground where they really count.* [13]

Hearings were held in the U.S. Senate on August 4, 1982, presided over by Senator Malcolm Wallop (R-WY). Several senators sent statements supporting the Trails Act amendments that strengthened volunteer roles along the trails and clarified issues of landowner liability. It also provided that whole tracts could be purchased (with income from the sale of surplus lands to be returned to the Land and Water Conservation Fund) and strengthened the role of cooperative agreements in supporting the Trails System. In these now more conservative times, Department of the Interior testimony offered support for additional trail studies but insisted they would not be carried out until specific funds were appropriated for such studies. Mary Lou Grier, Deputy NPS Director, went on to testify, *We do not recommend . . . the provision . . . requiring the submission of a National Trails System plan every two years to the Congress. We believe the present system whereby certain trails are designated for study is far preferable, in that limited staff and funds can be concentrated on those specific trails which Congress singles out. A nationwide plan every two years would of necessity be very general. We have no estimate of the cost of this provision.*

Additional endorsements for the proposed amendments were given by the American Hiking Society, the National Parks and Conservation Association, Sierra Club, Wilderness Society, Friends of the Earth, the

---

13. Keith Sebelius, 1980, *Congressional Record*, September 22, 1980, p. 26465.

National Trails Council, the Appalachian Mountain Club, the Pacific Northwest Trails Association, and the Sign Post Trails Association. [14]

One excellent analysis of the ideas that became embedded in the 1983 amendments (P.L. 98-11) is contained in the report of the Senate Committee on Energy and Natural Resources. Letters from the Forest Service and the Department of the Interior were included in the report. They endorsed the package (with a few suggested changes) and applauded the greater visibility and authorities given to volunteers. The House of Representatives Committee on Interior and Insular Affairs issued its own report on March 9, 1983, and the two versions were reconciled in conference so that the bill quickly passed and was signed into law March 28. [15]

Another perspective on the evolution of the 1983 amendments was provided years later by Agriculture Department solicitor Jim Snow:

In those amendments, if you go look at them, there are some interesting elements to those that particularly dealt with cooperative agreements between everybody. If you look at the '83 amendments, actually the Forest Service took the lead in pushing that along. That's where Cleve Pinnix came in, because Cleve was able to help push that through the Democratic-controlled Congress. Frankly over here, we persuaded the Administration that this is a pretty benign piece of legislation, so nobody opposed it. In some respects then, we played off one another's strengths and weaknesses. When the Park Service couldn't act, a few of us over here kind of stepped up to the plate. The '83 amendments really were never embraced by anybody officially high up, it was mainly those who were most interested in the project.

There was an amendment here that required that feasibility [of a proposed trail] *be determined on the basis of whether or not it was physically possible to build trail. We thought that was important because a lot of people were advocating a lot of crazy things. . . . It allowed for the establishment of side trails on privately owned lands with the agreement of the landowner, because we had trail clubs that wanted to have properties that were part of that. . . . It dealt with amendments to the trail location; it dealt with . . . interpretative sites; it dealt with inter-governmental relations. One of the most important things it allowed is the Park Service to provide financial assistance to the Appalachian Trail Conference through cooperative agreements. That was very*

---

14. U.S. Senate Committee of Energy and Natural Resources, August 4, 1982, *Hearing on Amendments to the National Trails System Act*, etc., in NTSAHA.
15. U.S. Senate, January 31, 1983, *National Trails System Act Amendments*, 98th Congress, First Session, Report 98-1, in NTSAHA.

important from a trail maintenance perspective, because it's one thing getting it on the ground, and it's another thing to go out and build it and maintain it. The '83 amendments also had provisions in there for donations. There were a lot of juicy little things in there that were quite helpful to the Park Service.

At the time, we were thinking if we could rewrite this act, what would we put in there. I remember one meeting very distinctly. I was this young buck lawyer sitting at a table, and Cleve Pinnix says, "Okay, you guys, you're writing the law of the land, what do you want it to say?" And at that moment, I realized just how funky Congress operates, because here we are writing the law of the land, and this guy is asking me, "What do I want put in it?" And so we gave him several things. You can see in there what some of the things were. I do remember that there was interesting jockeying between Agriculture and Interior. Interior was very backseatish on the '83 amendments. As far as the AT goes, it was the '78 amendments and the '83 amendments that really made the difference as to making that project [the Appalachian Trail] *work.* [16]

Important administrative changes were also part of the 1983 Trails Act amendments in P.L. 98-11. Several of these passages were suggested by Appalachian Trail or AHS activists but worded so that they would apply anywhere in the National Trails System. One entirely new section of the Act (Section 11) listed the full range of activities that volunteers could carry out for these trails — including planning, development, maintenance, and management. Coupled to this was an amendment to Section 7(h) that extended the Volunteers in the Park and Volunteers in the Forests programs to volunteers working on national trails (but without the stimulatory grant program originally proposed by Representative Burton). Language in the committee report on the bill also clarified that this status could even be conferred to private landowners hosting NSTs and NHTs on their lands to help reduce their personal liability when engaged in trail activities.

The 1983 amendments requested that a national trails plan be submitted by the Interior Department to Congress every other year. This was based on the National Trails Assessment issued in late 1980. (However, the

---

16. Jim Snow, 2007, NPS Oral History interview, NTS 40th Anniversary Oral History Project, pp. 6–7.

requested plans were never conducted, so this requirement was removed from the NTSA in 1996.) [17]

After this issue was discussed in the 1982 hearings, Jeannette Fitzwilliams, on behalf of the National Trails Council, wrote to NPS's Mary Lou Grier to try to change the Department of the Interior's attitude toward a biennial planning effort.

I, personally, attended five of the HCRS meetings . . . to evaluate trail problems for the recent [National Trails] *Assessment. In every one of them, participants said, loud and clear, "National Trails are of minor importance; what we are interested in is a network of trails to meet local needs and the measures needed to get them." This did not get through to HCRS and, now apparently, to NPS which still seems to concentrate on "National Trails." . . . A trails network is the sum total of the efforts of individual citizens and clubs; cities, counties and states; and federal agencies.* [18]

The 1983 amendments clarified land protection authorities and management transfers that would be useful to the Appalachian NST — and added a section of definitions (NTSA Section 12). The new law included a requirement that any NRT nomination for a trail crossing private lands had to include written permission from affected private landowners. Similarly, it refined the process for nominating connecting-and-side trails, allowed for regulations pertaining to national parks and national forests to be applied to the trails, and identified acceptable trail uses. These amendments also stipulated that any land interest donated for these trails would qualify for conservation tax credits under the Internal Revenue Service code. [19]

With the establishment of the Florida NST in 1983, the House Parks and Public Lands Subcommittee developed a compromise known as the "willing-seller" clause that opened the door to acquisition by federal agencies outside the boundaries of existing federal areas when conducted "with the consent of the owner." Previously, starting in 1978, the Section 10(c) restrictions severely limited federal funds to acquire lands for certain

17. P.L. 104-333, Sec. 814 (D) (e).
18. Jeanette Fitzwilliams in letter to Mary Lou Grier, August 11, 1982, attached to U.S. Senate Committee of Energy and Natural Resources, August 4, 1982, *Hearing on Amendments to the National Trails System Act*, etc., in NTSAHA.
19. GPO, Washington, DC, March 28, 1983, Public Law 98-11 (97 Stat. 42), *An Act to Amend the National Trails System Act*, etc., in NTSAHA.

NSTs and NHTs. The new "willing seller" language was embedded in almost every NST and NHT establishment bill between 1983 and 2009.

BECOMING AN NST WITHOUT A STUDY

How did the Ice Age NST become part of the National Trails System without a feasibility study? NPS's Tom Gilbert explained later:

The Ice Age Park and Trail Foundation . . . wanted to have that trail and link up those areas [that had already been declared Ice Age Reserves] *as much as possible. So they began working on it. They created a separate organization called the Ice Age Trail Council in the late 1960s. And their patron in Congress was Henry Reuss from Milwaukee* [recent author of *On the Trail of the Ice Age*]. *There's some great early pictures of Justice William O. Douglas up here walking the Ice Age Trail with Henry Reuss and Ray Zillmer. . . . By the fall of 1979 . . . ten established segments of the Ice Age Trail had been designated by the Secretary of the Interior as National Recreation Trails. . . . Henry Reuss thought that the whole trail should be designated, not just ten pieces.* [He] *. . . prevailed upon the Wisconsin Department of Natural Resources to file an application for an additional National Recreation Trail designation for the entire trail. . . . Well, I was doing the National Trails System planning effort in HCRS at the time. That application ended up on my desk in Ann Arbor, Michigan. I looked at that, and I had to get familiar with it. . . . I looked at it and I said, "Phew, it doesn't qualify." It doesn't meet the NRT criteria because more than half of the route of the trail was road walking. And [NRT] criterion number one . . . says that the trail must exist and be available for public use. That's one of the shortcomings we've always talked about for National Recreation Trail designation. It doesn't create new trails, it only designates what exists.*

So I said to my supervisor, Bob Martin, "Bob, this trail doesn't exist. We can't designate this whole thing as a National Recreation Trail." And he says, "Hmm, they aren't going to be happy with that answer." I said, "I know." He says, "Think about it." So I thought about it, and I don't know over what period of time — a day, a week, I don't remember. I looked at this thing and became more familiar with the geology and whatever else was in that big application package from the DNR. I looked at the length and I said, "You know, in terms of significance and length, it could be a national scenic trail." And then I said, "Oh, when Congress authorizes a national scenic trail they authorize the creation of a trail, not that it has to already exist." I said, "This is perfect."

Henry Reuss and Gaylord Nelson, c. 1980.
Photo Courtesy Ice Age Trail Alliance.

So I went to Bob Martin and said, "Bob, we really can't designate this as a National Recreation Trail. But you know what? We could propose this as a national scenic trail. The fact is that it is underway, that pieces exist at various places along the route. I don't think we even have to talk about doing a feasibility study. Is the trail feasible? Well heck, it's being built! Why spend taxpayer dollars [for a study]?" I said, "This could be instantly designated. There's nothing in the trails act to prevent it." He said, "Are you sure?" I said, "There isn't, Bob." He then worked through everything with me and said, "You're absolutely right." So we contacted the DNR since they had filed the application and asked the question. And they said, "Call Congressman Reuss and see if that's okay with him."

*Well, when we talked with Congressman Reuss (and we may not have talked to him directly, probably just his staff) the response that came back to us was, "Oh, you mean we can have the same status as the **Appalachian Trail** for our trail? Oh, by all means, and draft us the legislation." So I drafted the amendment to the National Trails System Act, and we sent it off to Congressman Reuss. Very quickly, in about May of 1980, he introduced the bill, and it was passed on October 3. So that's how that came about.* [20]

20. Tom Gilbert, 2007, NPS Oral History interview, NTS 40th Anniversary Oral History Project, pp. 11–2. See also U.S. House of Representatives, September 10, 1980, Report 96-1314, *Establishing the Ice Age National Scenic Trail and for Other Purposes,* in NTSAHA.

CHAPTER 9
MAKING THE SYSTEM OPERATIONAL 1984–1990

The value of the trails within the National Park System and the National Trails System is limitless. Today and in the future, trails are needed to meet America's trail activities; they protect access to backcountry and close-to-home areas; they promote tourism; and they provide solitude and enjoyment to users. Trails are important and the need to develop and protect them is unquestionable. (William Penn Mott, 1986) [1]

President Ronald Reagan, no date.
Photo courtesy National Archives
II, College Park, Maryland.

1. William Penn Mott, 1986, "National Trails – Their Value and Management Within the National Park Service," *International Congress on Trail and River Recreation Proceedings,* May 31–June 4, 1986, Vancouver, BC, p. 102, in NTSAHA.

After his reelection in 1984, President Ronald Reagan called for a President's Commission on Americans Outdoors. Created by Executive Order 12503, the charter of this commission focused on a review and update of outdoor recreation opportunities in the United States, building on the findings and trends of the 1962 ORRRC Report. The new commission's 1987 report, titled *Americans Outdoors*, recommended among many other points:

- A nationwide system of greenways within easy access of all Americans, and
- Decisions made between then and the year 2000 would "determine the fate of America's remaining land and water resources." [2]

After 1985, a number of National Trails System Act (NTSA) amendments resulted in the establishment of trails from the earlier feasibility studies. Table C shows the trails established, studies requested, and other NTSA amendments passed between 1986 and 1990. These amendments remained centered around national historic trails, confirming that the System had shifted away from creating new national scenic trails.

TABLE C
Legislative Actions of the 99th, 100th, and 101st Congresses

DATE	PUBLIC LAW	TRAIL ACTION
10/6/1986	99-445	Established Nez Perce (Nee-Me-Poo) NHT
5/6/1987	100-35	Established Santa Fe NHT
12/11/1987	100-187	Requested study for DeSoto Trail
12/16/1987	100-192	Established Trail of Tears NHT
10/4/1988	100-470	Authorized retention of federal interest in abandoned railroad and other rights-of-way
12/28/1988	100-559	Requested study for Coronado Trail

---

2. National Park Service, 1990, *Trails for All Americans*, p. 1.

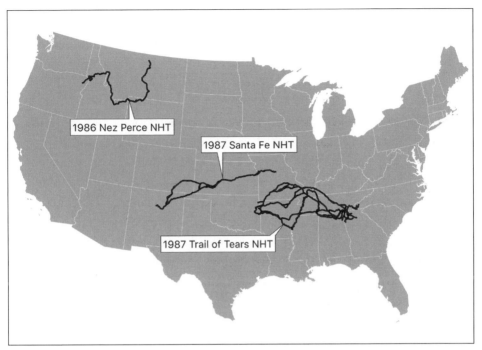

Trails Added 1986-1987.

    The Reagan administration's support for the proposed Santa Fe NHT shows how it balanced popular support for heritage and tourism while avoiding the controversies of land acquisition. In offering support for the proposed Santa Fe NHT, Bill Horn, Deputy Assistant Secretary for Fish and Wildlife and Parks at the Department of the Interior, stated:

We believe that the Santa Fe Trail fully qualifies for designation as a national historic trail. The historic significance of the trail is unquestioned. Its potential for historic interest can be developed through the planning process for designated national historic trails required in section 5 of the National Trails System Act. . . . Under such a plan, we would identify specific trail segments that could be marked and administered by private and public agencies. We would not propose additional land acquisition by the Federal Government. [3]

---

3. William P. Horn, 1987, letter to Hon. J. Bennett Johnson, in U.S. Senate Report 100-39, *Santa Fe National Historic Trail*, April 10, 1987, p. 5, in NTSAHA.

One proposal from this era that did not make it into PL 100-470 was a "Trails Fund" in the U.S. Treasury deriving its revenue from donations, appropriations, and sales of surplus trail corridor lands. This fund would have been used for land acquisition, trail construction and reconstruction, as well as loans to states and local agencies, federal agencies, and qualified organizations. [4]

Now responsible for a number of newly created national historic trails (NHTs) and facing budgetary and staffing cuts under the Reagan administration, the National Park Service considered setting up a consolidated Western Project Office for National Historic Trails in Denver, Colorado. The main reason was that where NHTs overlap, they need to be administered consistently. The newly released comprehensive plans for the Oregon and Mormon Pioneer NHTs — conducted by different regional offices and both released in 1981 — offered divergent management policies for the same corridor, confusing and irritating both partners and affected state agencies. The idea of a unified center was widely circulated, but it was not enacted due to objections by the affected NPS regional offices. [5]

The newly established Oregon-California Trails Association (OCTA) took the matter to a new level in 1985 by accusing the NPS of negligence regarding NHTs.

Through a lack of foresight and planning, the National Park Service has abdicated its responsibilities for the wise and careful management of these resources. Today, seven years after the legislation established National Historic Trails, there still is no policy for consistent planning for, management of, or interpretation of historic trails. Rather, ad hoc solutions have been adopted on a case-by-case basis until the present situation resembles nothing more than mass confusion. . . . I also think you can see why the governors of Wyoming and Nebraska are fed up. We echo the sentiments of [Nebraska] Governor Kerrey's Chief of Staff: "Further planning of trails is absolute insanity . . . " until these regional directors are overruled and some order is introduced to the situation. [6]

---

4. U.S. House of Representatives, June 10, 1987, H.R. 2641, *To amend the National Trails System act to provide for State and local governments for the improved management of certain Federal lands and for other purposes,* in NTSAHA.
5. Dr. John A. Latschar, January 10, 1984, letter to Gregory M. Franzwa, Oregon-California Trails Association and attached *Proposal for the Establishment of Western Project Office, National Historic Trails, National Park Service,* and related correspondence in NTSAHA.
6. Gregory M. Franzwa, OCTA, letter to William Penn Mott, NPS Director, July 15, 1985, in NTSAHA.

Meanwhile, in 1984 ATC had succeeded in negotiating an unprecedented 10-year agreement with the NPS for trail management responsibilities. In what has become known as the "delegation agreement," NPS turned over to ATC management responsibilities for NPS-acquired lands outside the boundaries of federal parks, national forests, and state parks. This was "the first time the Park Service had entrusted day-to-day stewardship of such a large unit of the national park system to a private organization." It worked well enough to be renewed in 1994. [7]

In the winter of 1987, after a year of back-and-forth among the NPS regional directors, Director William Penn Mott issued a memo outlining the major responsibilities of NST and NHT administrators and clarifying conflicting and ambiguous practices. "I have decided that these trails must be mainstreamed into the normal operational channels of the Service" and be treated as other NPS units. The memo established criteria for assigning new trails to regional offices, requested identifying administrators for each trail, urged the submitting of budget requests for operational funding, urged support for required advisory councils and the completing of comprehensive plans, and encouraged ongoing coordination with affected partners. [8]

In this struggle, several ideas that emerged and that have helped NPS-administered trails in later years include budget line items for each trail and a consistent agency-wide policy statement. (In fact, during later organizational consolidations and to foster consistency, all nine NHTs in the former Southwest and Rocky Mountain Regions have eventually come to be administered under one superintendent located at NPS's Santa Fe, New Mexico, office.)

One new provision in P.L. 98-11 of 1983 would revolutionize trail making across America: the recycling of abandoned railroads for use as recreational trails. The Department of the Interior had pioneered this concept about 1970 with its booklet *Establishing Trails on Right-of-Way: Principally Railroad Abandonments*, listing hundreds of possibly available corridors in 47 states. In 1975, the Citizens' Advisory Council on Environmental Quality issued a thought-provoking report, *From Rails to Trails*, explaining how

---

7. Bob Proudman, 1984, "The AT: 30 Years of Making NTSA Effective," *Pathways Across America*, Spring 1998, Vol. 11., No. 2, 8.
8. William Penn Mott, NPS Director, March 1987 memo to NPS regional directors, *National Park Service Administration of National Scenic and National Historic Trails*, in NTSAHA.

abandoned railroad beds could be converted to recreational trail use. Two members of this Advisory Council were Laurence S. Rockefeller, chair of the ORRRC in the early 1960s, and Tom McCall, former governor of Oregon and speaker at the second National Trails Symposium in 1973. [9]

The 1976 Railroad Revitalization and Regulatory Reform Act had further opened the door for preserving abandoned rail corridors intact by establishing funding through BOR for converting abandoned railroad corridors to recreation or conservation purposes. A 1985 evaluation of nine projects thus funded explored the complex legal issues surrounding such conversions, the resource conservation opportunities such conversions can create, and numerous court cases that grew from such conversions. This evaluation mentions the P.L. 98-11 amendment: "The key finding of this amendment is that interim use of a railroad right-of-way for trail use, when the route itself remains intact for future railroad purposes, shall not constitute an abandonment of such right-of-way for railroad purposes." [10]

Proponents of the idea of recycling abandoned rail lines into recreational trails (at least on an interim basis) included the newly created AHS and the American Recreation Coalition. In a single paragraph (Section 8(d)) the Trails Act now authorized the Interstate Commerce Commission (later the Surface Transportation Board) to preserve abandoned railroad rights-of-way for use as trails on an interim basis. This amendment gave birth to the "rails-to-trails" movement, launched first in the United States, and now found worldwide. A few years later, in 1986, this innovative form of recycling resulted in the founding of the Rails-to-Trails

David Burwell speaks at the 25th anniversary celebration of the Rails-To-Trails Conservancy in 2011. Photo courtesy RTC.

---

9. U.S. Department of the Interior, BOR, undated, *Establishing Trails on Right-of-Way: Principally Railroad Abandonments,* Washington, DC: GPO; "Washington Scene," *Parks & Recreation,* April 1975, p. 16, both in NTSAHA.

10. NPS Recreation Grants Division, August 1985, *Rails-to-Trails Grant Program, an evaluation of assistance provided under Public Law 94-210 to assist in the conservation of abandoned railroad rights of way to park and recreation use,* in NTSAHA.

Conservancy (RTC) by David Burwell and Peter Harnick. This new non-profit organization sought to foster the conservation of abandoned railway lines as trails by organizing a nationwide network of activists and quickly grew into the nation's largest trail organization. [11]

From its beginning, RTC worked with communities to preserve unused rail corridors by transforming them into recreation trails for health, economic benefits, and increased quality of life at the local level. RTC helped pass P.L. 100-470 on October 4, 1988, to provide for federal retention of interests in abandoned railroad rights-of-way on federal lands for use as trails in national conservation areas and national forests. The new law also expanded secretarial control of rights-of-way, especially abandoned railroads, and reverted federal rights-of-way back to the federal government unless used for highways. As a strong advocacy organization, RTC was instrumental in building Congressional support for funding National Park Service trail programs. [12] Today, RTC has more than 108,000 members and supporters and aspires to create and promote a nationwide network of trails recycled from former rail lines.

Another development in the early 1980s strengthened trail volunteerism. In 1983, the Richard King Mellon Foundation approached the Appalachian Mountain Club (AMC) in Boston with $600,000 to spread its decades-long success with volunteerism beyond New England. The project became known as the "National Volunteer Project." A small AMC team, in partnership with the Forest Service, brainstormed successful principles of good volunteer management and then took it on the road to benefit trail and conservation groups nationwide — eventually working with 14 different groups. One group, Volunteers for

The cover of the Appalachian Mountain Club's *Organizing Outdoor Volunteers*, published in 1992 as the result of the National Volunteer Project.

---

11. Susan Henley, 2007, NPS Oral History interview, NTS 40th Anniversary Oral History Project, p. 7.
12. Robert Karotko, May 8, 2008, email message to Steve Elkinton.

Outdoor Colorado, has become a great model for developing statewide volunteer networks. Another success was the Florida Trail Association. Coming out of this training, FTA learned how to imaginatively capitalize on the waves of new retirees coming to Florida. The Washington Trail Association was another group that benefited from this grant. Lessons learned were condensed into the handy guidebook, *Organizing Outdoor Volunteers.* [13]

To help lay the foundation for a National Trails System plan, as requested in P.L. 98-11, NPS issued a *National Trails Assessment* in late 1986. It was a snapshot of trails across America. The assessment examined the feasibility study process for NSTs and NHTs, the railroad abandonment process, the valuable role of technical assistance by agencies, the need for more urban trails, ways to lessen user conflicts, and the universal need for greater funding. In urging the need for strong user-based trail organizations, the assessment noted,

The long, linear nature of long-distance trails further argues strongly for user participation. Extended trails inherently involve many governmental jurisdictions and many types of public and private land ownerships; these fragmented patterns of responsibility present significant obstacles to long-distance trail projects. Assembling long, continuous corridors of land across public and private holdings is extremely difficult, as is routine maintenance and management of the trail. . . . Involvement of users [as organized groups] *in securing easements, rights-of-way, or other permission for long trails to cross private lands has proven to be effective and often less costly than similar efforts by public agencies.* [14]

This assessment identified many issues and obstacles facing trails and their consistent management, including the fact that there were no standard trail data systems, that the roles and authorities for volunteers varied among agencies, that trail use conflicts created safety problems, that there was wide variation among state trail programs and trail planning, and there were few easy answers on how to make trails accessible for physically disabled persons.

---

13. National Trails Council, *Trail Tracks*, Vol. XII, No. 3, September 1983, p. 6; Roger L. Moore, Vicki Lafarge, and Charles L. Tracy, *Organizing Outdoor Volunteers* (Boston: Appalachian Mountain Club, 1992.
14. U.S. Department of the Interior, NPS, 1986, *National Trails Assessment*, p. 23, in NTSAHA.

Several people noticed that 1988 marked the 20th anniversary of the NTSA. NPS's Bill Spitzer, Chief of the Recreation Resources Assistance Division, used the anniversary to ask some pointed questions:

- How can we best identify and satisfy the needs of the trails community?
- How can we provide an action framework that will help us meet the trail needs of the future?
- Do the processes, the criteria, and even the definitions of NST, NHT, and NRT in the Trails Act still make sense today? [15]

In fact, by the end of 1988, several remarkable changes helped move the trails system forward. Within NPS, the desire to embed rivers and trails technical assistance in agency operations led to the founding later that year of the NPS's River and Trails Conservation Assistance Program (RTCA). Over the next decades, some of the most valuable staff who served in the NPS administration of trails had developed their partnership skills with the RTCA program.

Also in 1988, the National Trails Council, organizer of the biennial National Trails Symposia, merged with the American Trails Network, a recently developed group that aspired to connect all of the state capitals via a network of trails. [16] These two groups formed American Trails, a nonprofit organization intended to enhance all types of trails in the U.S. — both motorized and non-motorized — by promoting cooperation and encouraging resolution of common trail issues. People instrumental in helping with the merger were NPS's Bill Spitzer, Colorado State Trail Coordinator Stuart Macdonald, and AHS's Susan "Butch" Henley. Since 1988, American Trails has coordinated the biennial National Trails Symposia (more recently called International Trails Symposium) and promotes new trails and trail issues through its magazine, *American Trails*, a quarterly that continues to improve in coverage and relevance to all trail managers. [17]

15. William T. Spitzer, January 14, 1988, letter to Peggy Robinson, American Trails Network, in NTSAHA.
16. American Trails Network, *An Action Plan for Creating an Interconnected Network of Trails Across America: Report on a Conference Held October 1986 at Rensselaerville Institute*, in NTSAHA.
17. Susan Henley, 2007, NPS Oral History interview, NTS 40th Anniversary Oral History Project, p. 19.

This merger occurred during the ninth National Trails Symposium, held in Unicoi, Georgia, in early September 1988. Issues discussed at the Symposium covered a wide spectrum, focusing on creating and improving trails at the local level. Many sessions shared current trail-related research. Only a brief mention was made of the status of the components of the National Trails System. All of these efforts faced the "lacks" of available land corridors, consistent information, funding, training, vision, planning tools, and strong constituencies. Yet NPS's Bill Spitzer offered this vision: *I'd like for most Americans to be able to reach a trail within walking distance of their home and workplace. I would like us all to have available a significant natural corridor where we can stroll, exercise, or socialize with friends. I would like to see the National Trails System be as myriad and diverse as the American people. I would like to see us being committed to preserving enough significant corridors that we could have a trail system that is reflective of various communities of interest — so we are not confused by some as serving a single activity group.* [18]

The newly organized America Trails immediately went to work on a manifesto, *Trails for All Americans: The National Trails Agenda Project.* The task force who compiled this document started out at the ninth symposium with the endorsement of the NPS (in the spirit of Bill Spitzer's "action framework") and was chaired by ATC's Dave Startzell. It articulated contemporary trail issues and made recommendations to address America's current and future need for trails, reaffirming the impor-tance of reliable, efficient, and inexpensive trail recreation. (In fact, it fleshed out Bill Spitzer's

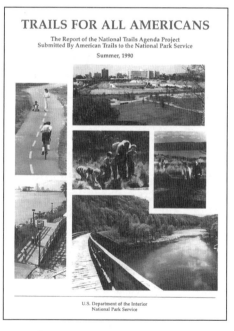

Cover of *Trails for All Americans.* In NTSAHA.

18. *Ninth National Trails Symposium Proceedings*, September 11–14, 1988, p. 46, in NTSAHA.

vision stated at the Symposium.) Eventually published by NPS in 1990, the *Trails for All Americans* report suggested that trails, like highways, be viewed as part of America's infrastructure. It reemphasized the goal that all Americans be able to reach a trail within 15 minutes of home to enjoy the health, economic, resource, educational, and transportation benefits of trails. It laid out a compelling vision of a "national system of trails" and offered 19 recommended actions. [19]

However, as the 1980s drew to a close, some agencies were still reluctant to commit adequate resources to the NSTs and NHTs for which they were responsible. Until 1989, one NPS observer noted,

. . . the attitude in Washington at that point, was that since these trails were to be done through partnerships, and since all [sic] of these trails had been authorized with this proviso that no federal agency may spend funds to acquire land for the trails. Well then it wasn't going to be like the Appalachian Trail, where we were buying lands and opening it (and the Appalachian Trail is even a unit of the National Park System). So with that proviso, the Washington Office's attitude was that once we get the management plans done and basically pass them out through all the various stakeholders and whatever, our [agency's] job was done. [20]

Early copies of *Pathways Across America*. In NTSAHA.

Yet, public awareness of the National Trails System was increasing. The launching in 1988 of *Pathways Across America* — the only periodical devoted exclusively to NSTs and NHTs — was one major tool that

---

19. National Park Service, 1990, *Trails for All Americans*, p. 1, in NTSAHA.
20. Tom Gilbert, 2007, NPS Oral History interview, NTS 40th Anniversary Oral History Project, p. 6.

assisted in promoting the National Trails System. For more than a decade, *Pathways* was produced, printed, and distributed through a cooperative agreement between NPS and AHS. In 2001, the agreement moved over to the Partnership for the National Trails System once it had the capacity to produce a magazine. A few years later, it went from black-and-white to color and has offered a faithful and comprehensive chronicle of National Trails System activities ever since.

Many of the participants who attended the first NST-NHT Conference at Camp Whitcomb near Hartland, Wisconsin, 1988. NPS photo courtesy PNTS.

Another important milestone occurred in late September 1988. At that time, the administrator of the Ice Age and North Country NSTs and the Lewis and Clark NHT was Tom Gilbert in the NPS Midwest Regional Office in Omaha. He and Gary Werner, an employee of the Ice Age Park and Trail Foundation in Madison, Wisconsin, organized the first-ever conference to bring together NST and NHT staff and activists. It was held at Camp Whitcomb near Hartland, Wisconsin. The Ice Age Trail NST advisory council was curious to know how other NST and NHT partners addressed certain issues. They invited representatives from each of the NSTs and NHTs to come together to discuss the status of their trails — as well as common problems and challenges — and share successes and solutions. One major challenge was getting Appalachian Trail representatives to attend, but with cajoling on several fronts, both NPS's Chuck Rinaldi and ATC's Dave Startzell came. At this meeting, a surprising number of commonalities were found, and the participants pledged to meet again when possible. [21]

At the Hartland conference, Leo Rasmussen, an Iditarod NHT enthusiast from Alaska, challenged the group to organize a nonprofit coalition; his challenge would slowly become a reality over the next decade. As he described it years later,

In 1988 someone fortuitously got a bunch of the Federal partners together in Hartland, Wisconsin, for a gathering of all these people. And there were darn few volunteers there — I can tell you that — most of them were Federal people. . . . I was not a trail person in the true sense that you knew who was doing this and what agency was doing that. I went through the whole session of meeting people and trying to know first names, and the whole process. We were in the last session together, and I could sense that there was something that would be far better if we were all working together instead of all these little separate trails that belonged to the Park Service, and the Forest [Service], and pieces of it to the BLM. We were all working in the same direction. We had so many things that were common. However, if you stay separate, your common problems are worse than someone else's — which is rarely ever true. I could see that if we got together, we could solve these problems in a far more efficient manner. So I stood up at the end of that session and suggested that — and apparently there were some people that were listening. But the majority of them thought, "Who's this little turkey from Alaska who's a volunteer and doesn't even belong to the Federal Government, sittin' back, telling us what to do?" [22]

In fact, this seminal conference of 77 participants produced a number of long-term tangible initiatives, including:

- Better promotion of NSTs and NHTs in special events, postage stamps, a slide show or video, an updated brochure, and marketing through the outdoor equipment industry.
- An inter-trail communications network.
- A follow-up meeting, hopefully near an NHT.

---

21. *Ibid.*, 27–9; Gary Werner, 2007, NPS Oral History interview, NTS 40th Anniversary Oral History Project, p. 5.
22. Leo Rasmussen, 2008, NPS Oral History interview, NTS 40th Anniversary Oral History Project, pp. 4–5.

- Increased status within the administering agencies.
- Improved networking to supportive beneficial legislation

A nine-member steering committee was appointed and approved to coordinate these efforts. [23]

The year 1989 opened with the release of an analysis of the nation's trails by the Congressional Research Service. It emphasized the 102,500-mile trail system managed by the USDA Forest Service and the growing importance of challenge cost-share funding within that agency. Regarding NPS involvement with the National Trails System, the CRS report's author notes:

The growth of the National Trails System to 16 long-distance components has resulted in some policy and program perplexities. The two categories (i.e., National Scenic and National Historic) and the individual trails themselves have different authorities, which has led to confusion. At the Federal level, the trails are administered by three agencies: the National Park Service, Forest Service, and Bureau of Land Management. There is a need for much improved coordination among these agencies and among the individual trail managers. The development and implementation of clear policy guidance from the NPS Policy Office to trail managers and the Regional Offices responsible for the trails is essential. [24]

Also, in early 1989, the Rails-to-Trails Conservancy, with NPS funding assistance, identified 19 locations where abandoned railroad corridors might help fill some of the missing gaps along the North Country NST. This was an imaginative study combining several of the authorities of the newly amended NTSA. [25]

In the fall of 1989, the National Park Service established a National Trails System program leadership position in its Washington, DC, headquarters. In part, this occurred in response to the earlier NPS struggles over whether to have a dispersed program or a centralized office to administer national historic trails. A line item for this program position

23. *National Conference on National Scenic and National Historic Trails – A Summary*, typescript MS in NTSAHA.
24. George Siehl, January 1989, *Trails Programs in Federal Agencies: A Data Compilation*, Washington, DC: Congressional Research Service of the Library of Congress, p. 47, in NTSAHA.
25. Bonnie Nevel, March 1989, *Closing the Gaps*, Washington, DC: GPO, in NTSAHA.

for $400,000 was mentioned in internal documents as early as 1986. [26] Landscape architect and park planner Steve Elkinton (the author of this book) was hired. A few months later, he coordinated a seminal meeting of NPS trail administrators and their supervisors in Kansas City, Missouri. It was the first of a series of annual trail administrator-level meetings to enhance coordination and operational consistency. A few years later, these meetings were expanded to include interagency counterparts. The Kansas City meeting yielded a prioritized task list. Staff task forces were organized to explore policy and legislation, trail logos and graphics, and trail compliance responsibilities. The group also resolved that each NPS-administered NST and NHT should have, as all authorized NPS park units did, a line-item in the annual NPS budget documents. [27]

In early 1990, the first court case challenging National Trails System Act authorities was decided by the U.S. Supreme Court unanimously in favor of reserving railbanked railroad corridors intact for interim recreational use. The amount of compensation from such takings would be determined under other authorities. Over the next few decades, many court challenges have questioned various authorities in the NTSA, with almost all concerning railbanking and its consequences or the use of eminent domain along the Appalachian NST. None has concerned the NHTs or NRTs so far. [28]

The second term of President Ronald Reagan (1985–1989) and much of his successor, George H. W. Bush's term in office (1989–1993) were seminal for the National Trails System — not because of White House leadership (other than the President's Commission on Americans Outdoors) but because other trends bore fruit. The challenges of the new category of NHTs, the excitement and enthusiasm around recycling abandoned railroad corridors into trails, a strengthened Appalachian Trail community, the formation of American Trails, the clarion call of *Trails for All Americans*, the first-ever meeting of NST and NHT advocates, and even the start-up of *Pathways Across America* — all of these

26. Bob Karotko for William T. Spitzer, August 19, 1986, memo to NPS Director with attachments, in NTSAHA.
27. William C. Walters, January 18, 1990, memo to NPS Directorate, etc., *Meeting Report: Long-Distance Trails Policy Meeting, November 8–9, 1989*, in NTSAHA.
28. Supreme Court of the United States, *Presault et ux. v. Interstate Commerce Commission et al.*, decided February 21, 1990, in NTSAHA.

factors laid the groundwork for the National Trails System's equivalent to "The Roaring '90s!"

"20TH ANNIVERSARY CRITIQUE"

Jackson's 1988 article, The Long Way 'Round . . ."
In NTSAHA.

Excerpts from Jackson, Donald Dale, "The Long Way 'Round: The National Scenic Trails System and How It Grew. And How It Didn't," in *Wilderness*, Summer 1988.

But on paper, at least, [in 1968] *the country now had a handsome blueprint for a grand coast-to-coast network of trails. MacKaye, hunkered down in Shirley Center, pronounced himself pleased — his radical precepts had now been validated in both the wilderness and trails bills. There was something unmistakably American — a certain raw grandeur, perhaps, or maybe hubris — about a foot-path that disappeared into a pine grove and emerged two or three thousand miles later in a blackberry thicket. The whole idea of a national trails system is characteristically American, in the opinion of the Wilderness Society's Ron Tipton, "It goes with our notion of the West, it's an American idea. Whatever's wrong with the system — and there's a lot wrong with it — it's still a great thing, a success story in its own way."*

No one realized it at the time, but the Herbst-Carter years turned out to be the lone bright interval — in the idiom of English weather forecasts — in the otherwise bleak twenty-year history of the national trails system. The money that would transform designated trails from lines on a fetching map into reality was still hard to find, to be sure, but the administration was still friendly from the idea. Two more scenic trails — the Ice Age and North Country — made it into the paper network in 1980. . . .

Worse times were ahead. When Ronald Reagan's Interior Secretary James Watt disbanded the Heritage Conservation and Recreation Service he eliminated the trails system's only effective sponsor in the government. Only once in seven years did the Reagan administration request appropriations for trails, though Congress regularly voted funding anyway. Most of the money went to the Appalachian Trail, and when new scenic trails were designated, as three more were in 1983 (Potomac Heritage, Natchez Trace, and Florida), private land acquisition was specifically prohibited.

The AT's success also derives from the constancy and effectiveness of its support troops; no other trail, putative or partial, has anything approaching the organized constituency of the ATC. The conference's most stunning coup was snaring a share of the responsibility for managing the trail, an exploit ratified in a 1984 agreement between the ATC and the Park Service. "That never happened before," a Park Service man marvels. "Government agencies don't willingly give up their authority."

Can a national trails constituency be organized? . . . The drawing-board trails of the South and West are more remote from big cites than the AT is, and the pool of potential trail activists is smaller. Rallying trail advocates is a job awaiting a leader, a latter-day MacKaye or Avery. . . . The national trails system is in the position of a hiker stranded alone in a storm, looking in vain for a signpost and all out of gorp; it's clearly in seven kinds of trouble. The trails system is the spurned and neglected stepchild among the extended family of 1960s environmental laws. Its friends are unorganized. At the moment at least, it's up against a hostile administration, a stingy Congress, and an ill-equipped and too-often indifferent bureaucracy . . . [29]

---

29. Donald Dale Jackson, "The Long Way 'Round: The National Scenic Trails System and How It Grew. And How It Didn't," *Wilderness*, Summer 1988.

CHAPTER 10
THE ROARING
1990S – PART I

In the National Trails System Act, I clearly see a vision: a network of trails spanning America, celebrating and cherishing our historic and scenic resources. These trails — both long and short — will cater to all appropriate types of uses, including hiking, horseback riding, motoring, cycling, and skiing. The long-distance interstate trails are the backbone connecting together the regional and local trails. When in place, they will bring recreational opportunities within easy reach of most Americans — linking them to our precious parks, forests, rivers, mountains, and historic sites. (James Ridenour, 1991) [1]

I n 1990, following the National Park Service's lead, the Forest Service established oversight of its National Trails System activities in its national office in the Dispersed Recreation Program. (And in 1996, the Bureau of Land Management created a similar full-time job in its national headquarters to coordinate NSTs and NHTs as they crossed BLM lands.)

Also in 1990, roughly following the route followed by HikaNation in 1981, the American Hiking Society (AHS) coordinated new public interest in hiking by laying out a coast-to-coast trail that became known as the American Discovery Trail (ADT). The exploratory team was led by Eric Seaborg and Ellen Dudley who fell in love during the year-long trek and were married soon after. On the heels of their cross-country trek, Reese Lukei became ADT national coordinator and selected volunteer state coordinators who promoted the route in each of the states it passed

---

1. James M. Ridenour in NPS, January 1991, *Report on America's National Scenic, National Historic, and National Recreation Trails – 1989–1990*, p. 18, Washington, DC: NPS, in NTSAHA.

through. A feasibility study act for the ADT was passed in 1993. As the NPS study team explored the proposed route, they found that much of this innovative trail followed low-volume roads as a right-of-way — while connecting many urban areas — thus it did not fit well into either the NST or NHT categories. Yet its supporters promoted it as "the backbone of the National Trails System." In 1997, NPS issued the feasibility study report asserting that it might be the first of a new category of "national discovery trails." However, neither popular nor political support has been sufficient in subsequent congresses to have the ADT added to the National Trails System. [2]

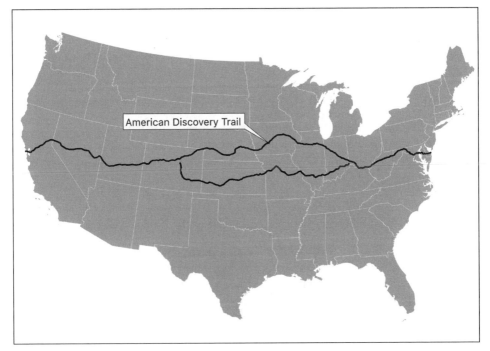

Proposed Route of the American Discovery Trail.

Also in 1990, the first two connecting and side trails were designated by the Secretary of the Interior Manuel Lujan under the previously unused Section 6 of the National Trails System Act. The 14-mile Timm's Hill Trail in Wisconsin connected the Ice Age NST to Wisconsin's highest

2. Reese Lukei, October 17, 2017, personal communication with the author.

point, and the-86-mile Anvik Connector linked the Iditarod NHT in Alaska to an important trail-related village. [3]

Early in 1991, NPS published its first attempt at an "in-progress" report on the status of various types of trails created under the NTSA almost 25 years before. Each of the NSTs and NHTs established thus far, as well as the two new connecting and side trails, were profiled. A graph in this report showed the number of NRTs recognized each year — with more than 200 annually in the late 1970s, but generally a dozen or less added most other years — totaling 780 by 1991. The report concluded with a discussion of current National Trails System issues, including the need for policy consistency within and among federal agencies, inadequate promotion and funding, patchy resource protection, and the challenges of adding additional trails then under study. [4]

As various agency field offices geared up to operate the NSTs and NHTs assigned to them, these staff gradually came to appreciate the complexity of these long, often interstate, trail resource corridors. Even without funding for land acquisition for the newer trails, identifying a trail corridor required environmental compliance and intricate partnerships. Defining roles and responsibilities seemed a never-ending challenge. Even determining the "federal interest" in such partnership projects proved difficult. The formal mapping and publishing of trail rights-of-way, as the NTSA requires, had fallen out of practice by the early 1990s, and trail offices sought new ways to establish definitive trail maps and resource inventories. And in NPS, the question festered, "Should NPS-administered trails be considered units of the National Park System?" [5]

In 1991, the ground shifted nationwide for trails funding. For the first time, a federal transportation funding law included provisions for trail projects. A broad coalition of new transportation partners, including RTC, the National Trust for Historic Preservation, the American Recreation Coalition, Scenic America, and AHS, worked with Senator Daniel Patrick Moynihan (D-NY) to craft the Intermodal Surface

3. "First Connecting Trails Designated," *Pathways Across America*, Summer 1990, p. 6.
4. NPS, January 1991, *Report on America's National Scenic, National Historic, and National Recreation Trails – 1989–1990*, Washington, DC: NPS, in NTSAHA.
5. NPS, September 30, 1991, "Discussion Paper: *Should National Scenic and National Historic Trails Administered by the National Park Service Be Considered "Units" of the National Park System?*; Thomas L. Gilbert, February 4, 1992, Memo to Regional Director, Midwest Region, both in NTSAHA.

Transportation Efficiency Act of 1991 (ISTEA). The Highway Trust Fund was expanded to benefit more than just roads and highways. As the Federal Highway Administrator, Tom Larson, described it to a group of trail advocates in 1992:

[ISTEA] is truly a landmark bill, the most significant transportation act since 1956, when funding for the Interstate Highway System was approved. . . . It's a broad bill that addresses all aspects of surface transportation — not just highway commuting and goods movement. . . . Ten percent of surface transportation funding must be used for transportation enhancement activities specified in the law [including] facilities for pedestrians and bicycles; acquisition of scenic easements and scenic or historic sites; . . . historic preservation; . . . preservation of abandoned railway corridors; . . . [etc.]. The ISTEA [also] includes the Symms National Recreational Trails Act of 1991. . . . [This new fund] *has opened Federal Highways to a vast new partnership. If it is to succeed, we will have to be partners, because we in Federal Highways can't do it alone.* [6]

The new transportation partnerships continued with their support on other fronts as well. The Recreational Trails Program (RTP) required participating states to establish multi-modal trail advisory committees. Within a few years, such committees were organized in all 50 states and the District of Columbia. Each committee advised designated state officials on recommendations for projects to receive funding.

The most significant development in the 1990s affecting NSTs and NHTs as a coherent nationwide network of trails was the formation of the Committee of 17. This nationwide coalition of NST and NHT groups — building on the vision of the 1988 Hartland Conference — was formed specifically to enhance the federal administrative base budget of each trail. In addition, it sought to have the federal agency administering each trail assign at least one full-time staff person to that trail. The Committee of 17 was founded at the 2nd Conference on National Scenic and Historic Trails, held at the Menucha Conference Center overlooking the picturesque Columbia River Gorge at Corbett, Oregon, in November 1991. Another aspect of this seminal conference was the release of the first edition of the *National Trails System Map and Guide*, which has proven to be a compact and

---

6. Thomas D. Larson, American Trails, etc., 1992, Proceedings – *11th National Trails Symposium, September 19–22, Missoula, Montana*, pp. 8–16, in NTSAHA.

effective marketing tool for informing the public about the many resources and routes associated with national scenic and historic trails.

Two key participants described the Menucha Conference this way:

. . . at that meeting, we managed to get both the scenic and historic people there together. And Reese Lukei and I and Gary were up until the wee, wee hours of the morning with some of the people in the historic trails community, convincing them to come and be a part of that coalition, and we were successful at it. [We were] *lobbying other trails people. I did more of that than I have lobbied Congress. But I was proud to be a part of that. That's what made this whole thing come together, and work, and it has worked beautifully ever since.* [7]

At that conference a group of us, Susan Henley and Reese Lukei from American Hiking Society, and myself, and a couple of others were determined that we were going to come out of that conference with some kind of an organized effort to work together beyond the conference. One of the things that we came up with (what the people getting together there and talking about) was what should we do together. We came up with two basic goals: one was to get annual, operational funding in the federal budget for each of the national scenic and historic trails, and second was to get at least one full-time person responsible for each of the trails in the given agency that had responsibility.

Most of us who were there at that second conference in 1991, the one at Menucha, have a soft spot sort of in our hearts and souls for that event because there was a kind of a magic about it. I was one of a handful of people who were determined to have that conference result in something that was going to carry on afterwards. A number of people made the effort, very selflessly, to come up with something that would work and then take it back. We ended up with a charter that we made up for ourselves, calling ourselves the Committee of 17 because there were 17 trails. But the responsibility was for each of the representatives to go back to their organizations and get our organizations to endorse this concept: that we would go to Congress and request funding. Then we were talking about $250,000, average, per trail. That was what we pulled out as a formulaic amount, plus at least one person per each agency to be full-time responsible for each of the trails. I'm very proud of the fact that most of the people did go back, and

---

7. Susan Henley, 2007, NPS Oral History interview, NTS 40th Anniversary Oral History Project, p. 10.

they actually got this charter that we had adopted endorsed by their organization board of directors. [8]

The one NST group not represented at the Menucha Conference (and not an original member of the Committee of 17) was the Appalachian Trail Conference (ATC). However, Reese Lukei, former ATC activist and by 1991 the principle AHS staffer coordinating the American Discovery Trail, felt so strongly that ATC should be involved that he leaned on the ATC leadership soon after the conference, and within a few months they, too, joined the fledgling Committee of 17. [9]

To move forward in its quest for adequate funding, the Committee of 17 sent Gary Werner to Washington, DC, for the budget hearings in early 1992. As he describes it,

In the spring of 1992, I had a mandate from them to go to Congress and testify, to make our case. The interesting thing was that we didn't get any immediate results, we didn't get any more money in '92. So we had another meeting — not at our own conference, but at the National Trails Symposium that fall in Missoula, Montana . . . and basically I said, "Okay this is what happened. What do you want to do?" And George Cardinet . . . who had a great booming voice, from the back of the room said, "We go back, and we go back, and we go back, and we keep going back until we get what we want!" And the follow-up was that the leadership basically said, "We've got to stick together. Let's keep working together. The fact that we didn't succeed right away, that's no reason not to keep doing it." [10]

The 11th National Trails Symposium, held in 1992 in Missoula, Montana, was energized by the recent passage of ISTEA and the new programs in it providing funds for trail projects. Most of these funds were to be distributed through state agencies and transportation planning organizations. States were encouraged to have statewide trails councils, and a national Recreational Trails Advisory Committee was established to help guide the new Recreational Trails Program. The promise of new funding and the vision of *Trails for All Americans* seemed to catalyze new discussions

8. Gary Werner, 2007, NPS Oral History interview, NTS 40th Anniversary Oral History Project, p. 11.
9. Reese Lukei, October 16, 2017, personal communication with the author.
10. Gary Werner, 2007, NPS Oral History interview, NTS 40th Anniversary Oral History Project, p. 20.

about trails and tourism, multi-use trails, economic impacts of trails, the roles of land trusts, better access for the disabled, environmentally sustainable trails, and getting citizens successfully organized around trails. In addition, NPS and the Bicycle Federation of America announced a nationwide series of citizen seminars devoted to getting the most project success out of ISTEA. [11]

Also in 1992, NPS and Pennsylvania State University released a study called *The Impacts of Rail-Trails*. It examined three very different rail-trail projects (one each in Iowa, Florida, and California) and determined that each trail brought in hundreds of thousands of dollars of "new money" to the communities served by these trails. This was one of just a few comprehensive examinations of the economic impacts of trails associated with the National Trails System, especially since rail-banking was added to the Trails Act in 1983. [12]

In January of 1993, the NPS administrators of various NSTs and NHTs continued their new pattern of annual gatherings to discuss mutual issues — this time in Tucson, Arizona. Many issues were discussed, and the ones that proved most important were 1) embarking on a modified strategic planning process to link to an agency-wide strategic planning process already underway and 2) recommending that with the recent establishment of the California and Pony Express NHTs, all four NHTs which overlap in Nebraska and Wyoming should be administered from one centralized office somewhere in the NPS Rocky Mountain Region. Other long-simmering topics included management policy, logos and trail markers, wayside exhibits, and the American Discovery Trail. [13]

January 1993 also marked another transition in the federal government from Republicans to Democrats, with William J. Clinton taking the helm as president. About this time, the former Interagency Trails Task Force was reestablished (since its original MOU charter had never been abolished) as the Federal Interagency Council on Trails to better coordinate multi-agency issues, standards, policies, and initiatives. This group then met on a regular basis for many years, serving as a model for

---

11. American Trails, etc., 1992, Proceedings – *11th National Trails Symposium, September 19–22, Missoula, Montana*, in NTSAHA.
12. "Rail-Trail Case Studies," *Pathways Across America*, Fall 1990, p. 5.
13. NPS Long Distance Trails Program, *Long Distance Trails Managers Meeting, Tucson, Arizona, January 26–28, 1993, Meeting Report*, in NTSAHA.

interagency cooperation helping coordinate funding, mapping, policy, and information exchange. Its role evolved over the years in a series of interagency MOUs and annual reports discussed in later chapters.

AHS launched National Trails Day (NTD) in 1993 in part to celebrate the 25th anniversary of the National Trails System and to give communities a chance to showcase their trails. NTD aspired to involve a million Americans positively with trails on that day, to promote the principles of *Trails for All Americans*, to promote recreation industry support, and to strengthen grassroots trails organizations. AHS sought financial support from NPS, Recreation Equipment Inc. (REI), and other sponsors and was able to report after June 1993 on 2,000 events in all 50 states engaging an estimated 750,000 participants. [14]

Clinton and Gore campaigning, Fall, 1992. Photo from the Robert McNeely Collection courtesy Clinton Library, Little Rock, Arkansas.

Butch Henley, then AHS Executive Director, later gave this account of the origins of NTD:

[Someone] *planted the idea for National Trails Day in my head many years ago. I kept pushing for AHS to take it on as a project for six years before I finally convinced them to do it. And then I didn't get any credit for it. I twisted their arm for six years to get them to include that in developing their long-range plan, back 20 years or so ago. Finally it ended up that we had two people from Backpacker* [Magazine] *on our board at that time, and they liked the idea. They thought it was a good idea. Then I ended up staffing AHS . . . and brought in a draft and put it into the final thing. I ended up drawing it up, so I included it. And a couple of years later Backpacker come up and said, "We'd like to support that." So I started National Trails Day, which I think is a great thing!* [15]

14. Susan "Butch" A. Henley for AHS, July 15, 1992, letter to William T. Spitzer, NPS; David Lillard, June, 1993, *National Trails Day 1993 Program Report*, both in NTSAHA.
15. Susan "Butch" Henley, 2007, Oral History interview, NPS 40th Anniversary Oral History Project, p. 19.

Although National Trails Day events can occur any time in the year, most occur on the first Saturday in June each year. Through its website, AHS has developed an online toolkit and tracking system to document the thousands of events that occur each year highlighting trails. In many communities, National Trails Day has become a key moment for building public awareness of local trails and involving local businesses and institutions to support and promote their trails.

AHS has remained strongly committed to key principles of the National Trails System such as volunteerism. Each year it organizes volunteers in dozens of locales on public lands through a program called Volunteer Vacations. AHS has also proven a strong advocate for trails by helping sponsor Hike the Hill every winter.

In May 1993, Trail Lobby Week (later known as Hike the Hill) was organized for 25 representatives from various trails organizations to make their case for increased funding before Congress. The first one was hosted by the National Trails Coalition (AHS, Sierra Club, Wilderness Society, National Audubon Society, and National Wildlife Federation) supported by a grant from REI. This advocacy was evident in the next House Appropriations Committee markup that included a $750,000 increase for NPS trail operations (plus a one-third earmark of NPS's new Challenge Cost-Share program), a $4 million increase for BLM recreation programs, and increases for Forest Service trail programs. The Hike the Hill tradition quickly evolved into a midwinter advocacy week that has continued ever since. [16]

The National Trails Coalition's lobbying was successful in 1993, and new funds were appropriated for NPS-administered trails. This enabled NPS (as field staff had already recommended) to add a line-item to the official FY 1994 NPS budget for every NST and NHT with a completed comprehensive plan. One NPS staffer responsible for NHTs remembered it this way:

*So it was a thrill to see instead of 'Can you provide some money this year?' to see a **budget line** [emphasis his] in the Park Service budget for the Oregon Trail just as there was for the San Antonio Missions, or Yellowstone, or Gettysburg. And so in that budget, still very modest, but nevertheless something that you could depend upon — as*

16. "Long-Distance Lobbyists Advocate Trails Funding," *Pathways Across America*, Summer 1993, p. 10.

a superintendent — was a budget item for the Pony Express, or the California Trail, or the Santa Fe Trail, whatever. [17]

President Clinton appointed Bruce Babbitt as Secretary of the Interior in 1993. One of his first acts as secretary was to join Forest Service Chief Dale Robertson and trail partners to celebrate the "completion" of the Pacific Crest NST at Soledad Canyon, California, at a "Golden Spike" ceremony on National Trails Day, 1993. Despite rain, hundreds of people attended. Because of popular interest, CNN TV ran the story for a week afterward. [18]

For the 25th anniversary of the National Trails System in 1993, NPS and the Oregon-California Trails Association teamed up again to host the third conference on NSTs and NHTs in Kansas City, Missouri. The Committee of 17 tried out a new name, "The Committee for the National Trails System." Keynote speaker Bill Spitzer, Chief of NPS's Recreation Resources Division, highlighted the political nature of the NSTs and NHTs:

In 1968 a political act happened that affects the business we are here for today. The Appalachian Trail was "adopted" politically by the Federal Government — the beginning of the National Trails System. And as another political act, it was realized that there was no way that just the Appalachian Trail could be brought into the national system — a panoply of trails would have to be brought in. So there were a number of other trails that were brought in for study. It took ten years for a number of these other trails to come in. And I suggest to you that happened because "Congressmen favor parks close to home." The question is, how do we turn it into something higher, how do we turn it into something else? We must be political if for no other reason than what we chose to have happen will not happen without us having a political base. . . . So I suggest to you that if we are going to have a vision of bringing the real trail network together, a real network that is inclusive of our cities, of our values, of our people, that is supporting the human and natural world, we will have to sell that — and we will have to sell it in every congressional district across America. [19]

17. Jere Krakow, 2008, NPS Oral History interview, NTS 40th Anniversary Oral History Project, p. 13.
18. "World Watches Story of a Border-to-Border Trail," *Pathways Across America*, Summer 1993, p. 9.
19. NPS and OCTA, 1993, *Connection – '93: The Third National Conference on National Scenic and National Historic Trails, Proceedings*, pp. 16–8, in NTSAHA.

THE NATIONAL TRAILS SYSTEM

A year later, the 12th National Trails Symposium was held in Anchorage, Alaska, in the fall of 1994. It addressed many aspects of trails at all levels — national, state, regional, and local (including successful ISTEA-funded projects, accessibility for the disabled, research, economic impacts, greenways, the ambitious TransCanada Trail — even navigability of water trails). But very little was said about the status of the National Trails System and its components. From this time on, it appears that American Trail's biennial symposia and supporters of NSTs and NHTs largely diverged in their interests and meeting schedules. [20]

In 1994 — more than 10 years after the Section 10(c) prohibitions against federal funding for land acquisition for certain NSTs and NHTs had been superseded by the generic willing seller clause available to all the trails established later — the first efforts were made to correct this inequality. (In fact, this effort would take another 15 years.) On October 7, 1994, Senator Carl Levin (D-MI) offered this observation as he introduced S. 2549 (a bill that never passed):

Providing the Federal Government with acquisition authority to purchase land from willing sellers for these trails will help address increasing development pressures that threaten the long-range continuity of the National System in many areas. With voluntary acquisition as an additional tool, the Federal Government can more efficiently participate in the trail building process . . . . This country's scenic beauty and precious natural resources deserve protection. [21]

In the face of federal government restructuring and agency budget cutbacks, the spring 1995 edition of *Pathways Across America* was devoted to testimonials by trail advocates about how small federal investments in NST and NHT funding and staff can be multiplied many times for public benefit. Tullia Limarzi, editor of *Pathways Across America*, observed: Most of the responses can be summed up this way:

Our organization puts thousands of volunteer hours per year into the trail, and we're glad to do it. But our contributions could not be sustained without federal funding and organizational commitment that pay for staff coordination and supplies. More ardent respondents would like to tell Congress, "Do your duty! National long-distance trails

---

20. American Trails, etc., 1994, *Proceedings [for] 12th National Trails Symposium, "Connecting Our Communities," September 28–October 1, 1994, Anchorage, Alaska,* in NTSAHA.
21. Carl Levin, October 7, 1994, in *Congressional Record – Senate*, p. S 14860, in NTSAHA.

were created by Congress to provide a common good — don't let fiscal starvation kill them." [22]

At the next conference for NSTs and NHTs held in 1995 in Chevy Chase, Maryland, the Committee of 17 officially changed its name to the Partnership for the National Trails System (PNTS). In 1997, it formalized a leadership council and executive committee structure and in 2001 obtained 501(c)(3) nonprofit status. In 1997, PNTS took over editorship and production of *Pathways Across America*, which has served as a major communications tool for PNTS ever since. The Partnership's primary goal remains achieving better funding for the NSTs and NHTs. However, its scope and structure have gradually expanded following strategic plans completed in 2007 and 2017.

The 1995 conference was remarkable for another reason. It was the first time that the federal agency trail administrators had met together (before this they had met at separate agency meetings — if they had met at all). After a day of discussing many common issues, they also met with their nonprofit counterparts from the newly renamed PNTS,

. . . and were not surprised that nonprofit partners want less red tape, more money to support volunteers, reliable links for federal protection, better interagency cooperation, clear understanding of roles, and a focus on the educational value of the trails. Federal partners hope for strong volunteer and political support, appropriate trail promotion, and well-informed on the ground "eyes and ears" to help protect and monitor trails. One immediate result of this interagency gathering . . . is a listing of electronic mail addresses for faster and broader communication. [23]

This Chevy Chase conference capitalized on being in the Washington, DC, area, not only for learning lobbying skills but for tapping many of the conservation and historic preservation organizations with offices there. Secretary Babbitt's Assistant Secretary, Bonnie Cohen, offered this advice to the attendees: "We must all redouble our efforts to demonstrate the value of these trails to the American people . . . and demonstrate to

22. Tullia Limarzi, editor, "What Does Your Trail Want from Congress?," *Pathways Across America*, Spring 1995, Vol. 7, No. 2.
23. Steve Elkinton, "At Last, a Full House: Federal Trail Administrators Get Together," *Pathways Across America*, Summer 1995, Vol. 7, No. 3, p. 8.

Congress just how cost-effective the trails community is in forging partnerships with federal agencies and others." [24]

DO WE NEED A NATIONAL TRAILS SYSTEM PLAN?

IN THE 1983 AMENDMENTS, there was a requirement for a biennial National Trails System Plan. Congress wanted a report on what would make this a system, rather than just a collection, of trails. [After the 1986 National Trails Assessment,] *the closest anyone came to doing that was an effort that NPS's newly established Rivers, Trails, and Conservation Assistance (RTCA) program embarked upon in 1988 that lasted about four or five years. It had a very interesting twist — which caused them to run out of money in doing it — and that was to break the country down into a series of regions and to look at those regions and do an inventory of all the major trails in that region and publish an atlas of those trails as a public document. The most impressive of these was the first one,* Trails of the Mid-Atlantic States, *that included Virginia, West Virginia, Pennsylvania, Delaware, Maryland, and New Jersey. It brought together a dynamic network of people. I remember when the rail-trail people and the hiking trail people in West Virginia got together for the first time ever. This was before the days of state trail coordinators in some states, before the days of ISTEA. All kinds of synergies happened when people from the same state who were working on trails but had never met each other got together. So the atlas was useful and was sold through the Government Printing Office. The complex and gorgeous graphics were done by Virginia Commonwealth University. But it was before the days of websites, it was before the days of simplified graphics. I don't think that you'd ever see a document like that again.*

---

24. Bonnie Cohen, Assistant Secretary of the Interior for Policy, Management, and Budget, April 11, 1995, *Pathways Across America*, Summer 1995, Vol. 7, No. 3, p. 8.

Trails of the Mid-Atlantic States, 1992, as issued by NPS. Photo by author.

Trails Tomorrow: A Call to Action, the follow-up New England region
trail report from Trails Today, A Heritage at Risk?

*NPS then replicated this in New England and was getting ready to do it again in
the Midwestern States and the Great Lakes, and even the Northwest, when the
whole program fell apart. The idea was to take these eight or nine regional trail
atlases, region by region, and build on the grassroots brainstorming sessions of trail
planning (documenting existing trails, identifying missing links to get them to work
better together, and fleshing out dream trails, future trails that are needed). One
of the reasons it fell apart was that just in those days as the Mid-Atlantic plan
was underway, the American Discovery Trail kind of shot through like an arrow
from west to east. And it's like "Whoa! Here's a backbone trail for the whole
region, and we didn't even know it was coming." So it showed the weakness of a
piecemeal trail plan.*

This region-by-region effort, one or two regions every year, was cumbersome, taking 10 or 12 or 14 years to put it all together, to stitch together all these regions. And, still you didn't really have a coherent national plan. I don't think that's what Congress intended anyway, so eventually the requirement for that plan was thrown out of the law by the elimination of various unused report requirements . . . [in 1996].

Without a national plan, the National Trails System becomes vulnerable to continue to be built piece by piece rather than systematically. In the Atlas of the United States *published in 1970, there are many pages of routes of exploration and conquest and settlement that were officially documented as historic trails—the Butterfield Overland Stage, the Goodnight-Loving Trail, the voyages of Fremont. There are many historic routes important to American history that are not yet in the National Trails System as historic trails. I think there is basically an unlimited number of potential ones.*

The bottom line is: which of those trails are going to garner the public interest sufficient to organize a group around it? Most of the historic trail organizations that I know of right now are dropping in membership even though the population is growing. Many of these groups don't know how to reach out to youth or to young people. Many of them may seem a little old-fashioned or esoteric to the average citizen. But a trail without such a group is very vulnerable. So I don't know how many more trails there will be in this system. So far it has depended more on the intensity of citizen interest (and political leverage) than on any systematic approach. [25]

25. Condensed from Steve Elkinton, 2007, NPS Oral History interview, NTS 40th Anniversary Oral History Project, pp. 14–5.

CHAPTER 11
THE ROARING
1990S – PART 2

America's national trails are among our least known national treasures. They uniquely provide a way to significantly link together a great wealth of scenic resources, historic sites, and local communities. Your work in making these trails come together is itself historic in importance and will have far-reaching effects on Federal agencies, future visitors to the trails, and the Nation as a whole. (Robert Stanton, NPS Director, 1999) [1]

As the number of NSTs and NHTs increased, so did the number of citizen organizations dedicated to supporting these trails. Building on the successful networking that occurred at the 1988 and 1991 NST/ NHT trail conferences, various federal agencies (NPS, Forest Service, and BLM) provided financial assistance and organizational help for the next set of biennial conferences in the period approaching the new millennium. NPS first organized these conferences in partnership with one or more nonprofit host groups, such as the Oregon-California Trails Association. Conference planning fully passed to the Partnership for the National Trails System (PNTS) in 1999. The location of each conference featured mobile workshops (educational field trips) to one or more nearby NSTs and NHTs.

---

1. Robert Stanton, NPS Director, September 14, 1999, letter to Participants [at the] Sixth National Conference on National Scenic and Historic Trails, Zephyr Point, Nevada, in NTSAHA.

TABLE D

Sequence of National Scenic and Historic Trail Conferences, 1988–2018

YEAR	LOCATION	FEATURED TRAILS
1988	Camp Whitcomb, Hartland, WI	Ice Age NST
1991	"Menucha," Corbett, OR	Oregon and Lewis and Clark NHTs Pacific Crest NST
1993	"Mo-Kan," Kansas City, MO	Oregon, California, Santa Fe, and Lewis and Clark NHTs
1995	National 4-H Center, Chevy Chase, MD	Potomac Heritage and Appalachian NSTs
1997	Canterbury Retreat Ctr., Oviedo, FL	Florida NST
1999	Zephyr Point, Lake Tahoe, NV	California and Pony Express NHTs Pacific Crest NST
2001	Casper, WY	Oregon, California, Mormon Pioneer, and Pony Express NHTs
2002	Fort Smith, AR	Trail of Tears NHT
2003	Skagit Valley Resort, Bow, WA	Pacific Northwest Trail
2005	Las Vegas, NV	Old Spanish NHT
2007	Duluth, MN	North Country NST
2009	Missoula, MT	Continental Divide NST Lewis and Clark and Nez Perce NHTs
2011	Abingdon, VA	Overmountain NHT Appalachian NST
2013	Tucson, AZ	Juan Bautista de Anza NHT
2015	Franklin, TN	Natchez Trace NST
2018	Vancouver, WA	Oregon and Lewis and Clark NHTs Pacific Crest NST

Significant anniversaries helped foster public awareness and involvement in the trails. In the years leading up to the Oregon Trail Sesquicentennial in 1993, many new trail partners became involved in that trail. The wagon trains, reenactments, improved visitor sites, and new state programs designed to enhance the trail's historic legacy inspired the BLM to become fully involved in NSTs and NHTs.

Building on this momentum, the BLM followed the example of NPS and the Forest Service in 1996 by establishing a full-time National Trails System position, first stationed in Washington, DC, then later in Riverside, California, and Whitefish, Montana. Deb Salt has held this position from

1997 to this writing. Within BLM, this program now falls under the National Landscape Conservation System (NLCS). [2]

In March 1996, Art and Marge Miller published the first-ever guidebook to all the NSTs and NHTs. After four years of touring 19 trails, the 308-page *Trails Across America: Traveler's Guide to Our National Scenic and Historic Trails* was published by Fulcrum Press. It was officially launched at the 13th National Trails Symposium held that year in Bethesda, Maryland. [3]

Art and Marge Miller meet with Representative Karen McCarthy (center) during the March, 1996, National Trails Symposium where the Millers launched their book *Trails Across America*. Photo from *Trail Tracks*, Summer, 1996.

The mid-1990s was the era when websites first appeared and quickly proliferated. Overnight, it seemed, every office had access to computer technology. Soon, many people converted from postal mail service to e-mail. And major attempts were made (often for the first time) to map trail and trail corridors using satellite Global Positioning System (GPS) and Geographic Information System (GIS) software. On the one hand, these were seen as systematic, comprehensive, and more easily shared than paper maps. On the other hand, their complexity, ever-changing software, sophisticated technology, and unexpected high costs created major challenges. [4]

Another aspect of the NSTs and NHTs that had been neglected for a long time was the standardization of trail marker logos that were authorized in Section 7 of the NTSA and graphically established by the Interagency Trails Task Force in the early 1970s. Since the disbanding of that task force in 1981, each trail office and agency had gone off on its own direction. All used the rounded triangle shape — but some had wide borders while others had none. Font types also differed. None of the agencies

2. BLM, 2006, *National Scenic and Historic Trail Strategy and Work Plan.*
3. "Millers 'Write the Book' on Trails," *Pathways Across America*, Spring 1996, Vol. 9, No. 2, p. 11.
4. "GPS Revolutionizes Trail Mapping," *Pathways Across America*, Summer 1996, Vol. 9, No. 3, p. 3.

had established rules for the design, placement, use, or protection of these logos along the trails.

A uniform system of logos would ensure that national trails were easily recognizable and protected and that Trails System graphics harmonized. By the mid-1990s, there were places — especially along the Platte River Valley in Nebraska and Wyoming — where as many as four NHTs followed overlapping or braided routes, and their logos in different fonts and styles did not look good together. To untangle and standardize these logo issues, NPS (in close cooperation with Forest Service and BLM) hired graphic designer Paul Singer, noted for the Audubon Guide logos. His firm examined the entire set of National Trails System logos and made recommendations for graphic consistency and future expansion. Under the contract, Paul Singer & Associates adjusted most of the trail marker logos, developed a replacement for the Ice Age NST, and crafted new ones for the recently created California and Pony Express NHTs. As follow-up, NPS published all of the logos for the NPS-administered NSTs and NHTs as official federal insignia in the *Federal Register*, formally alerting the general public that these insignia were protected against unauthorized uses. (Logos associated with Forest Service-administered trails are considered service marks by their solicitors and are registered with the U.S. Patent Office.) [5]

Cover of *The Economic Impacts and Uses of Long Distance Trails* conducted by North Carolina State University. In NTSAHA.

Another project in the mid-1990s was the first research on the economic impacts of NSTs and NHTs. Inspired by the earlier study of the economic benefits of rail-trails (*The Impacts of Rail-Trails* in 1992), NPS staff contracted with North Carolina State University to undertake a survey of visitors at sites along the Overmountain Victory NHT to look at visitor spending patterns. The results were impressive. First, an extensive literature review was conducted. Then, using the ImPlan economic model,

---

5. *Federal Register*, Vol. 64, No. 71, April 14, 1999, p. 18444, and Vol. 65, No. 60, March 28, 2000, p. 16412–8; Steve Elkinton, 2007, NPS Oral History interview, NTS 40th Anniversary Oral History Project, pp. 7–8.

almost $16 million a year spent by an estimated 1.1 million visitors in 1995 was calculated to be coming into counties along the Trail. Visitors were recorded from all over the world (but primarily from states along the trail) and spending money on overnight lodgings, site visits (often going to three or four sites), or following the trail from end to end. Their total spending along the trail far outstripped the minimal investment NPS made each year in that trail. [6]

In May 1996, AHS and RTC (with support from NPS, the Federal Highway Administration, and the Sporting Goods Manufacturers Association) issued a manifesto called *Trails and Trailways into the 21st Century* as a call to action based on the 1991 *Trails for All Americans*. With suggestions from five public forums held nationwide, involving hundreds of individuals, this manifesto offered six basic principles for alternative transportation systems:

- Be accessible to all Americans,
- Create a truly nationwide infrastructure of trails,
- Provide diverse experiences while respecting the natural and built environments,
- Provide numerous benefits simultaneously,
- Encourage local empowerment, and
- Work through creative partnerships.

The report then made specific recommendations for legislative amendments and refinements in such new programs as DOT's Recreational Trails Program. [7]

One result of agency reorganizations that occurred during the Clinton administration was that the NPS Trails Branch was assigned to the NPS Directorate of Cultural Resources. This turned out to be a boon for bringing attention to the fragile cultural resources associated with America's NHTs. One manifestation of this was an issue of NPS's *CRM* Bulletin that highlighted the cultural resource challenges associated with these trails. Articles in that issue addressed resource studies, significance criteria,

---

6. Roger Moore and Kelly Barthlow, *The Economic Impacts and Uses of Long-Distance Trails*, NPS, 1998; Steve Elkinton, 2007, NPS Oral History interview, NTS 40th Anniversary Oral History Project, p. 11.
7. American Hiking Society and Rails-to-Trails Conservancy, May 1996, *Trails and Trailways into the 21st Century: The Trails Policy Report of Trails for All Americans '94*, in NTSAHA.

visitor centers, education, aerial surveys, archaeology, reenactments, historic sites along NHTs, and even Switzerland's international perspective developing and protecting routes of both recreation and history. [8]

Another development in the late 1990s was a meeting of NHT partners to discuss the special challenges and issues associated with these long and vulnerable historic routes. Coordinated by PNTS, the first such group met in Kansas City in October 1998 and was inspired by a talk on "The Living Significance of Historic Trails" by Lewis and Clark College History Professor Stephen Dow Beckham. One outcome of this gathering was a stirring vision and goal statement for national historic trails:

Our Vision
National Historic Trails will be forever preserved by the American People to commemorate the stories of those who passed over them and profoundly shaped the United States. These trails will provide the opportunity to experience a deep sense of the past on the lands and water where the events occurred. From this shared vision we will endeavor to foster cooperative efforts that will promote and further the spirit and intent of the National Trails System Act.

Our Goals
- *To preserve and protect lands, resources and stories of the National Historic Trails to ensure that the opportunity for a quality trail experience is available for ourselves and posterity.*

- *To strengthen the management and protection of the National Historic Trails through effective communication, cooperation, and partnerships.*

- *To foster stewardship and ensure the continuing legacy of the National Historic Trails by emphasizing trails education.*

- *To increase support for the National Historic Trails by developing effective outreach strategies.* [9]

---

8. NPS, 1997, "CRM and the National Trails System" issue of *Cultural Resource Management*, Vol. 20, No. 1, 1997, Washington, DC, NPS, in NTSAHA.
9. Ross Marshall, "Groups Craft Vision for NHTs," *Pathways Across America*, Fall-Winter 1998–1999, Vol. 11, No. 4/Vol. 12 No. 1, p. 6.

In 1997, the often under-appreciated category of national recreation trails (NRTs) received some attention in an examination by two University of Maine researchers and a Forest Service colleague. In their comprehensive survey of NRTs (perhaps the first ever conducted), they observed that most NRT managers are unaware that their trail has this designation and that resource damage is the most common problem. They concluded, "This study suggests no clear advantage to NRT designation and raises the question: Do we still need them?" [10]

Meanwhile, as the agencies and nonprofit groups involved in the National Trails System in this period became better organized and built membership and organizational capacity, a steady stream of amendments to the NTSA requested additional trail studies and established some new trails. Table E provides a list of these amendments.

TABLE E
Legislative Actions 1990–2000 (101st through 106th Congresses)

DATE PASSED	PUBLIC LAW	ACTION
7/3/1990	101-321	Requested study for the Selma to Montgomery voting rights march route
8/15/1990	101-365	Established the Juan Bautista de Anza NHT
8/3/1992	102-328	Established the Pony Express and California NHTs
10/23/1992	102-461	Requested studies for the Ala Kahakai and American Discovery Trails
11/17/1993	103-144/5	Requested studies for El Camino Real de Tierra Adentro and El Camino Real para los Tejas
11/12/1996	104-333	Established the Selma to Montgomery NHT and requested studies for the Old Spanish and Great Western Trails
12/07/1999	106-135	Requested study for the Star-Spangled Banner Trail
10/13/2000	106-307	Established El Camino Real de Tierra Adentro NHT
11/09/2000	106-473	Requested study of the Washington-Rochambeau Revolutionary Route
11/13/2000	106-509	Established the Ala Kahakai NHT

---

10. Joanne F. Tynon, Deborah J. Chavez, and James A. Harding, *National Recreation Trails: A Comprehensive Nationwide Survey*, July 1997, in NTSAHA.

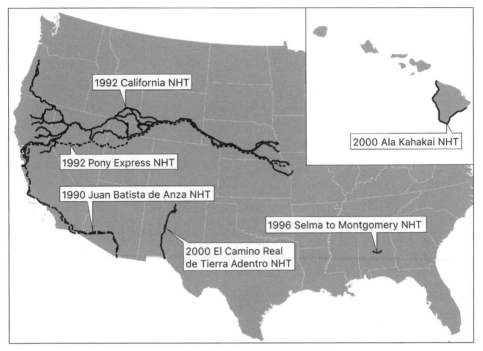

1992 California NHT

2000 Ala Kahakai NHT

1992 Pony Express NHT

1990 Juan Batista de Anza NHT

1996 Selma to Montgomery NHT

2000 El Camino Real
de Tierra Adentro NHT

Trails Added 1990-2000.

This narrative by no means reflects the complex and often hidden politicking associated with all the bills that led to these successful pieces of legislation. For each bill that was eventually signed into law, there were numerous preliminary versions, hearings, letters and statements of support and opposition, and behind-the-scenes negotiating. Although the AHS and PNTS were working hard in these years to alter some of the administrative authorities of the NTSA (such as the need for uniform willing-seller land acquisition authority for all NSTs and NHTs created after 1983), this period is remarkable because the only bills that did succeed involved either new trails or additional trail studies (despite varying political agendas and the remarkable suggestions in *Trails and Trailways Into the 21st Century*).

By the late 1990s, various ISTEA programs — such as Transportation Enhancements (TE) and the Recreational Trails Program (RTP) — were providing millions of dollars a year for trails and trail-related facilities of all kinds. TE projects were funded out of a 10% set-aside for qualifying non-pavement transportation-related projects. With ISTEA, the Federal Highway Administration became a major player in trails nationwide

— and the National Trails System specifically. Christopher Douwes, the RTP program coordinator, quickly became an essential member of the Federal Interagency Council on Trails.

The Iron Ore Heritage Trail along the North Country NST in Marquette County, Michigan, developed in part with Transportation Enhancement funds. Photo courtesy Mike Smith, Michigan Dept. of Transportation.

ISTEA programs pertinent to trails were retained, strengthened, and expanded in 1998 by the funding law that succeeded ISTEA, the Transportation Equity Act for the 21st Century (or TEA-21). Federal surface transportation funding has historically been authorized in six- or seven-year cycles. Advancements in computer-related technologies during the 1990s helped groups such as RTC maintain databases to track the thousands of trail-related projects that these new funds made possible. Various NSTs and NHTs tapped a small portion of these funds, mostly for facilities such as visitor centers, bridges, and sign systems. Rail-trail projects were successful in being awarded a much larger percentage of TE and RTP funds. And the Rails-to-Trails Conservancy has succeeded better than others in tracking all the projects benefiting from RTP, TE, and other FHWA funding programs.

Other new sources of funds for trails also appeared during these years. For example, in the early 1980s, Congress authorized the Forest Service to leverage appropriated funds through challenge cost-share (CCS) matching so that government funds could be matched at least one-to-one by partners. BLM received authorization for similar funding in 1985, as did NPS in 1993 — with one-third of its annual CCS appropriations specifically earmarked for NST and NHT projects. For NSTs and NHTs, the availability of challenge cost-share funds to build and nourish partnership proved invaluable. Hundreds of projects and programs have been conceived and carried out through cost-sharing.

Meanwhile, within the federal agencies, the complexity of administering NSTs and NHTs became increasingly apparent. And recognition of trail leadership — at least within NPS — emerged. As newly minted trail superintendent, Jere Krakow, later described it:

And to the credit of the regional directors of this [the NPS Intermountain] *Region, beginning in 1995, this superintendent of the trails was accorded the same recognition and rank as the superintendent of major national parks or smaller national parks, national monuments and national historic sites, and so on. Having said that, how ever, there's still a kind of second class aspect to it, because there are the traditionalists who say that what the National Park Service is all about are those gems of national parks and especially the large western parks (and you can name them as well as I). So there's an ongoing need to raise awareness in the outfit itself, the National Park Service, about the importance of national trails and getting support from them. Often times you hear (or it's implied) that the trail's budget is taking away from the budget, say, that Grand Teton might have or that Big Bend might have. The importance of being able to demonstrate that a trail should be accorded equality or equity, is based upon not only Congressional authorization of the trail (just like it authorized Big Bend, or Grand Teton), but that it also has a constituency, and that constituency can be one that supports a whole National Park System and not just the trails. When you measure up, say, the volunteer hours of folks like the Watsons or members of the Santa Fe Trail Association or OCTA, you can demonstrate to the upper management of the National Park Service or your colleagues who are superintendents in the Intermountain Region here that there is value added by the National Trails to the overall support for the National Park Service.* [11]

A similar situation existed in the Forest Service where there was now a full-time NST/NHT coordinator at the national level, but a fragmented approach in field offices. Longtime ATC staffer Robert Proudman

---

11. Jere Krakow, 2008, NPS Oral History interview, NTS 40th Anniversary Oral History Project, pp. 13–4.

eloquently appealed to an incoming Rocky Mountain Regional Forester in the Forest Service to develop consistent NST management practices from region to region and forest to forest:

[I urge] you and your peers to recognize and adopt common standards of administration, management, and protection for these nationally significant recreation resources, staff them with FS personnel who understand and are sympathetic to their unique values and vulnerability, and take bold steps to fully involve and nurture their related citizen advocacy groups and individual volunteer maintainers. The Forest Service has already proved the efficacy of its approaches in the Appalachian National Scenic Trail; now it is time to ensure that the unique values of other national scenic trails are nurtured in a similar way, and not fractured by competing local interests. Their national designations by Congress and their obvious national significance require nothing less. [12]

The revived Federal Interagency Council on Trails steadily fostered coordination among all the federal agencies involved with trails. Council attendance grew as more federal agencies committed specific staff to National Trails System issues. For many years, the council served largely as an information exchange without making many decisions or recommendations. However, it stimulated a variety of initiatives — such as GIS mapping and standards coordination, NRT submission packages, training opportunities, conferences and workshops, an executive order, and a sequence of interagency agreements — that have strengthened the entire National Trails System.

The agencies participating in the Council have signed a series of non-financial interagency agreements called memoranda of understanding (MOUs). These MOUs have formalized and helped in multi-party collaborations. The first MOU, signed in 1995, focused just on NHTs. Building on that MOU, a new agreement was signed in 2001 by five agencies (BLM, FHWA, FS, NPS, and the National Endowment for the Arts) fostering the interests of both NHTs and NSTs. A five-year summary report titled *National Historic and Scenic Trails: Accomplishments 2001–2005* describes its successes. [13] In 2006, a ten-year MOU that enlarged on both the scope and number of signatories was signed to address the entire National Trails

12. Robert Proudman, ATC, October 20, 1997, letter to Lyle Laverty, Director of Recreation, Forest Service, in NTSAHA.
13. BLM, FHWA, NEA, NPS, and USDA-FS, 2006, *National Historic and Scenic Trails: Accomplishments 2001–2005,* in NTSAHA.

System, including NRTs. (This chain of agreements proved its success and effectiveness so that a successor MOU was signed again in early 2017.) [14]

A unique event occurred on Earth Day 1998, when it was arranged that President Bill Clinton and Vice President Al Gore come to Harpers Ferry, West Virginia, to highlight trail volunteerism and conservation. They joined other volunteers moving rocks and planting shrubs before conducting a ceremony overlooking the

On Earth Day, 1998, President Clinton and Vice President Gore worked with ATC volunteers to build stone steps along the Appalachian NST at Harpers Ferry. Photo courtesy William J. Clinton Presidential Library/NARA, Little Rock, Arkansas.

confluence of the Potomac and Shenandoah Rivers with ATC leadership thanking members and volunteers and promising to support full funding for the Land and Water Conservation Fund to complete the trail's protection program by 2000. [15]

In 1998, NPS was fully immersed in conducting the comprehensive management plans (CMPs) for the newly established California and Pony Express NHTs. In the same document, the planning team attempted to update the earlier out-of-date plans for the Oregon and Mormon Pioneer NHTs. Longtime trail advocates Bill and Jeanne Watson described this process: *Covering more than 11,000 miles of overland trails through 13 states, the plan outlines procedures for preservation and interpretation of these four important 19th-century routes. . . . A trail planning project of this magnitude is unprecedented according to NPS personnel who spoke to the . . . OCTA Board of Directors meeting in March. . . . The 175-page CMP includes identification and justification of hundreds of historically important 'high potential sites and segments' along the trails.* [16]

14. Search "2006 National Trails System MOU" on NPS publications website and 2017-2027 MOU posted on NPS' "National Trails System" website.
15. "Trail Notes," *Pathway Across America*, Spring 1998, Vol. 11, No. 2, p. 11.
16. Bill and Jeanne Watson, 1998, "The New CMP Most Complex Ever," *Pathways Across America*, Spring 1998, Vol. 11, No. 2, pp. 3–4.

Interagency collaboration continued to improve. In 1999, at the invitation of BLM, the Interagency Trails Council agencies and 13 nonprofit trail organizations joined together to form the National Trails Training Partnership (NTTP). Convened by BLM, funded largely by the Federal Highway Administration, and coordinated by American Trails, the NTTP network aspired to be an information clearinghouse for trail-related training and skill-building nationwide. PNTS staff worked hard to make sure that NTTP offerings benefited their members groups and federal counterparts. Even today, the NTTP website provides a continuously updated calendar for upcoming training events as well as in-depth technical information about all types of trails. [17]

Also in 1999, NPS staff wishing to tighten up the significance criteria for NHTs held a symposium in Santa Fe, New Mexico. Papers were presented by a wide variety of scholars and trail administrators from various agencies, especially looking at similar procedures for determining significance, such as those for

Mike Bullington teaches Universal Trail Assessment skills at an NTTP-related training course. Photo courtesy American Trails.

the National Historic Landmarks and the National Register of Historic Places. Flip charts from the meetings articulate great principles to guide the NPS Advisory Committee that rules on the significance of proposed NHTs. However, it took more than ten years for these suggestions to be incorporated into agency policy. [18]

As the 1990s drew to a close, the Clinton administration sought ways to prepare for the coming new millennium. Humanities and arts agencies in the executive branch suggested that since trails connect all Americans to their heritage, a trail recognition program might be an appropriate

17. See National Trails Training Partnership website.
18. John Conoboy, August, 2, 1999, email to meeting participants, "Thanks and flip chart notes," in NTSAHA.

means of ushering in the new millennium. Developed in close partnership with the U.S. Department of Transportation, the Clinton administration launched the Millennium Trails Program in 1998 to recognize, promote, and stimulate trails that "honor the past and imagine the future." Between 1998 and 2001, the Clinton White House officially recognized 16 national millennium trails (most of these were already-established NSTs and NHTs), 51 state millennium legacy trails, and nearly 1,000 self-nominated local millennium trails. [19]

Transportation is about more than asphalt, concrete, and steel. The Millennium Trails connect our nation's landscape, heritage, and culture. They demonstrate our national commitment to improving the quality of life for all Americans. What legacy will this generation of Americas leave behind for our children and our children's children? I can think of no better gift — no finer legacy — than this network of historic trails. When our story is told, these Millennium Trails will resonate through history as our generation's gift to the ages. [20]

For one of the NHTs established in 2000 — El Camino de Tierra Adentro NHT — international authorities were included for the first time in the NTSA to foster cross-border consultations with Mexico in order to offer to the public a more complete intercultural story of this remarkable and ancient trail.

One indicator that NPS and other federal agencies were taking seriously the cultural resource challenges posed by trails was a symposium titled "Preserving Historic Trails" held in October 2000 at Acadia National Park in Maine. Timed

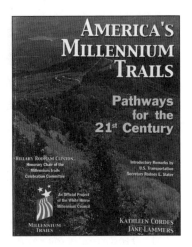

Kathleen Cordes' book on the Millennium Trails. Photo by author.

to celebrate a recently completed in-depth study of that park's hiking trails (some dating back to prehistoric times), the conference looked at both

19. "Millennium Trails," *The White House,* accessed June 18, 2018, https://clinton2.nara.gov/Initiatives/Millennium/trails.html.
20. Rodney Slater, Secretary of the U.S. Department of Transportation, as quoted in Kathleen Cordes and Jane Lammers, 2002, *America's Millennium Trails: Pathways for the 21st Century,* American Association for Leisure and Recreation, p. 1.

domestic and international trails. This was the first time that trails within national park units were examined for their cultural resource values. [21]

By the end of 2000, at the close of the Clinton administration, the BLM's National Landscape Conservation System (NLCS) was established under instructions from Interior Secretary Bruce Babbitt. Starting with the 14 national monuments administered or co-administered by BLM, this system of special landscapes also included 11 national conservation areas, a forest reserve, portions of wild and scenic rivers, wilderness study areas, and BLM-managed segments of national scenic and historic trails — in total, over 25 million acres of lands and waters. Facility development would largely occur outside these areas in neighboring gateway communities. Planning occurred under BLM's governing authority, the FLPMA. "These landscapes and public treasures will, for the first time, begin to receive the extra attention they need and deserve." This reorganization finally gave BLM-managed segments of NSTs and NHTs a logical place to fit within that agency. (The organic act for NLCS was finally established in law, almost ten years later, in 2009.) [22]

And, during the 1990s, also for the first time, enough records were kept to offer a quantitative perspective on how the National Trails System had changed (and, hopefully, improved) each year. One set of data tracked volunteer hours and financial contributions made by NST and NHT groups each year. For just the six years between 1995 and 2000, these statistics show remarkable growth.

---

21. Friends of Acadia, etc., *Preserving Historic Trails: Conference Proceedings*, October 17–19, 2000, in NTSAHA.
22. Deb Salt, "BLM's New National Landscape Conservation System," *Pathways Across America*, Fall 2000, Vol. 13, No. 4, pp. 6–7.

TABLE F
Volunteer Contributions for NSTs and NHTs 1996–2000 [23]

YEAR	VOLUNTEER HOURS	VOL. HOURS' VALUE	FINANCIAL CONTRIBUTIONS
1995	369,941	$4.3 million	$2.7 million
1996	473,066	$4.5 million	$4.1 million
1997	439,299	$5.7 million	$4.2 million
1998	498,702	$6.9 million	$4.4 million
1999	533,905	$7.4 million	$5.8 million
2000	593,392	$8.8 million	$6.6 million
	(60% increase)	(104% increase)	(144% increase)

Another data set, published in 2002 by a group of federal trail program leaders, offered a ten-year analysis of National Trails System accomplishments since 1991 when the Committee of 17 was first organized.

TABLE G
Key Indicators of National Trails System Growth – 1991–2000 [24]

FACTOR	1990	2000	% CHANGE
Annual federal operating funds (in $millions)	$2.5	$13.2	+428%
Number of paid organizational staff	31	93	+200%
Number of NST and NHT volunteers	4,785	13,966	+192%
Number of federal operating staff	13	37	+185%
Membership in partner organizations	35,105	67,508	+92%
Number of partner trail organizations	18	25	+39%
Number of NSTs and NHTs	17	22	+30%
Number of completed comprehensive plans	14	18	+29%
Number of registered NRTs	784	825	+5%
Number of completed challenge cost-share projects	0	350	---

23. "Contributions Sustaining the National Scenic and Historic Trails Made by Partner Trail Organizations," *Pathways Across America*, Spring/Summer 2002, Vol. 15, No. 2, p. 9.
24. Adapted from Steve Elkinton, with Helen Scully, Jim Miller, Jamie Schwartz, Deb Salt, and Gary Werner, "What Have We Accomplished in 10 Years?," *Pathways Across America*, Spring/Summer 2002, Vol. 15., No. 2, pp. 7–10.

In retrospect, it is clear that during the 1990s and the Millennium Trails period, the National Trails System moved beyond the experimental stage to become a fixture of the American landscape. One indicator was that several successive editions of the *National Trails System Map and Guide* had to be published during the 1990s to accommodate the ever-increasing number of NSTs and NHTs. Meanwhile, new trail groups were founded, and existing ones strengthened. In retrospect, the 1990s had indeed been a roaring decade!

SISTER PROGRAMS

During the 1990s, a variety of federal designation and funding programs in various federal agencies either were established or strengthened, reflecting practices and values similar to those in the National Trails System Act. All of these programs explored ways for Americans to protect large (and often endangered) landscapes. Three programs of special interest to (and sometimes intersecting with) national trails were National Scenic Byways, National Heritage Areas, and Wild and Scenic Rivers.

NATIONAL SCENIC BYWAYS

Under ISTEA in 1991, a National Scenic Byway program was established and funded under the U.S. Department of Transportation. Groups supporting this system of remarkable roads and highways included Scenic America, the American Recreation Coalition, and even the American Automobile Association. Roads that exhibited one or more of these "intrinsic qualities" were eligible: natural, cultural, historic, archaeological, recreational, and scenic. The most unique roads and highways with two or more of these qualities were eligible to be "All-American Roads," considered to be destinations in their own right. The first designations were made in 1998, and by 2010 (when the program was defunded), 210 national scenic byways and 31 All-American Roads had been designated by the Secretary of Transportation. Similarities to national trails included a) corridor management plans, b) seed funding from federal agencies, and c) grassroots organizations conducting the work on the ground. For example, the Selma to Montgomery NHT is congruent with an All-American Road of the same name. Most scenic byways became known as billboard-free corridors. Today, many states and some federal agencies (such as the Forest Service) have their own scenic byway, road, or drive programs. For those interested, the all-volunteer National Scenic Byways Foundation, based in Denver, Colorado, provides training and networking for these specially recognized road corridors. [25]

NATIONAL HERITAGE AREAS

To quote the NPS website on this subject, these are "designated by Congress as places where natural, cultural, and historic resources combine to form a cohesive, nationally important landscape. Through their resources, NHAs tell nationally important stories that celebrate our nation's diverse heritage." This sounds very similar to national historic trails. However, their organizing elements are not necessarily routes of travel but rather discrete landscape units united by past industrial or other land use themes. The first of these, the Illinois & Michigan Canal National Heritage Corridor, was established in 1984. Since then, 48 other areas and corridors have been designated in 32 states (all without an umbrella "organic act" at the federal level). The emphasis of these areas is community-led historic and landscape conservation and tourism development assisted by federal funding and technical help. All are coordinated through NPS, but the land and water resources comprising these areas are generally not owned by NPS. Like NHTs, these corridors are linear in extent and sometimes interstate in length. Most involve multiple overlapping themes. They receive federal funding assistance, require comprehensive corridor planning, and rely on grassroots volunteer efforts to be a success. [26]

25. "National Scenic Byway," *Wikipedia*, last modified May 26, 2018, https://en.wikipedia.org/wiki/National_Scenic_Byway; related sites.
26. "National Heritage Area," *Wikipedia*, last modified May 17, 2018, https://en.wikipedia.org/wiki/National_Heritage_Area; related websites.

WILD AND SCENIC RIVERS

This federal program was created the same day as the National Trails System (October 2, 1968). Senator Gaylord Nelson (D-WI) was perhaps even more enthusiastic about river protection than trails. The key to understanding Wild and Scenic Rivers is the concept of "outstanding and remarkable values," be they scenic, recreational, geologic, historic, cultural, or rich in fish and wildlife. The purpose of these designations is to protect these river segments from inappropriate development (especially dams) and to leave them free-flowing for recreational uses. In fact, this is the highest level of river protection offered in the United States.

As with NSTs and NHTs, the federally administered rivers are established by Congress after a feasibility study. They receive some federal funding and technical assistance and are subject to corridor management plans. River segments on federal lands are managed by the appropriate federal agency. In fact, these are the same agencies responsible for the National Trails System: BLM, FS, NPS, and the USF&WS. Some Wild and Scenic Rivers may also be designated and managed by states. In 1968, eight rivers were designated. Today, there are 208 in 38 states totaling 12,700 miles in combined lengths. They are classified on a spectrum from "wild" (most primitive) through "scenic" to "recreational" (most developed). A subcategory of Partnership Wild and Scenic Rivers was developed to vest as much control and ownership with local communities as possible, shaped by networks of cooperative agreements. [27]

27. "National Wild and Scenic Rivers System," *Wikipedia*, last modified April 9, 2018, https://en.wikipedia.org/wiki/National_Wild_and_Scenic_Rivers_System; related websites.

CHAPTER 12
THE NEW MILLENNIUM
2001–2008

Federal agencies will, to the extent permitted by law and where practicable — and in cooperation with Tribes, States, local governments, and interested citizen groups — protect, connect, promote, and assist trails of all types throughout the United States. (President William Jefferson Clinton, 2001) [1]

The dawning of the new millennium in 2001 brought several changes — an executive order signed by outgoing President Bill Clinton, a new administration in Washington, DC, and a new multiagency agreement supporting National Trails System activities. Inspired by the success of the Millennium Trails Program and just before departing the White House in January 2001, President Clinton signed Executive Order 13195, *Trails for America in the 21st Century.* This "EO" was crafted by Jeff Olson, the Millennium Trails Program Coordinator at the U.S. Department of Transportation, and reviewed by the Federal Interagency Council on Trails. It outlined clear directives for federal agencies that oversee trails, promoted interagency collaboration, and reauthorized the Federal Interagency Council on Trails.

Another innovation early in 2001 was a memorandum issued by outgoing Interior Secretary Bruce Babbitt on his last day in office directing that both BLM and NPS co-administer the newly established Camino Real de Tierra Adentro NHT. This was the first time two agencies were

---

1. President William J. Clinton, January 18, 2001, *Executive Order 13195: Trails for America in the 21st Century*, in NTSAHA.

assigned to jointly administer one trail. (It happened once again in 2003 when both NPS and BLM were directed by Interior Secretary Gale Norton to co-administer the Old Spanish NHT.) [2]

As the Clinton administration came to a close in early 2001, five federal agencies (BLM, NPS, Forest Service, FHWA, and the National Endowment for the Arts) signed a five-year memorandum of understanding (MOU) agreeing to carry out joint goals and tasks associated with NSTs and NHTs. This was the first National Trails System interagency agreement of such broad scope — previous interagency agreements had just addressed NHTs. Building on months of drafts and negotiations, the 2001 MOU laid out several worthy purposes and principles and then listed 20 specific tasks to be accomplished jointly including regular participation in the Interagency Council on Trails, coordination of policy, coordination of planning and compliance, collaborative training, a unified data tracking system, and coordinated budget submissions. [3]

Following the inauguration of the new MOU, representatives of each signatory agency met in Denver in May 2001 to discuss ways to implement it. They were joined by staff from the Colorado Trails Program, the National Geographic Society, and the U.S. Geological Survey. They agreed that only GIS mapping and training should be carried out through national coordination; all other joint interagency functions (planning, budgeting, compliance, etc.) should be carried out through existing regional and state offices, by agency. [4]

After the presidential election of 2000, it was clear that the nation would move in a more conservative direction under Republican President George W. Bush. Typical of Republican administrations, funding became tighter, agency business practices received greater scrutiny, and environmental programs were de-emphasized. However, in these early months, by coincidence, PNTS received increased financial support for its programs and *Pathways Across America* from the Federal Highway Administration, the Bureau of Land Management, and the

---

2. Steve Elkinton, January 25, 2001, memo to National Park Service NST and NHT administrators, *Monthly Message No. 8*, in NTSAHA.
3. *Memorandum of Understanding for the Administration and Management of National Historic and National Scenic Trails Among* [the five listed agencies], January 2001, in NTSAHA.
4. Steve Elkinton, May 21, 2001, memo to NPS NST and NHT administrators, *Monthly Message – May 25, 2001,* and *Monthly Bulletin –* June 2003, both in NTSAHA.

Forest Service, who joined NPS through cooperative agreements to support PNTS's activities.

PNTS started off the new millennium hosting another conference for NSTs and NHTs in Casper, Wyoming, with the theme "Strong Partnerships Make Great National Trails." Special emphasis was given to the ways NSTs and NHTs can link together disparate cultures. Sacred sites along the trails were highlighted along with multicultural sensitivity on interpretive materials. In addition, the new multiagency MOU was discussed as a model partnership. [5]

One participant, Mike Dahl, from the Overmountain Trail Association, left some notes from the Casper conference that show how important these face-to-face gatherings can be — and how surprised struggling trail groups are when their accomplishments are given recognition: [We] *got absolutely outstanding responses on the* [Overmountain Victory NHT] *video and trail protection presentation. In fact, Ross Marshall, President of the Santa Fe Trail Association, just came up a minute ago and said we had the best preservation policy statement he has seen from any group and wants copies of our scope and prospectus. Isn't that a reassuring thing? We go out there to learn how to do this stuff and find out that the little bit of work that we have already done is valued so highly.* [6]

With the signing of the five-agency MOU in 2001, the Federal Interagency Council on Trails began a tradition of issuing annual reports to document successes associated with their collaborations. The first one, issued in early 2002, included as accomplishments interagency planning for the pending Lewis and Clark Bicentennial, support for the National Trails Training Partnership, and the formation of a trail data standards team. It concluded: "Because of their partnership nature and long-distance geography, national trails are a laboratory for innovation." [7]

As the Bush administration took root, it emphasized funding accountability and fostered agency reorganizations for greater efficiencies. Within NPS, the National Trails Program was moved from Cultural Resources to a new directorate with the ungainly title of Partnerships, Interpretation,

5. PNTS, 2001, "Strong Partnerships Make Great National Trails," The 7th Conference on National Historic and National Scenic Trails, Casper, Wyoming, August 17–21, 2001, *Conference Program and Information*, in NTSAHA.
6. Mike Dahl, Aug. 20, 2001, email to ovta-list@ovta.org, in NTSAHA.
7. Federal Interagency Council on Trails, March 2002, *Annual Report for CY 2001 . . .*, in NTSAHA.

Education, Volunteerism, and Outdoor Recreation. In addition, the pressure was on for greater accountability and periodic reporting on accomplishments. Newly appointed Deputy Interior Secretary Lynn Scarlett, an avid hiker, offered to give the keynote speech at the Eighth National Conference on NSTs and NHTs in Fort Smith, Arkansas. She came, was welcomed, and spoke from the heart about the importance of America's national trails. [8]

In this era of transition into the new millennium, three guidebooks were published specifically about national scenic and historic trails. Recreation professor Kathleen Cordes, then teaching at Miramar College in San Diego, wrote *America's National Historic Trails* in 1999 and its counterpart, *America's National Scenic Trails*, in 2001 (both published by the University of Oklahoma Press with photographs by Jane Lammers). A few years later, following an NPS field staff suggestion for a "field guide to the National Trails System," author

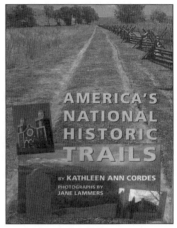

Cover of Kathleen Cordes' book, *America's National Historic Trails*, published 1999. Photo by author.

Glenn Scherer, with funding and support from NPS and AHS, published *America's National Trails: Journeys Across Land and Time* with Globe Pequot Press, profiling 20 of the NSTs and NHTs. (Curiously, no more trail system-wide guidebooks have been published since.)

The new Bush presidency did not look promising for trails, especially after the terrorist attacks of September 11, 2001, and the start of the Iraq War. However, in March 2003, First Lady Laura Bush announced the "Preserve America" program. It was promoted by John Nau, newly appointed chairman of the President's Advisory Council on Historic Preservation. He believed that the National Trails System could serve as a centerpiece of national efforts to foster heritage tourism. (Earlier in his

---

8. PNTS and others, Oct. 17–21, 2002, "Telling Our Trail Stories – Educating the World About the National Trails System," *Conference Program and Information* booklet, in NTSAHA.

career, Mr. Nau had ably promoted historic trails in Texas as a catalyst for statewide heritage tourism efforts.) [9]

Other trends that started in the George W. Bush administration and continued forward included increasing restrictions in federal staff travel, less flexibility in grants and cooperative agreements, tightening rules about advisory councils, and Congressional delays in appropriating funds for each fiscal year. All of these factors inhibited creative public-private partnerships. Yet, despite pressure to reduce funding, PNTS and its network of allies were able to bring about substantially increased individual trail and program budgets in various agencies during this administration.

For the tenth anniversary of National Trails Day on June 7, 2003, AHS estimated almost 100,000 participants in events in all 50 states, a Congressional resolution in appreciation of trail volunteers, broad media coverage, a brochure issued by the U.S. Centers for Disease Control on the health benefits of trails, and strong corporate sponsorships. After a decade, it was clear that National Trails Day had become an event embedded in hundreds of communities, bringing positive attention to trails nationwide. [10]

The bicentennial commemoration of the Lewis and Clark Expedition of 1803–1806 was another outstanding example of interagency collaboration related to national trails. Taking place from 2003 to 2006, it remains to date the largest and most iconic interagency set of events within the National Trails System. Starting in 1993 and moving into high gear with the publication of Stephen Ambrose's *Undaunted Courage* and the establishment of the National Council on the Lewis and Clark Bicentennial — both in 1996 — almost two dozen federal agencies worked together to assure that the bicentennial of this remarkable expedition would be a success. At first, Department of the Interior leadership drew together 12 federal agencies in 1998 to sign an MOU fostering bicentennial coordination. Ten additional agencies joined later. This agreement yielded a variety of benefits, such as safe boating programs on affected rivers, a federal expedition map and brochure, commemorative coins, and educational traveling trunks with replica expedition artifacts.

---

9. NPS, *National Trails System Program Monthly Bulletin* – May 2003, in NTSAHA.
10. AHS, August 2003, *National Trails Day 2003 Final Report*, in NTSAHA.

Behind the scenes, House and Senate Lewis and Clark Caucuses kept members of Congress alert to issues and opportunities associated with this massive undertaking. State tourism councils banded together and carried out two rounds of market research to predict public attendance at signature events. And even though more visitor centers already existed along this route than along any other NHT, several new ones were inaugurated and built in time for the celebratory years. Conservation partners banded together and helped protect many sites and scenes important to preserving the story of these early explorers. The conservation organization American Rivers led a partnership effort to restore 45 river-related sites along this route. [11]

Bringing all interested state and federal agencies to the table in planning this commemoration was important. As the federal administering agency for the Lewis and Clark NHT, NPS also launched a traveling visitor center called the Corps

The Tent of Many Voices set up on the Lewis and Clark Landing, Omaha, Nebraska, July, 2004. NPS Photo.

of Discovery II: 200 Years to the Future, with its accompanying Tent of Many Voices, a spacious performance tent. NPS collaborated closely with American Indian tribal groups, giving dozens of Native-American communities the opportunity to tell their stories to a wide public audience. Their perspectives and stories were coordinated by the Circle of Tribal Advisors, a coalition of 40 tribal groups. Corps II became the centerpiece for many of the events that took place up and down the Lewis and Clark NHT in the first years of the new millennium. [12] In addition, NPS was put in charge of overseeing $5 million per year for Lewis and Clark NHT-related challenge cost-share projects just before and during the bicentennial years.

11. *Pathways Across America*, Spring 2000, Vol. 13, No. 2, is largely devoted to bicentennial issues and activities.
12. Circle of Tribal Advisors and Lewis and Clark Bicentennial, *Enough Good People: Reflections on Tribal Involvement and Inter-Cultural Collaboration 2003–2006*, Grand Junction: Colorado Printing Company.

As the 2001 interagency National Trails System MOU matured and trail offices figured out ways to measure some of their progress each year, the MOU partners agreed on various means to jointly report their accomplishments. For example, in the "Year 3 Report," a number of impressive annual statistics for all 24 NSTs and NHTs during 2003 were collectively listed, including:

- 8,048 acres acquired by federal agencies
  to protect trail corridors
- 877 acres acquired by nonfederal
  partners to protect trails
- 579 miles of new NHT auto route established
- 240 compliance actions underway or completed
- 210 trailwide public/private meetings
- 101 miles of new NST trail opened during the year
- 93 new supplemental agreements at the local level

This was the first time that systemwide statistics at this level of detail had been collected. The "Year 3 Report" concluded:

As we passed the half-way mark last summer of this MOU's 5-year life, collaboration — rather than exclusive command and control — has generally become the watchword in moving forward with trail system activities. Although not yet finalized, interagency standards, policies, and best practices have moved forward significantly (sometimes against great odds). Meanwhile, actions throughout the trails — both in administration and management — have been characterized by innovation, partnership, and leveraging. The spirit of Lewis and Clark, proceeding valiantly on, pervades the entire National Trails System. [13]

Meanwhile, an effort that started back in 1999 — first by NPS and then on an interagency basis — became a system-wide multiagency approach to electronic mapping services, or Geographic Information System (GIS). An interagency working team was formed in 2004 to develop data standards for trail-related information. Before this, every state and federal agency had separate data standards and graphic symbols for trails. This

---

13. Federal Interagency Council on Trails, February 26, 2004, *YEAR 3 REPORT on Interagency Collaboration in the Administration and Management of National Scenic and Historic Trails*, p. 11, in NTSAHA.

team produced a matrix of trail data attributes called the Interagency Trail Data Standards (ITDS). The ITDS was based on ten years of work by the Forest Service which had been developing universal codes and values for trail data. Despite its complexity and many setbacks due to lack of funding, changes in personnel, and shifting priorities, the ITDS was eventually adopted government-wide in 2008 with help from the Federal Geographic Data Committee. Today it is known as the Federal Trail Data Standards (FTDS) and is used by many federal agencies, state governments, and local jurisdictions. [14]

In parallel with other efforts to standardize databases and mapping for trails across agency boundaries, the NPS office for NHTs in Salt Lake City, Utah, compiled a sophisticated handbook for historic trail components. Its breakthrough concept was disentangling three layers for NHT corridors: (1) the Congressionally mapped route, (2) the location of actual sites and remnants, and (3) modern recreational facilities and access points. This handbook was addressed to volunteer crews who could then survey NHT routes and resources and upgrade data and mapping associated with them on a consistent basis. This approach was soon incorporated into the larger ITDS/FTDS effort. [15]

One festering inequality in this period was the fact that the first two NSTs, created in 1968, had access to the full array of federal land acquisition authorities in the NTSA. Then the next nine trails had minimal access to funds for land protection outside of federal boundaries due to the Section 10(c) restrictions introduced in 1978 and 1980. And the trails established after 1983 had full access to federal land acquisition from willing sellers only. Starting in the early 1990s, PNTS and its member organizations worked hard with members of Congress to rectify this disparity

Representative Richard Pombo, photo courtesy High Country News.

---

14. NPS National Trails System Program, *Monthly Bulletin – June 24, 2008*, in NTSAHA.
15. Kay Threlkeld and Adam Sobek, November 2005, *Historic Resource Database for the National Historic Trails: GPS Level Data Instructions, Features and Attributes*, in NTSAHA.

and to give all NSTs and NHTs at least the "willing seller" clause that had become standard for all trails established since 1983. [16]

However, from 2003 to 2007, Representative Richard Pombo (R-CA) served as chairman of the House Resources Committee. As a strong property rights advocate and skeptic about rail-banking, he blocked almost all legislation involving trails throughout those four years, especially the American Discovery Trail. Even so, during the first eight years of the 21st Century, the following amendments to the National Trails System Act were successfully enacted into law:

TABLE H
Legislative Actions 2001–2008

DATE	PUBLIC LAW	ACTION
8/21/2002	107-214	Requested study for the Long Walk Trail
12/4/2002	107-325	Established the Old Spanish NHT
12/16/2002	107-338	Requested study for the Metacomet-Monadanock-Mattabessett Trail
10/18/2004	108-342	Established El Camino Real de Los Tejas NHT
8/2/2005	109-54	Requested study of the Captain John Smith Chesapeake Historic Water Trail
12/1/2006	109-378	Requested study of two additional major routes plus the collection routes associated with the Trail of Tears NHT
12/19/2006	109-418	Established the Captain John Smith Chesapeake NHT
5/8/2008	110-229	Established the Star-Spangled Banner NHT and requested study of Lewis and Clark Eastern Legacy routes

Two of these amendments were passed in unusual ways. After the establishment bill for El Camino Real de los Tejas NHT passed the Senate in 2004, its main sponsor, Senator Kay Bailey Hutchison (R-TX) knew it would never get through Representative Pombo's House Resources Committee for consideration and hearings. So, she asked her Texas colleague, Representative Tom DeLay, House Majority Leader, if he could

16. Steve Elkinton, Oral History interview, NPS 40th Anniversary Oral History Project, p. 13.

just bring it up for a floor vote and assure its passage. He succeeded, and the bill then went directly to another Texan, President George W. Bush, for signature. Thus, this important Southwestern historic trail was added to the Trails System without a House committee hearing.

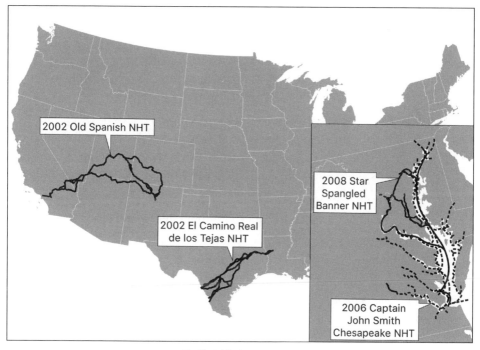

Trails Added 2002-2008.

Another unusual legislative story in this period involves the study and establishment acts for the Captain John Smith NHT. Both occurred during the 109th Congress — the only time in 50 years that a trail's study and establishment acts both occurred during the same Congress. This happened due to the smart and diligent efforts of the trail's advocates, especially Pat Noonan of the Conservation Fund and Gilbert Grosvenor of the National Geographic Society. They were able to attach the study bill to a must-pass appropriations bill early in that Congressional session, then effectively pressured NPS to carry out the feasibility study in record time. They then worked hard to get the establishment bill passed by the same 109th Congress just before it adjourned. [17]

Immediately before the 17th National Trails Symposium in Austin, Texas, in October 2004, PNTS held its first organizational strategic planning meeting. One result was a prioritized set of actions, and another was a two-tiered leadership structure: a leadership council comprised of representatives from all its affiliated member groups and a smaller board of directors who would concentrate on fiduciary and administrative responsibilities. Then, during the week of the Symposium, the establishment act for the Camino Real de los Tejas NHT, the System's 24th trail, was passed, and Texas was formally welcomed into the National Trails System.

On July 26, 2005, House National Parks Subcommittee Chair Stevan Pearce (R-NM) held an oversight hearing on the National Trails System Act (the first NTSA-related hearing since 1976). Although most who came to testify spoke to various facets of this Act, it became clear in the course of the hearing and in his follow-up questions that Chairman Pearce was only interested in the use of eminent domain in federal land acquisition along the Appalachian NST. The testimony of PNTS Executive Director Gary Werner was particularly eloquent:

*The culture and spirit of volunteerism for public benefit runs deep and strong throughout the organizations within the National Trails System family. The Appalachian Trail Conservancy, the oldest and largest of the National Trails System collaborating organizations, has a number of volunteers who have been contributing their "sweat equity" to sustain the Appalachian National Scenic Trail **for more than 50 years**. (emphasis his)* [18]
Fortunately, no Congressional action regarding NTSA administrative or resource protection authorities resulted from these hearings.

One indicator that programs that supported trails of all kinds were becoming stronger was reflected in the passage of the Safe, Accountable, Flexible, Efficient Transportation Equity Act – A Legacy for Users (SAFETEA-LU). In 2005, following the end of the TEA-21 era, SAFETEA-LU was passed to provide surface transportation funding through 2009. Its authorization of $244.1 billion was then the largest surface transportation investment to

17. Patrick F. Noonan, May 16, 2006, testimony in *Hearing Before the* [Senate] *Committee of National Parks of the Committee on Energy and Natural Resources* [on eight bills], Senate Hearing 109-547, Washington, DC: GOP, pp. 51–7, in NTSAHA.
18. Gary Werner, July 26, 2005, Statement . . . on Implementation of the National Trails System Act, in NTSAHA.

date in U.S. history. And under SAFETEA-LU, hundreds of millions of additional dollars became available through RTP and TE for trail projects associated with the National Trails System. These programs lasted from 1991 to 2012 when the Moving Ahead for Progress in the 21st Century Act (or MAP-21) realigned transportation enhancements and reduced the span of eligible projects. The next round of transportation funding after MAP-21, the Fixing America's Surface Transportation Act of 2015 (or FAST), made funds for trails generally available only through renamed block grants or discretionary set-aside funding sources. [19]

On May 4, 2006, PNTS was awarded one of 13 U.S. Department of the Interior Cooperative Conservation Awards. Among all the awardees, PNTS was the only group that was national in scope. The award was made by Deputy Interior Secretary Lynn Scarlett, and the accompanying text stated: *The Partnership has drawn all 22 of the nonprofit organizations that work to support America's national trails into its affiliate membership. In 2005 the Partnership['s] member organizations] contributed more than 690,000 volunteer hours, fostered dozens of community-based conservation projects along the trails, collaborated on 42,000 miles of trail, raised millions of dollars to protect trail corridor lands and established effective communications networks, training, and events to foster cooperative conservation.* [20]

Arising from NST and NHT caucuses at the 2005 PNTS conference held in Las Vegas, both interest groups offered to host and organize special skills workshops for each type of trail the following year. The first NHT workshop was held in Kansas City, Missouri, in May 2006, and a counterpart NST workshop was held that fall in Nashville to discuss land trusts and trail corridor protection.

The major wrap-up product of the 2001-5 MOU was a five-year report about interagency accomplishments under the MOU. Most of the report highlighted successes and innovations along each trail. Summary statistics indicated that a great deal of work had occurred throughout the NSTs and NHTs during those five years, including:

- 786 miles of new NST trail opened for use,
- 659 miles of marked NHT auto tour route marked, and
- 159 miles of new NHT trail opened for use. [21]

---

19. Christopher Douwes, FHWA, September 24, 2017, email to author.
20. NPS National Trails System Program, *Monthly Bulletin – May 24, 2006*, in NTSAHA.
21. Bureau of Land Management and four other agencies, 2006, *National Historic and Scenic Trails: Accomplishments 2001–2005*, in NTSAHA.

The five-year, five-agency MOU was replaced by a ten-year, six-agency MOU, signed in 2006. The first annual report to be issued under the new MOU offered a more sophisticated format than earlier reports. Among the top findings for the new MOU's first year (2007) were:

- $11.5 million base operating funds
  for 25 NSTs and NHTs,
- $6.4 million supplemental funds (including challenge
  cost-share projects and land acquisition).
- 6,260 acres of trail corridor protected
  by federal agencies.
- 1,795 acres of trail corridor protected
  by non-federal partners.
- 360 miles of trail improved or reconstructed.
- 321 trail-related structures installed,
- 290 compliance actions and reviews,
- 116 miles of new NST trail created,
- 68 new partnership agreements,
- plus dozens of innovative actions by
  individual trail partnerships. [22]

Once it was certain that BLM's new National Landscape Conservation System — in which BLM-managed segments of NSTs and NHTs were now embedded — would survive the new administration, BLM leadership held an NST/NHT workshop in Riverside, California, in March 2004. BLM Director Kathleen Clarke offered an inspiring opening talk. The goal was to gather in partners and listen to their perspectives and suggestions — and then begin to craft an internal BLM strategy for National Trails System activities and responsibilities. PNTS's Gary Werner noted after attending this event, "Our other two federal partners [NPS and Forest Service] have some work to do to catch up with the BLM in regard to this level of recognition, integration, and coordination within their agencies of the scenic and historic trails." [23]

22. Federal Interagency Council on Trails, January 2008, *National Trails System Annual Report for FY 2007*, in NTSAHA.
23. NPS National Trails System Program, *Monthly Bulletin* – April 23, 2004, in NTSAHA.

After two years of in-depth deliberations and consultations, BLM issued its *National Scenic and Historic Trails Strategy and Work Plan* in early 2006. This remarkable document set a ten-year time horizon to embed NSTs and NHTs into BLM operations. After an overview of issues and authorities, goals were framed for trail administration and management, resource protection, partnerships, training, and visitor experience. Each was then discussed and broken into actions set against an ambitious time-frame, with priorities given for the most important actions. [24]

As the 40th anniversary of the National Trails System Act approached in 2008, PNTS began to lay a foundation for both the anniversary and for ways of using it to strengthen the the National Trails System as a whole. During Hike the Hill in February 2007, PNTS inaugurated a process that named the years 2008 to 2018 as "A Decade for the National Trails" and brainstormed a set of compelling goals and objectives. These goals guided PNTS and its partners over the next ten years:

- *GOAL 1 – Increase public awareness of the National Trails System and its component trails so that it becomes well known to every citizen and community in the United States.*

- *GOAL 2 – Complete and enhance the designated National Trails for public appreciation and enjoyment.*

- *GOAL 3 – Build the capacity of the organizations and federal agencies involved to better administer, manage, and sustain national scenic, historic, and recreation trails.* [25]

Meanwhile, trail-related educational services began to gear up on several fronts. The newly formed NTTP network helped organize a week-long course called "Trail Management – Plans, Projects, and People." At first, it was offered through BLM's National Training Center in Phoenix, Arizona. Then, about 2007, it was moved to the U.S. Fish & Wildlife Service and offered at that agency's National Conservation Training Center in Shepherdstown, West Virginia, through 2011.

---

24. See web entry "BLM National Scenic and Historic Trails Strategy and Work Plan."
25. See PNTS website, search under "Decade for the National Trails Goals and Objectives."

Along the Appalachian NST, a program for teachers called "A Trail to Every Classroom" was initiated. Teachers were invited in summer workshops to develop curriculum materials that met their school needs and state standards — and used some aspect of the Appalachian Trail to "teach." Once developed, these curriculum materials were widely shared in states up and down the trail. If the students had access to the trail, sometimes they could actually experience adventures and learning opportunities along it. This trail-related educational service soon spread to other national trails in Colorado, Alaska, and other states.

The year 2008 proved to be a busy year on many fronts ramping up to the 40th anniversary of the NTSA. One unexpected surprise was that PNTS was included in the President's Advisory Council for Historic Preservation Chairman's Award given out by Council Chairman John

Virginia teachers developing "A Trail to Every Classroom" curricula in 2011. Photo courtesy ATC.

Nau in St. Louis to the Secretaries of Agriculture and the Interior — and other groups such as PNTS — for historic preservation efforts along America's national historic trails. [26]

Soon afterward, PNTS received the Kodak American Greenways Award that was given jointly by The Conservation Fund, the National Geographic Society, and Eastman Kodak Company. The Partnership "was honored for its strong voice in advocating for the National Trails System, a vibrant system of trails that connects people, landscapes, cultures, and histories across the country." [27]

On October 2, 2008, the actual 40th anniversary of the National Trails System Act, a commemorative event was held in Washington, DC,

---

26. NPS National Trails System Program, *Monthly Bulletin – August 26, 2008*, in NTSAHA.
27. PNTS, September 15, 2008, "News Release: Partnership for the National Trails System Receives National Honor for Outstanding Achievement in Greenways Preservation," in NTSAHA.

at the Smithsonian Institution's Museum of Natural History. AHS hosted the morning symposium, with participation by NPS, BLM, Conservation Fund, and other staff. Noted speakers included Pat Noonan, Gary Werner, and Lynn Scarlett. One high point was an exhibition of photographs by Bart Smith, who had just completed hiking all eight NSTs.

The 19th National Trails Symposium was held in Little Rock, Arkansas, in November, 2008, just after the anniversary. PNTS hosted an NST workshop immediately before it, and there, Forest Service program leader Jonathan Stephens proposed the idea of youth apprentice scholarships. At the Symposium's opening reception, dozens of NST and NHT advocates commemorated the 40th anniversary with a parade of trails. NPS handed out a free a 50-page booklet called *The National Trails System – A Grand Experiment*, the first-ever attempt at a comprehensive history of the National Trails System. The Symposium itself focused on the health benefits of trails, featuring Little Rock's Medical Mile Trail along the Arkansas River. [28]

October 2, 2008 Gary Werner speaks at the 40th anniversary symposium, Smithsonian Institution, Washington, DC. Photo by author.

The year 2008 also marked the emergence in many states of major wind and solar energy projects — as well as the massive transmission infrastructure to carry that energy to distant cities. In more than 60 places, these projects — if built — would severely impact whatever remained of NST and NHT scenic quality. NPS review comments to the U.S. Department of Energy for the Westwide Energy Corridors EIS included this statement: "[T]hese corridors, if built, would constitute the gravest threat to the resources and integrity of the resources of the National Trails System since its creation in 1968." This was followed a few months later

28. Steven Elkinton, 2008, *The National Trails System – A Grand Experiment*, Washington, DC: GPO for National Park Service.

by a similar proposal (and environmental assessment) for the Eastwide Energy Corridors in the rest of the Nation. [29]

And 2008 closed out with another publication by the Federal Interagency Council on Trails, a profile of the entire system called *The National Trails System at 40*. It opened with this portrayal of the trails:

National trails are complex. Some are long, some short. Many involve built elements such as bridges and steps, restrooms and visitor centers, markers, blazes, and highway signs. Many include a land corridor of cherished views or rare and sacred cultural sites. Some trails cross large amounts of Federal land, while others mostly involve private landowners, local park authorities, public road rights-of-way, and state and tribal reservations. These trails involve complex organizational issues: partnership agreements, fund raising, volunteers, and special events. Some are a single route, while others form complex braided networks.

And it concluded by making these recommendations:
- Foster volunteerism,
- Conduct research,
- Define uniform data standards,
- Build new partnerships,
- Establish a Federal Lands Trails Program for reliable multi-year funding, and
- Open a National Trails Resource Center. [30]

Between 2000 and 2008, the National Trails System continued to expand, growing from 20 to 26 NSTs and NHTs with combined trail corridor lengths mushrooming from 38,000 to almost 50,000 miles. The number of NRTs rose from 825 to 1,070. The increase in interagency collaboration and the growth and sophistication of nonprofit, volunteer-based trail organizations became crucial to this success, strengthening the System through a nationwide system of active partners. This was mirrored by increased interest on the part of many federal agencies and a widening network of active staff.

---

29. NPS National Trails System Program, *Monthly Bulletin – October 21, 2008*, and *November 25, 2008*, both in NTSAHA.
30. Federal Interagency Council on Trails, November 2008, *The National Trails System at 40*, pp. 1 and 11–12, in NTSA.

CHALLENGE COST-SHARE PROGRAMS

The concept of matching financial and volunteer labor contributions that assist federal government agencies has a long history. Specifically, in the 1980s, the Forest Service demonstrated how such programs leveraged appropriated dollars very effectively — and by then, that agency had the authority to match any appropriated funds at least one-to-one with outside contributions.

Congress gave NPS its first specific Challenge Cost-Share (CCS) authority in 1993, and the first awards were announced in 1994. Thanks to Committee of 17 lobbying, one-third of the designated CCS funds (about $800,000 most years) was to be devoted to National Trails System projects. That first year, 52 projects were funded. Most went to NPS-administered NST and NHT projects, while some went to selected NRTs. By 1995, 80 trails projects leveraged $1 million of outside funding, and in 1996 $1.2 million. That same year, the Omnibus Parks Act allowed the use of any appropriated funds for challenge cost-share projects. By 1999, NPS could announce that CCS funds were being matched one-to-two or better for 72 projects occurring along 16 of the NSTs and NHTs. [31]

Once fully up and running (and understood by potential and active partners), the CCS program as administered by NPS proved a very effective way of building trail-related partnerships and leveraging tightly-budgeted appropriated funds. Priorities and project selection occurred in field offices, not centrally. Starting in 2001, through special appropriations, NPS was also asked to award as much as $5 million per year for projects associated just with the Lewis and Clark NHT and bicentennial. For 2003, $4.9 million funded 130 Lewis

---

31. "NPS Announces Cost-Share Awards for Trails," *Pathways Across America*, Spring 1994; Steve Elkinton, 2000, "Challenge Cost-Share Program: Summary of Issues and Observations," in NTSAHA; and Steve Elkinton, "Benefits of Challenge Cost-Share Growing," *Pathways Across America*, Winter 2000, Vol. 13, No. 1, pp. 5 and 8.

and Clark projects attracting over $30 million in outside investment (a one-to-six match!). These ranged from visitor center displays to educational services and resource preservation. The funds only lasted through 2006 and averaged over 95 projects per year, often being leveraged as high as one-to-ten for multi-partner projects. [32]

Then, especially in years 2004 to 2006, NPS's CCS funds were increased and broadened to more programs throughout the agency. However, in 2009, the Interior Department's Office of Inspector General issued a negative report about CCS as practiced within various Interior agencies (largely BLM and NPS), highlighting lack of competition, weak program oversight, and apparent favoritism to the same partners year after year. Within a few years, these negative findings gave appropriators an excuse to largely shut down the program.

In June 2010, NPS issued a five-year report on its CCS program for the years 2004–8. During that period, 390 trail projects were funded with $3.6 million, helping a wide variety of efforts in construction, signs, interpretation, resource protection, youth activities, publications, mapping, and other needs. For every federal dollar, partners provided an average of $2.60 in leveraging. [33]

CCS for national trails continued strong through 2012 at almost $400,000 a year. Over the next two years, it was restructured to remove it from the NPS Consolidated Call for projects, to streamline the application process, to be more responsive to administration priorities, to increase leveraging, and to use a third party — the Outdoor Foundation — to do the paperwork. NPS staff continued to select the projects. By 2016, only two projects benefited components of the National Trails System. [34]

32. Steve Elkinton, "Challenge Cost-Share Aids 130 Lewis and Clark Projects," in NTSAHA.
33. Steve Elkinton, 2010, *NPS Challenge Cost-Share Projects – 2004 to 2008*, in NTSAHA.
34. NPS memo, 2016, "NPS Challenge Cost-Share Program: Update," courtesy Stefan Nofield.

CHAPTER 13

A DECADE FOR THE NATIONAL TRAILS SYSTEM 2008–2018

The setting at South Pass is not pristine, but it is still evocative of the emigrants' journey. A power line crosses the trail a few miles west of the pass and an old railroad grade lies parallel to the trail. Wind farm sites are being studied on the adjacent ridges. I am not certain that future visitors will be able to replicate the experience at South Pass that means so much to me. . . . There are three aspects of the preservation of a historic trail. First, . . . the story itself: the challenges, failures and successes of the emigrants themselves. Second, there are the physical remnants (the ruts and swales). Third is the experience which can only be found by visiting an undisturbed trail site. We have done a good job on the first (history), less well on the second (physical remains), and very little on the third (setting). As another friend noted, once part of the trail and the setting is lost, a part of the story is lost as well; the loss is irreplaceable. (David Welch, OCTA, 2010) [1]

As 2009 began, "A Decade for the National Trails" was well underway. PNTS's three Decade goals structured the reporting on NST and NHT accomplishments throughout the Decade as described in numerous issues of *Pathways Across America*. [2] This era also marked the beginning of a new presidency. Democratic President Barack Obama and Vice President Joe Biden took the reins of government. There was a new

---

1. David Welch, "The Importance of Setting," *Pathways Across America*, Winter 2009–10.
2. For a sample, see *Pathways Across America*, Winter 2010–11.

mood of optimism in conservation and preservation circles, with a clear commitment to youth.

Right on schedule, in February 2009, trail advocates organized by AHS and PNTS came to Washington, DC, for "Hike the Hill" to get to know new members of both Congress and the administration. By now, this well-regarded and effective event had also become a chance for federal agency trail administrators to gather and network as a group. (They did not lobby, as that is an activity prohibited for federal employees.) [3]

OCTA's David Welch and others explore the Juan Bautista de Anza NHT near Phoenix, Arizona, 2008. Photo by author.

Even though challenge cost-share funding (see sidebar above) had become an essential stimulus for trail partnerships, NPS inaugurated a new source of funds from which NSTs and NHTs benefited. The Connect Trails to Parks (CTTP) program was initiated in 2006 by departing NPS Director Fran Mainella and was eventually funded in 2008. At first, it was linked to the pending NPS Centennial, but later was identified with A Decade for the National Trails. For most of the decade, it remained at about $800,000 per year, funding 14 to 20 projects annually. Although intended primarily to better link national trails with the NPS units through which they passed, projects could also be proposed by other trail-related federal agencies. Unlike NPS challenge cost-share projects — where decisions selecting projects were made in individual trail offices — CTTP proposals were selected competitively on a national basis in NPS's national office. [4]

After three years, NPS issued a progress report highlighting the 40 CTTP projects in 28 states funded thus far with $2.5 million. The diversity of these projects illustrated the complex nature of America's NSTs and

3. NPS *National Trails System Program, Monthly Bulletin – February 25, 2009*, in NTSAHA.
4. *Ibid.*

NHTs — from educational outreach to trail crew leader training, from wayside exhibits to construction and rehabilitation projects. [5]

By 2013, CTTP had largely replaced NPS's Challenge Cost-Share Program as a significant source of partnership project funds for national trails within NPS. Total CTTP funds each year were about the same size as the former CCS earmark for trails, but funding requirements were more restrictive and benefited far fewer projects each year.

Early in the Obama presidency, conditions on Capitol Hill were at last ripe for passing an omnibus public lands bill made up of 160 elements that had been introduced by 53 senators and 75 representatives over the previous ten years, including organic language for BLM's National Landscape Conservation System. The resulting mega-bill was signed into law as P.L. 111-11 with eight sections pertaining to the National Trails System. [6]

TABLE I
Omnibus Public Land Management Act of 2009

3/30/2009	P.L. 111-11	Section 5201 – Establish Arizona NST
		Section 5202 – Establish New England NST
		Section 5304 – Establish Washington-Rochambeau Revolutionary Route NHT
		Section 5205 – Establish Pacific Northwest NST
		Section 5206 – Expand Trail of Tears NHT
		Section 5301 – Remove Section 10(c) giving willing seller authority to those affected trails
		Section 5302—Request for study of supplemental routes for four overland NHTs
		Section 5303 – Request for studies of the Great Western, Chisholm, and Butterfield-Overland Trails

Some of the amendments included in P.L. 111-11 had long and tortuous histories. For example, the Section 5302 study of supplemental routes for four NHTs originated with the Oregon-California Trails Association (OCTA) in reaction to what that group felt had been left out of the

---

5. NPS, January 2011, *Connect Trails to Parks: A Three-Year Program Report*, in NTSAHA.
6. NPS *National Trails System Program, Monthly Bulletin – March 26, 2009;* AHS, "Senate Omnibus Public Land Management Act Facts," both in NTSAHA.

combined comprehensive plan for the Oregon, California, Pony Express, and California NHTs completed in 1999. A bill to study these routes was first introduced in 2000, taking nine years to become law. [7]

Almost all of these amendments had been introduced and discussed in previous Congresses. Some issues, such as the willing seller authority, had been in play for many years. Senator Wayne Allard (R-CO), sponsor of the bill in the 110th Congress, summed up this change by saying: "The Willing Sellers Act restores consistency to the National Trail System by providing the means to complete the Trail Systems Act. S. 169 provides the authority for Federal agencies to help protect the sites and segments critical to preserving the integrity and continuity of nearly half of the National Trails System." [8]

In retrospect, P.L. 111-11 turned out to be the last set of amendments added to the NTSA for a full decade. Despite numerous other bills introduced in the 111th and subsequent Congresses, none received enough votes (or even committee attention) to become law. This post-2009 period has become the longest without any changes to the NTSA since the original act was passed in 1968.

In July 2009, PNTS held the 12th National Conference on NSTs and NHTs in Missoula, Montana. One new feature was a scholarship program inviting 32 young adults (18-25 in age) as "trail apprentices," funded by federal agency cooperative agreements. Not only did this emphasis on youth reduce the average age of conference goers, but it started a successful tradition of youthful involvement that has continued at every PNTS conference and most workshops since that time. Many of these young people later secured jobs with trail organizations nationwide. [9]

7. U.S. House of Representatives, July 2, 2000, 106th Congress, 2nd Session, H.R. 5014, "To amend the National Trails System Act to update the feasibility and suitability studies of four national historic trails and provide for possible additions to such trails," in NTSAHA.

8. Senator Wayne Allard, April 26, 2007, Statement in *Hearing Before the* [Senate] *Subcommittee on National Parks of the Committee on Energy and Natural Resources in Miscellaneous National Parks Bills*, Senate Hearing 110-88, p. 5, in NTSAHA.

9. PNTS, 2009, *12th Conference on National Scenic and Historic Trails: Gearing Up for the Decade for the National Trails: Outreach, Protection, and Capacity*, registration booklet in NTSAHA.

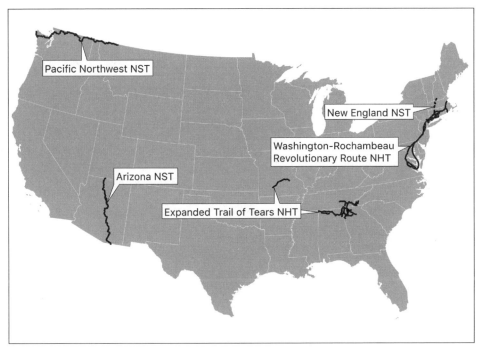

Trails Added 2009.

Also in July 2009, the Surface Transportation Board (STB) held hearings on the success of rail-banking after 25 years. As lead witnesses, RTC's Marianne Fowler and attorney Chuck Montaigne stated that in those 25 years, the STB and its predecessors had issued 698 rail banking orders of which 301 were activated preserving 2,700 miles of rail trails. (This compared to 9,000 miles of abandoned rail corridor lost for such purposes due to various factors.) The successful projects ranged in size from Nebraska's 320-mile Cowboy Trail to New York City's now famous High Line. Both witnesses asserted that most abandonments have already occurred and that it was a shame that this authority hadn't exist back in the 1920s. Obstacles still facing rail-banking agreements included their voluntary nature, the usually short time frames available for reacting to abandonment notices, and potential liability to cover costs when trail routes might be reactivated for rail use. [10]

10. Surface Transportation Board, July 8, 2009, Hearings on 25 Years of Rail Banking, Ex Parte No. 690, accessed through STB website.

The Fall 2009 issue of *Pathways Across America* illustrated some of the new issues affecting national trails with reports on proposed pipelines, transmission lines, wind farms, and solar projects that could adversely impact the trail corridors. These resulted from new Obama administration initiatives to encourage alternatives to fossil fuel industries. This issue of *Pathways* also reported on the many flourishing youth projects springing up across the National Trails System, such as the Ice Age Trail's Summer Saunters. [11]

The year-end annual report for 2009 by the Federal Interagency Council on Trails offered these highlights for that one year for all 30 NSTs and NHTs:

- 8,975 acres trail corridor protected by nonfederal partners
- 3,670 acres trail corridor protected by federal agencies
- 451 compliance actions and reviews
- 216 miles of NST opened for public use
- 154 NHT high potential sites and segments experiencing resource threats
- 83 energy projects impacting NSTs and NHTs

And it went on to conclude:

Despite the economic turndown — the worst nationwide economic conditions and highest unemployment since the 1930s — several new sources provided much-needed funds for National Trails System projects. Under the American Recovery and Reinvestment Act (ARRA), numerous National Trails System projects received funding, including over $6 million for projects under BLM's jurisdiction. One is a multi-state project developing a systematic inventory and assessment process for cultural and visual trail resources within trail corridors. At the same time the USDA Forest Service received $22 million . . . specifically for projects along the Pacific Crest and Continental Divide NSTs, the Nez Perce NHT, and Forest Service segments of the Iditarod NHT. In addition, NPS continued a second year with the Connect-Trails-to-Parks Program, distributing $837,000 to 14 projects in 14 states, ranging in scope from educational outreach for teachers to new wayside exhibits . . . [12]

---

11. *Pathways Across America*, Fall 2009.
12. Federal Interagency Council on Trails, 2010, *National Trails System Annual Report for FY 2009*, in NTSAHA.

After the 2008 stock market drop and subsequent economic recession, the ARRA pumped millions of dollars into NST and NHT projects. Over the next few years, BLM coordinated $7.7 million covering 26 projects. These ranged from trail assessments and repair projects to energy project mitigation. The largest was a multi-state GPS/GIS analysis of NHT-related cultural sites and landscapes. The Forest Service coordinated 11 projects (costing $22 million) in nine states for bridge replacement, trail repair, site interpretation, and youth crews. [13]

Sparked by a lawsuit on the Merced River in California, in March of 2010, an interagency working group on carrying capacity was organized, and the National Trails System became involved due to the NTSA requirements in Sections 5(e)(1) and 5(f)(1) that NST and NHT comprehensive plans address carrying capacity. This multi-agency group met for several years — sometimes stuck in a standoff between departmental lawyers who wanted exact quantified use limits and local agency managers who wanted as much flexibility as possible. Eventually the six-agency Visitor Use Management Council (and its attending lawyers) hammered out guidance for many aspects of visitor use management on public lands and waters, not just carrying capacity. This is a complex issue, since conditions can vary widely from one place to another and season by season. The Council's approved paper on "visitor capacity" specifically addressing rivers and trails was published in 2016. [14]

The 150th anniversary of the Pony Express as a mail route in the early 1860s was commemorated in 2010. Advocates for that trail organized an impressive event on Capitol Hill in Washington, DC, on April 15, before heading west where they held more anniversary events along the trail. [15]

By late 2010, as a result of a recent energy bill and the Obama administration's pursuit of alternative energy sources, major solar and wind projects were proposed — especially in the West. One in southern California was to be built on top of the alignment of the Juan Bautista de Anza NHT, and that proposal especially awakened the National Trails System community to the threat of industrial-scale solar and wind projects. Later, dozens of additional projects affecting the trails came into

13. *Pathways Across America*, Autumn, 2010, pp. 11–2.
14. *Interagency Visitor Use Management Council*, accessed June 20, 2018, https://visitorusemanagement. nps.gov/.
15. *Pathways Across America*, Winter 2009–10 and Summer 2010.

view. Pressure mounted in 2011 with review of two programmatic EISs: one for the western 11 states (Westwide) and the other for the rest of the nation (Eastwide). Trail staff became increasingly engaged in reviewing EISs and networking with partners about common issues relating to energy infrastructure projects.

The 500 kV Susquehanna to Roseland Transmission Project was proposed in 2008, enlarging an existing powerline that cut across several miles of the Delaware Water Gap National Recreation Area (DWGNRA) in Pennsylvania and New Jersey and crossing the Appalachian NST. After intense negotiations and an environmental and economic analysis by NPS, the utility companies agreed to establish a $56 million mitigation fund to be spent down over ten years through a multi-party memorandum of agreement. Most of these funds were spent by the DWGNRA for wetland restoration, an historic resource plan, and improvements to visitor experience. Most of the trail's share of funds are being used to acquire lands for the trail corridor in an adjoining wildlife refuge. The transmission line was completed in 2015.

Once the nation's economy had stabilized after the 2008 recession, the Obama administration wanted to build on the success of P.L. 111-11. Therefore, in 2010, after a White House conservation conference, the America's Great Outdoors (AGO) initiative was launched. To understand what citizens and organized groups nationwide desired, 50 listening sessions were held across America during the summer and fall of 2010. From these findings, the Obama administration strove to reorient federal conservation programs in many agencies with a special emphasis on empowering local communities.

As a small part of AGO, Interior Secretary Ken Salazar took a deep interest in water trails. Serious discussions started late in 2010 among Interior officials and key river partners about how to promote and foster high-quality water trails. Eventually, it was decided that the best existing authority to use was Section 4 of the NTSA authorizing National Recreation Trails. Thus, the secretary could officially recognize these special trails without any action required by Congress. The National Water Trail Program was officially launched in 2012. National Water Trails were to be exemplary models of partnership-driven river and shoreline recreational routes. Candidate routes were to be nominated through

NPS's RTCA program staff and had to meet both NRT criteria and an additional seven factors to be recognized by the Secretary of the Interior. To date, 21 such routes have been recognized in the National Water Trail System. [16]

More broadly, another White House conference, "Growing America's Outdoor Heritage and Economy," was held in Washington, DC, in March 2012. One fruit of this effort was an emphasis on large landscapes, which led to a multi-agency effort called Collaborative Landscape Planning (CLP). In the long term,

A boat launch along the Chattahoochee National Water Trail in Georgia. This 48 mile-long river was the first National Water Trail to be designated. NPS photo courtesy Robert T. Armstrong.

this initiative has greatly helped protect resources throughout the National Trails System. But in the beginning, it was a long shot. (See the sidebar at the end of this chapter for the details.)

On May 16, 2012, four new connecting-and-side trails thematically associated with the Captain John Smith Chesapeake NHT were formally recognized. All are water trails.

- Susquehanna River in Pennsylvania and New York (552 miles)
- James River in Virginia (220 miles)
- Chester River in Maryland (46 miles)
- Upper Nanticoke River in Delaware (23 miles)

These were the first connecting and side trails to be recognized since 1990 under NTSA Section 6. [17]

By the end of 2010, PNTS calculated that its constituent member organizations together had already exceeded the decade target of documenting one million volunteer hours that year for NSTs and NHTs. The value

16. National Water Trails System," *National Park Service*, accessed June 20, 2018, https://www.nps.gov/watertrails/.
17. *Pathways Across America*, Winter 2010–11, p. 4.

of this contributed time was estimated at \$24.4 million. [18] In May 2011, PNTS held its 13th national conference on NSTs and NHTs in Abingdon, Virginia, featuring the western end of the Overmountain Victory NHT, as well as an enjoyable Trail Fest Day in Damascus, Virginia, a beloved Trail Town festival along the Appalachian NST. Once again, a large group of trail apprentices helped lower the average age of conference participants and liven up many of the sessions.

About this time, Bob Ratcliffe replaced Rick Potts as chief of the NPS office responsible for the National Trails System, RTCA, and other related programs. Bob came from BLM's recreation programs and brought with him deep knowledge of interagency cooperation and an amazing network of recreation contacts. He became instrumental in strengthening interagency councils, such as those coordinating national trails, visitor use management, and outdoor recreation in general. He was also very supportive of using GIS and other forms of electronic data management to better coordinate agency effectiveness.

The spring 2012 issue of *Pathways Across America* was a special edition devoted completely to partnerships — federal, state, nonprofit, community, and private — along the NSTs and NHTs. It profiled all 30 trails, showing their funding sources as pie charts; federal support per trail varied from a high of 81% to a low of 12%, averaging 34% (worth about \$18 million for all the trails). This was matched by \$36.5 million, the combined value of more than one million volunteer hours and financial contributions totaling \$8.7 million. This issue of *Pathways* also noted that NSTs and NHTs cross or lie adjacent to 43 U.S. metropolitan areas with populations over 500,000 people, including New York; Los Angeles; San Francisco; Washington, DC; and Kansas City, Missouri. [19]

In May 2012, PNTS helped organize a stimulating NHT workshop in Socorro, New Mexico, to examine in some detail how undeveloped NHT corridor segments both in town and in backcountry settings might best be presented to the touring public. Discussion also covered strategies to minimize the threats of new energy projects along fragile NHT corridors. And one site visit looked at the futuristic SpacePort, built north of Truth

---

18. Federal Interagency Council on Trails, February 2013, *National Trails System Annual Report for FY 2012*, 35, in NTSAHA; Robert Campbell, NPS, November 17, 2017 email to author.
19. *Pathways Across America*, Spring 2012.

or Consequences, New Mexico, along a formerly remote segment of El Camino Real de Tierra Adentro NHT and now visible along the trail for many miles in either direction. Clearly, in addition to energy projects and transmission lines, new forms of industrial-scale development will increasingly threaten remote NST and NHT landscapes.

Participants examine a segment of El Camino Real de Tierra Adentro NHT, known as "La Jornada del Muerto," near Socorro, New Mexico, in 2012. Photo by author.

Mid-2012 provided an opportunity for the Federal Interagency Council on Trails to collectively report on the first five years of the 2006 interagency MOU. These impressive totals for 2007–2011 included:

- 48,580 acres of land and water protected by nonfederal partners and agencies,
- 11,986 acres of land and water protected (acquired) by federal agencies,
- 3,540 compliance actions,
- 2,151 miles of substandard trail brought up to standard,
- 1,852 miles of trails constructed or reconstructed,
- 967 trailwide meetings or conferences,
- 800 new structures (bridges, boardwalks, shelters, etc.) built or rebuilt,
- 676 miles of new trail built,
- 639 new partnership agreements,
- 180 trail sites and segments certified.

These five-year totals clearly reflected a tremendous amount of work by federal agencies and their many partners, enabled in large part by the advocacy for adequate funding brought about by PNTS and its constituent member organizations. [20]

---

20. Steve Elkinton, "5-Year Trends, a Federal Perspective," *Pathways Across America*, Summer 2012, p. 10.

Also in 2012, after many years of negotiations and refinements, and growing directly out of BLM's 2006 NST and NHT workplan and the tenth anniversary of the National Landscape Conservation Service in 2010, BLM issued three policy manuals that emphasized "the nature and purposes of the trails, identification of NHT high potential sites and segments, the continuous nature of NSTs, selection of official . . . rights-of-way, and establishment of National Trail Management Corridors at the local planning level." The policy manuals were numbered and titled:

- 6250 – National Scenic and Historic Trail Administration
- 6280 – Management of National Scenic and Historic Trails and Trails Under Study or Recommended as Suitable for Congressional Designation, and
- 8353 – Trail Management Areas: Secretarially Designated National Recreation, Water, and Connecting and Side Trails.

For the first time, a federal agency responsible for the administration and management of NSTs and NHTs had developed and approved at the highest levels comprehensive and legally binding policy governing its actions pertaining to these complex trail corridors. Soon, BLM resource planning practices and environmental reviews were adjusted to more closely follow the full legal intent of the NTSA. [21]

The next year, in May 2013, NPS Director Jon Jarvis approved Director's Order 45 clarifying National Trails System policy for the National Park Service. This DO was NPS's counterpart to the three BLM policy manuals issued the year before — and the culmination of 22 years of effort trying to state in the format of NPS policy statements the key issues pertaining to NSTs, NHTs, and NRTs. (The accompanying reference manual enumerating many of the nonpolicy aspects of trail administration and management not covered directly in DO 45 is still in draft as of this writing.) [22]

---

21. Federal Interagency Council on Trails, February 2013, *National Trails System Annual Report for FY 2012*, 35, in NTSAHA.
22. NPS, Chief, Office of Policy, May 28, 2013, memo to NPS National Leadership Council, *Director's Order #45: National Trails System*, in NTSAHA.

Meanwhile, PNTS Executive Director Gary Werner provided a cogent analysis of three important trends among the NSTs and NHTs:

The first idea, that national historic trails should be on-the-ground heritage resources that people can use for recreation, was explored in both urban and rural settings during the Historic Trails Workshop in May 2012 in Socorro, New Mexico. . . . [M]ost of the effort of the agencies and the trail organizations has been focused on "telling the story" of these trails and interpreting the significant sites along them. . . . This intent adds another dimension to the imperative to preserve the historic remnants of the trails: how to make trails that enable people to experience those remnants and the landscapes experienced by their historical travelers without destroying those historic artifacts. . . .

The second idea is that one of the essential characteristics of national scenic and historic trails is that they have two equally critical dimensions — length and width. The exceptional length of these trails has long been recognized, but except for the Appalachian Trail, there has not been any concerted effort to manage the national scenic and historic trails as environmental corridors of any width. That insufficient, damaging practice changed for parts of the trails during the summer of 2012 with the release by the Bureau of Land Management (BLM) of three Policy Manuals directing the administration and management of national scenic and historic trails within the National Landscape Conservation System. . . . The BLM Policy Manuals . . . recognize that it is not enough to protect the ruts and other historic artifacts of the historic trails. The landscape setting that provides the context for those historic features must be preserved, as well, to allow trail users to have a vicarious experience of the historic use of the trail. . . .

The third idea, that the 30 national scenic and historic trails of the National Trails System comprise a large landscape, is the newest, and perhaps the most profound, of the three. This idea arose in the process of the inter-departmental Federal agencies Collaborative Landscape Planning (CLP) initiative during the spring and summer of 2012. . . . Agency leaders with whom we talked about this CLP proposal during "Hike the Hill" in February were extremely enthusiastic about it because they understood that it combines resource conservation with recreation opportunities, just as Congress intended in the NTSA. They were also enthusiastic about the layers of interagency collaboration and public/private partnership — hallmarks of the National Trails System — manifest in the proposal; it is the way we work. Participating in the realm of large landscape planning put the National Trails System on the map of national resources as a true system rather than as a collection of trails. The intangible benefit of the National Trails

System as a large landscape is in becoming recognized as an iconic national resource system complementary to the National Park System, National Wildlife Refuge System, National Wild and Scenic Rivers System, and the Wilderness System. . . . These national resource systems in turn help define our common identity and shared heritage as Americans. [23]

In September 2013, after 16 years of negotiations and several rounds of public review, the U.S. Access Board published the *Final Guidelines for Outdoor Developed Areas* that included trails. These guidelines aimed to foster full compliance with the Americans with Disabilities Act at all rel-

This trail at Crotched Mountain in Greenfield, New Hampshire, was designed and built to the new trail accessibility guidelines. Photo by Peter S. Jensen, Trail Planner/Builder, courtesy Stuart Macdonald.

evant federal lands and facilities. They offered both clear instructions for projects that fully qualify as well as exceptions for those that do not for various reasons (difficult terrain, fragile cultural values, or circumstances where compliance would unduly alter the trail segment's function or purpose). The guidelines were mindful of trails with special purposes (such as primitive wilderness or fragile historic values). Representatives from the ATC ably and persistently represented the interests of the National Trails System throughout this lengthy process. [24]

In November 2013, PNTS held the 13th national conference for NSTs and NHTs in Tucson, Arizona, featuring the national trails of the American Southwest. As had become the tradition during this decade approaching the 50th anniversary, conference sessions reflected the three major goals of the Decade for the National Trails: public outreach, resource

23. Gary Werner, "Three Big Ideas Emerge in 2012 and Spawn Transforming Actions," *Pathways Across America*, Winter 2012–13, p. 4.
24. "Outdoor Developed Areas Accessibility Guidelines: Access Board Issues ABA Final Guides for Outdoor Developed Areas, including Pedestrian Trails, on Federal Lands," *Pathways Across America*, Autumn/Winter 2013–14, pp. 7–8; NPS National Trails System Program, *Monthly Bulletin – July 26, 2007*; Christopher Douwes, September 24, 2017, email to author, both in NTSAHA.

protection, and capacity-building. Keynote speaker Luther Probst, long-time director of the Sonoran Institute, spoke to "the power of place":

But we often don't effectively describe the economic benefits that natural and historic trails bring to local communities. . . . Many studies have demonstrated the power of place, and it is critically important that we tap into that power by showing that national trails are important, not only for recreation, culture, and conservation, but also as the backbone for regional smart growth and as a local asset. [25]

In early 2014, the Federal Interagency Council on Trails issued its last annual report relating to the 2006 MOU. The following table summarizes the major quantifiable statistics that had been collected for the five years between 2009 and 2013.

The Autumn 2014 issue of *Pathways Across America* highlighted youth programs throughout the National Trails System, especially PNTS's Trail Apprentice Program. On the educational side, ATC's A Trail to Every Classroom (TTEC), started in 2005, provided K-12 teachers the opportunity to develop curriculum materials linked to the Appalachian NST. As the years went on, it accumulated a database of remarkable programs for all levels of elementary and secondary education. In 2010, federal agency and local partners launched the Iditarod Trail to Every Classroom, using TTEC principles adapted to often-remote native Alaskan villages on and near the Iditarod NHT's route. Both programs reach thousands of school students each year. [26]

25. PNTS, *14th Conference on National Scenic and Historic Trails – National Trails: Weaving the Tapestry of America's Cultures, Histories and Landscapes*, [registration booklet], p. 10, in NTSHA.
26. *Pathways Across America*, Autumn 2014.

TABLE J
Five-Year Summary 2009–2013 [27]
Where steady trends are discernible from year to year
over this five-year period, they are so noted.

Goal 1	**Outreach, Youth, and Community Involvement**	
	Number of website hits	26.4 million (a shrinking trend)
	Number of publications distributed	3.6 million (a growing trend)
	Number of trailwide partner meetings	1,417
	New national recreation trails recognized	186
Goal 2	**Trail Protection and Completion**	
	Acres of land protected by partners	35,224 (a growing trend)
	Acres protected by federal agencies	8,175
	Compliance actions	3,320
	Miles of NHT auto routes marked	1,936 (just in 2012 and 2013)
	Miles of trail constructed or maintained	1,702
	New miles of NHTs opened to the public	1,305 (a growing trend)
	New miles of NSTs built and opened	591
	Major structures installed	543
	NHT high potential sites/segments protected	474 (a shrinking trend)
	Recreation facilities installed	293
Goal 3	**Capacity Building**	
	Hours of official volunteer time	3.9 million (peaked in 2011)
	New partnership agreements	657 (a shrinking trend)

One highlight in 2015 was the 50th anniversary commemorative civil rights march along the Selma to Montgomery NHT. March 7, 2015 marked the anniversary of Bloody Sunday, 1965, when 600 voting-rights marchers in Selma, Alabama, were blocked, beaten, and tear-gassed. Their subsequent march two weeks later to Montgomery, the state capital, took place under court order and was watched on TV by a national audience. For the 50th anniversary march, President Barack Obama gave a speech before 70,000 people by the Edmund Pettus Bridge in Selma.

27. Adapted from Federal Interagency Council on Trails, February 2014, *National Trails System Annual Report for FY 2013*, p. 5, in NTSAHA.

This was followed by a reenactment of the entire march. One feature was an NPS-sponsored Youth Educational Tour (known as the "Walking Classroom") for 66 high school-aged students who explored the many social justice themes embedded in this important event. [28]

Another development in early 2015 was the official launch of the National Trails System GIS Network. It sought to engage anyone interested in coordinated electronic mapping along the national trails — be they federal staff, nonprofit agencies, state partners, commercial service companies, or even interested citizens. Monthly conference calls were held to discuss a wide range of issues from interactive atlases to viewshed management. Such a network is essential to applying and implementing the Federal Trail Data Standards on a consistent basis. [29]

NPS had been preparing for its centennial in 2016 for at least a decade. The National Park Foundation engaged a prestigious public relations firm to refine messaging and public outreach. Internally in the agency, work groups were set up to build relevance, coordinate special projects, and foster youth engagement under "A Call to Action." The public message became "Find Your Park." PNTS was invited to send a representative to the Centennial Advisory Committee to make sure the story of the National Trails System was not forgotten as NPS's centennial unfolded. Later, the

Students participate in a "Find Your Park" event at City of Rocks National Reserve, Idaho, to commemorate the NPS Centennial. Photo courtesy Wallace Keck.

centennial's "Find Your Park" theme evolved into "Find Your Trail" for the National Trails System 50th anniversary in 2018. [30]

Preparing for the 50th anniversary of the Trails System — and occurring on the 25th anniversary of PNTS's predecessor, the Committee of 17 — Gary Werner embarked on an informative and detailed three-part history of the Partnership for the National Trails System in *Pathways Across*

28. *Ibid.*, Spring 2015, pp. 7–8.
29. *Ibid.*, p. 10.
30. *Ibid*, Spring 2016, p. 11.

America. In 2017, PNTS also launched its now well-attended series of monthly webinars on different aspects of trail partnership and operations. Some address technical matters, some address operational issues such as best practices in volunteer programs, and some have fostered information about the pending anniversary. [31]

Meanwhile, in early 2017, the various federal agencies involved with the National Trails System reaffirmed their collaboration by signing a successor agreement to the 2006 MOU. All six original agencies continued as signatories, with the addition of the Department of the Interior's Bureau of Reclamation. The new MOU's scope covered all parts of the National Trails System, including NRTs and connecting and side trails. In this agreement, the Federal Interagency on Trails was renamed the National Trails System Council, and it was identified as the primary organization for carrying out the purposes of the MOU. The MOU went on to encourage a system-wide annual workplan, better links to agency line authority, and rotating leadership. [32]

However, the 2016 presidential elections brought a new sea change to the federal government with the election of Republican Donald J. Trump as president and his inauguration in January 2017. As of this writing, it is too early to tell how the policies of this administration will

PNTS Leadership Council Meeting, Washington, DC, during the 2016 Hike the Hill. Photo by author.

directly or indirectly affect the National Trails System. Staff reductions or attrition, more restricted travel, and nit-picking scrutiny of agreements could all become obstacles to the complex partnerships that are so vital to the success of the National Trails System. Happily, the supporters of NSTs and NHTs fall along the entire spectrum of American politics, so they

31. Gary Werner, "25 Years of the National Trails Community Working Together," Parts 1, 2, and 3, *Pathways Across America*, Autumn-Winter 2016, 3–5, Spring 2017, 5–6, and Summer 2017, pp. 3–4; *Pathways Across America*, Spring 2017, p. 6.
32. See website "2017 National Trails System MOU."

can approach politicians of every kind. Such citizen support — including myriad volunteers on many fronts — is, in fact, pure democracy at work.

2018 is the golden anniversary for the National Trails System. Much work has occurred in preparation, and many accomplishments have already been noted under the three goals developed for A Decade for the National Trails. However, this anniversary year will soon pass by, but the value and importance of America's trails will remain a lasting legacy and heritage that will serve this nation far into its future.

COLLABORATIVE LANDSCAPE PLANNING (CLP)

This program started as a long shot for national trails, but by 2018 had proven an invaluable and significant source of help in protecting trail-related resources nationwide. It came about in gradual stages.

The story began with the Obama administration's America's Great Outdoors initiative (AGO) that grew from an April 2010 White House Conservation Summit. During the summer and fall of 2010, top-level administration officials hosted dozens of listening sessions to hear what Americans at all levels wanted in conservation and recreation. Several AGO sessions were directed at youth perspectives. NST and NHT supporters attended many of these sessions. [33]

The resulting AGO report, issued by the White House in February 2011, emphasized large landscape preservation and conservation. PNTS's Gary Werner, in referring to this report, stated: "The quality of the experience of our trails is wholly dependent on the quality of the landscapes through which they pass. The quality of those landscapes, as well as the treads and ruts, will be the measure of the quality of our stewardship." Each state was to propose two projects for special consideration under AGO. Among these 100 projects were several linked to NSTs and NHTs. [34]

---

33. *Pathways Across America*, Summer 2010, 10, and Autumn 2010, p. 10.
34. Gary Werner, "Our Heritage and Challenge of Nature Cultural Landscape Stewardship," *Pathways Across America*, Spring 2011, 14 ;and , Winter 2011–12, p. 5.

One result of the AGO report was the concept of protecting large landscapes (such as the Crown of the Continent or the Southern Long-Leaf Pine region) through concerted efforts at coordinating the effects of the many conservation partners and federal agencies associated with such areas. Funds would be provided from a dedicated portion of the Land and Water Conservation Fund. During Hike the Hill 2012, PNTS's Gary Werner asked "What about the National Trails System — is the whole nation a large enough landscape to qualify?" And the answer was, "Try it and see."

Soon after, in the spring of 2012, PNTS and its associated federal agencies were invited to submit a pre-proposal of pending resource protection projects for FY 2014. From 40 initial CLP pre-proposal packages, ten were selected for full submission — including the National Trails System package! The resulting $61 million request for dozens of projects benefiting a variety of NSTs and NHTs in 17 states and 31 Congressional districts was prepared by PNTS as it gathered information over the summer from field offices and trails groups. The project lists were then prioritized by federal agency trail program officials into a smaller formal list for the first cycle of CLP funding in FY 2014. Administration officials seemed impressed by the collaborative partnerships that characterized the National Trails System at all levels. [35]

The result? In May 2013, $25 million for National Trails System CLP projects appeared in the president's budget for FY 2015. As enacted by Congress, this became the first round of trail CLP projects funded at $27 million for 18 projects along 12 NSTs and NHTs.

Meanwhile, work proceeded on follow-up packages for succeeding years to build on this success. The needs were great. For example, the FY 2016 package resulted in $20.8 million for CLP benefiting five NHTs and three NSTs. And for FY 2018, $19.7 million was made available for CLP projects benefiting projects along six NHTs and four NSTs. [36]

---

35. Gary Werner, editorial in *Pathways Across America*, Summer 2012, 3, also CLP report, p. 8.
36. *Pathways Across America*, Winter 2014–15, Winter 2015–16, 3, Winter 2016–17, 3, and Gary Werner, personal communication to author, May 21, 2018.

Two examples of CLP projects along national trails include:

- Kauleoli Fishing Village on the Big Island of Hawaii along the Ala Kahakai NHT. It was the trail's first protection project consisting of 59 acres along a half-mile of trail at a cost of $3.5 million. The tract adjoins Pu'uhonua O Honaunau National Historical Park and includes both endangered cultural sites and habitat for threatened species. [37]

- Werowocomoco, Gloucester County, Virginia, along the Captain John Smith NHT. This 264-acre rural site along the York River, 15 miles northeast of Jamestown, was the native people's capital under Chief Powhatan. Captain John Smith met Powhatan here, and perhaps his legendary daughter, Pocahontas. Soon abandoned after English settlement and its importance long forgotten, the site was confirmed archeologically in 2003, entered onto the National Register of Historic Places in 2006, and acquired, first by the Conservation Fund, and then NPS in 2016, using CLP funds. [38]

By the end of the Obama administration, the CLP had funded projects along eight NHTs and six NSTs in 20 states for a total of $77 million from the LWCF. For each cycle, PNTS staff gathered the site information and arranged them in a spreadsheet for consistency and ease of comparison. Each year, the packages competed against many others. Federal agencies then narrowed the lists and set priorities. In total, this proved to be the largest investment by the federal government in the National Trails System in any four-year period. [39]

37. *Ibid*, Summer 2016, pp. 5–6.
38. Werowocomoco," *Wikipedia,* last modified March 25, 2018, https://en.wikipedia.org/wiki/Werowocomoco.
39. *Pathways Across America*, Summer 2017, p. 4.

CONCLUSION
PREPARING FOR
THE FUTURE

I fear . . . the increased bureaucratic mindset. There's going to be more of a move to have uniform policies and procedures and things on trails which probably aren't appropriate. . . . Let it be more flexible. It gives us the ability to respond to partners in a better way and keep them happy and get their things done. . . . I see more of a need for certain kinds of work with the partners, setting standards for the trail and trying to meet that. I think the Appalachian Trail model — letting the partners really take the lead, which apparently goes all the way back to Benton MacKaye — is a good way of doing it on both scenic and historic trails. (John Conoboy, 2008) [1]

B ack in 1993, coincident to the 25th anniversary of the National Trails System, NPS trail staff gathered in Tucson, Arizona, and came up with a vision statement for the next 25 years:

By the year 2018, when the National Trails System celebrates its 50th anniversary, we hope to see in place:

1. *A nationwide comprehensive network of national scenic and national historic trails that link many of America's significant resources.*

2. *Trails which provide a unique set of educational experiences through a chain of protected and interpreted resources. Trail corridors will be clearly and consistently marked and interpreted, with public information of the highest quality.*

---

1. John Conoboy, 2008, NPS Oral History interview, NTS 40th Anniversary Oral History Project, p. 23.

3. *Continuing popular support and shared vision in cooperative partnerships with state and local governments, nonprofit organizations, commercial interests, and individuals.*

4. *Full performance trail management, completely integrated through funding, staffing, and other administrative functions with the management of America's public lands.*

5. *Trail management which recognizes and cooperates with the tourism and recreation industries, as appropriate, to provide quality experiences and protect resources.*

6. *An international network of trails linked to trail systems in Canada and Mexico.*

7. *Shared funding between taxpayers and cooperators, volunteers, endowments, donations, etc.* [2]

The new southern terminus monument for the Pacific Crest NST was erected by PCTA volunteers in 2016. Photo by Michael Lewis.

How well have these vision statements been achieved? And how differently would such statements be framed today?

Since 1993, ten NSTs and NHTs and hundreds of NRTs have been added to the system. These new trails now fully stretch across the nation and provide enriching cultural and recreational experiences bringing NSTs and NHTs to almost every state. But none of the trails are full marked or protected. Some are well supported by the public, but many are not. In fact, most Americans are still unaware of this magnificent system of trail opportunities. Links with the tourism and outdoor recreation industries remain weak. Funding today compared to 1993 is much better, but still often uncertain (and not freely shared as envisioned above). And, due to anti-immigrant fears, it is actually more difficult to connect to Canada and Mexico now than it was 25 years ago.

---

2. Steve Elkinton, memo to Participants, Long-Distance Trails Meeting, Tucson, Arizona, January 26–28, in NTSAHA.

Founded on federal legislation, the National Trails System is a political construct. Birthed in the idealistic and troubled 1960s, it has weathered over five decades through ten presidential administrations and seven changes in party where there were often significant shifts in priorities and policy. It has witnessed a burgeoning outdoor industry economy, a widening gap between rich and poor, and an emptying out of rural areas. It has also been sustained by increasing public interest in heritage tourism and hiking. For the first time, publicly accessible interactive e-mapping aids are making access to the trails easier. And, with no new NSTs or NHTs added since 2009, there has been a stabilizing influence, letting agencies and partners alike adjust to the complexities of the trails already created by law.

Besides uncertain funding, inconsistent marking, and spotty community support, America's NSTs and NIITs face some other remarkable challenges, some long term and some that have emerged just recently. These include:

- Energy projects, transmission lines, and pipelines that disrupt fragile trail corridors,
- Suburban growth and sprawl,
- Lax local and state ordinances and statutes to protect endangered resources,
- Lack of awareness by the public of the benefits and opportunities offered by the trails,
- Weakening trail organizations with declining membership,
- Demographic changes, especially new generations who may volunteer less in the future,
- And new urgency to seek private-sector funds as federal funding programs become scarcer and more difficult to access.

In a 2007 oral history interview, PNTS Executive Director Gary Werner observed,

We're still not finished on our . . . quest to get really adequate federal [funding] *resources for the trails. We're a lot better off than we were in 1991. We have a widely disparate capacity among the nonprofit partners. On one end of the spectrum we have one organization, the Appalachian Trail Conservancy, with 40,000+ members and a*

$5 million annual operating budget. On the other end of the spectrum, we've got a couple of the historic and scenic trail organizations that barely exist. . . . And, in the next 10 years, a real challenge will be to both reach out and hold us retiring baby boomers, the biggest cohort in the nation's population. At the same time, we need to find a way to reach out and engage and inspire the youngsters who will carry on after we are gone. In both of those populations, we need to be sure that we're getting all of the ethnic and cultural mix that is embodied by the Trail System. That's a big challenge. If we succeed in doing that, our success will be assured. If we don't succeed in doing it, I don't know how this is all going to ultimately survive. . . .

And in the long run, I would like to see the model of the National Trails System — this public/private collaboration, this encouragement and even reliance on citizens to take an active role as stewards of our public resources — I would like to see that idea carried way beyond the Trails System and embraced by agencies for the stewardship of public lands in general, both as a way of bringing many more hands to all the necessary work to be done, but also, frankly, as a way of helping reconnect the people to the land and to our cultural and historical heritage as a country and as a country of many people. The tangible connections that you get with the experiences out there on the land and with other people, you can't duplicate with all of the slick electronic media we have now. There's no substitute. [3]

It is hard to predict where the National Trails System may be going in the future — as hard as it is to predict the nation's political future. In fact, the two are tied together. As this exploration of the Trails System history has shown, the broader political atmosphere and trends of the nation even have effects on a system as low-key as national trails. The Trails System is more likely to prosper and bring untold benefits to this and future generations if its supporters and partners share some common visions and principles. The emergence of a wide-ranging alliance of trail advocates — namely the Partnership for the National Trails System — and the experiences of preparing for A Decade for the National Trails and the 50th anniversary show that such collaboration over time is possible and effective.

The future may not necessarily be shaped by a coherent and action-oriented plan. Instead, perhaps, it is best directed by framing big questions

---

3. Gary Werner, 2007, NPS Oral History interview, NTS 40th Anniversary Oral History Project, pp. 27–8.

and following simple rules of thumb. One observer almost 30 years ago offered this advice:

*Without a constituency, without a **broad** capability to gather in committed people who are motivated out of an incredible emotional intensity . . . these . . . systems cannot be built and cannot last. And those kinds of constituencies you just can't create from scratch. . . . Have faith that this era of minimal expectations — particularly in our government — is not the last word, and we need to take great care and caution in inventing any system that relies on the federal government. I don't care whether it is a welfare system or a space system or a national trails system — to not design it on the cheap today, because that is the only way we can see to do it, when, if we have faith, there is a brighter tomorrow.*

. . . You've got to stop thinking (even though that is your mandate) just about the long-distance trails. . . . [Y]ou'd better think in a very embracing way about trails, and the uses of trails as a common focus that you are going to bring to get lots of people together. . . . [I]t's important to re-conceive the mission of the trail in the context of something that isn't linear, [but] that's big and round and has ecological wholeness to it.

*I would encourage you to be **really wary** of false alliances and alliances of convenience. . . . But alliances that are unnatural to begin with carry with them costs that probably you didn't think through completely before. [Yet] . . . you need to think long and hard about how to make the work of the long-distance trails — and, of course, all the other trails — a much bigger part of the business of a bunch of people who **already** built the infrastructure for political clout in this country, so that you don't have to waste your time doing that all over again. There is no point in trying to get bigger than (or as big as) the Wilderness Society or the Sierra Club or the Natural Resources Defense Council if you can sneak in and get your issue on their agenda. . . . It is the smartest kind of coalition politics to get your issues on other people's agendas . . . . Link to the big national groups, just because it's smart politics. (When you have to have a fight with them, have a fight with them.) But together, you will be so much more powerful than you will ever be alone. Share your issues with them and you share theirs, and there's real power in all that.* [4]

Certain questions haunt the National Trails System, and some of these have no easy answers:

---

4. Adapted from Doug Scott, 1991, *Keynote Speech*, Second National Conference on National Scenic and National Historic Trails, November 14, 1991, in NTSAHA.

- How many national trails are enough?
  When is the "System" complete?
- What kinds of trails are missing from the National
  Trails System and should be added to it?
- What new kinds of partnerships are
  needed to sustain these trails?
- Should state agencies be more involved in national trails?
- What are the incentives that will keep federal
  agencies cooperating together to foster the National
  trails System as a multiagency enterprise?
- Where will the funding come from in the long term to
  adequately protect, operate, and publicize national trails?
- How can more Americans be inspired to visit, appreciate,
  and volunteer to support America's national trails?

And, to close, no more fitting words than these of Gary Werner, PNTS executive director, can round out this historical chronicle of an experiment which has yielded so much more than the people who launched it ever expected.

I believe our trails are important to the long-term health of our Nation. I believe our trails and our organizations have an essential role to play in the conservation and preservation of key elements of our natural and cultural heritage. Our trails are pathways for citizens of all ages to use to tangibly discover their roots in our native landscape and our history. Perhaps, even more significantly, our organizations offer our citizens opportunities to become stewards of our cultural and natural heritage. We are pioneers in the endeavor of conserving and providing resources for public enjoyment through public-private partnerships. . . . We have a direct hand in educating new generations in the challenges of understanding and caring for the tangible reminders of our past and the ecosystems that must remain healthy to sustain us into the future. We do this day to day in direct, practical, hands-on work, most of it unsung. . . .

In a time of instant gratification provided by electronic entertainment and media, how do we capture the imagination of younger generations with the stories of our heritage embodied in our national historic trails?

Unless we are able to make connections to at least some of the supporters of like causes, I cannot imagine how we are going to finish our work of trail-making. We need to learn from and emulate the practices of successful organizations. We cannot afford to be unsung heroes in an age of such intense media bombardment. Financial resources and volunteers flow to heralded causes and projects. We must find ways to advertise our good work for public benefit much more actively than we have been. We must overcome our reticence toward asking for the money and attention required to complete the trails we cherish. [5]

It is very easy for us who live within this culture of collaboration and cooperative management — like fish in water — to take it for granted. We should not do so. Rather we should celebrate the legacy that we and our predecessors have created and strengthen our practice of cooperation, collaboration, and inclusion to ever perfect our culture of citizen stewardship. The shared responsibility at the heart of this culture has fostered amazing degrees of dedication, "ownership," knowledge, and skill among the tens of thousands of us living and practicing this culture. Our National Trails System culture of citizen stewardship has created a remarkable level of knowledge, expertise, dedication, and competence within the individuals and organizations that practice it. Long may we perfect its practice and may it flourish within the National Trails System! [6]

Along the Juan Bautista de Anza NHT near
Tumacacori NHS, Arizona, 2013. Photo by author.

5. Gary Werner, "Which Way for the National Trails System? A Call to Action," *Pathways Across America*, Winter 1996, pp. 1 and 6.
6. Gary Werner, "The National Trails System – A Culture of Citizen Stewardship," *Pathways Across America*, Autumn/Winter, 2013–14, p. 13.

APPENDIX

NATIONAL TRAILS
SYSTEM TIMELINE

YEAR	MAJOR EVENT IN HISTORY	SIGNIFICANT NATIONAL TRAILS SYSTEM EVENT
1905		U.S. Forest Service established
1906		Ezra Meeker starts first Oregon Trail retracement
		DAR starts monumenting historic trails
1916		National Park Service established
1917–18	World War I	
1920	Women's right to vote granted	
1921		Benton MacKaye envisions Appalachian Trail
1925		Appalachian Trail Conference founded
1929	Great Depression starts	
1930s		Catherine Montgomery and Clinton Clarke envision PCT
1935	Wilderness Society organized	
1940–45	World War II	
1945		First federal trails legislation introduced (not passed)
1958		ORRRC authorized (published in 1962)
1962		Bureau of Outdoor Recreation established
1963	President Kennedy assassinated	
	LBJ becomes president	
1965	President Johnson's Beautification Message	Senator Nelson's first trails bills
	Passage of the Outdoor Recreation Act	
	Vietnam War becomes unpopular	

YEAR	MAJOR EVENT IN HISTORY	SIGNIFICANT NATIONALTRAILS SYSTEM EVENT
1966		*Trails for America* published
		Florida Trail Association founded
1967		National Trails System Act hearings in both houses
1968	MLK and RFK assassinated	National Trails System Act passed (PL 90-543) Appalachian and Pacific Crest NSTs established
	Richard Nixon elected president	
1969		Federal Interagency Task Force on Trails established
1970	First Earth Day	
1971		First NRTs designated by Secretary of the Interior
		First National Trails Symposium, held in Washington, DC
1974	Nixon resigns and Vietnam War closes down	
1976	Jimmy Carter elected president	American Hiking Society founded
1978		PL 95-625 adds national historic trails to system Oregon, Mormon Pioneer, Lewis and Clark, and Iditarod NHTs plus Continental Divide NST established
1980	Ronald Reagan elected president	North Country and Ice Age NSTs plus Overmountain Victory NHT established
1981		Bureau of Outdoor Recreation abolished
		Hike-a-Nation captures popular interest in trails
1982		OCTA founded
1983		Natchez Trace, Florida and Potomac Heritage NSTs established
1986		Rails-to-Trails Conservancy founded Nez Perce (Nee-Me-Poo) NHT established
1987	Report by President's Commission on Americans Outdoors	Santa Fe and Trails of Tears NHTs established
1988	George H. W. Bush elected president	American Trails formed
		First NST and NHT conference in Hartland, Wisconsin
1989	Soviet Union breaks into independent republics	
1990	First Iraq War	Juan Buatista de Anza NHT established
1991		ISTEA offers transportation funding for trails

YEAR	MAJOR EVENT IN HISTORY	SIGNIFICANT NATIONAL TRAILS SYSTEM EVENT
		Second NST and NHT conference in Corbett, Oregon
		First edition of *NTS Map & Guide* published
1992	Bill Clinton elected president	California and Pony Express NHTs established
1993		Twenty-fifth anniversary of National Trails System Act
		Third NST/NHT conference in Kansas City, Missouri
1995		Fourth NST/NHT conference in Chevy Chase, Maryland
1996		BLM establishes NLCS, NSTs and NHTs are a part Selma to Montgomery NHT established
1997		Fifth NST/NHT conference in Oviedo, Florida
1999		Sixth NST/NHT conference in Lake Tahoe, Nevada
2000	George W. Bush elected president	El Camino Real de Tierra Adentro and Ala Kahakai NHTs established
2001	World Trade Center attacks	Executive Order 13195 promoting trails signed by Clinton
		Seventh NST/NHT conference in Casper, Wyoming
2002	Second Iraq War begins	Eighth NST/NHT conference in Fort Smith, Arkansas Old Spanish NHT established
2003		Ninth NST/NHT conf. in Bow, Washington
2003–6		Bicentennial of L&C Expedition
2004		El Camino Real de los Tejas established
2005		Tenth NST/NHT conf. in Las Vegas, Nevada
2006		Interagency MOU to foster coordination Captain John Smith Chesapeake NHT established
2007		Eleventh NST/NHT conf. in Duluth, Minnesota
2008	Major recession begins	A Decade for the National Trails System launched
	Barack Obama elected president	Star-Spangled Banner NHT established

YEAR	MAJOR EVENT IN HISTORY	SIGNIFICANT NATIONAL TRAILS SYSTEM EVENT
2009		Twelfth NST/NHT conference in Missoula, Montana P.L. 111-11 establishes the Arizona, New England, and Pacific Northwest NSTs and the Washington-Rochambeau Revolutionary Route NHT and enlarges the Trail of Tears NHT
2011		Thirteenth NST/NHT conference in Abingdon, Virginia
2013		Fourteenth NST/NHT conference in Tucson, Arizona
2014–8		CLP releases millions for trail land protection
2015	LWCF authorization extended	Fifteenth NST/NHT conference in Franklin, Tennessee
2016	Donald J. Trump elected president	
2018		Trails System's fiftieth anniversary on October 2
		Sixteenth NST/NHT conference in Vancouver, Washington

BIBLIOGRAPHY

* = Items found in the National Trails System Administrative History
Archive (NTSAHA), c/o NPS National Office, Washington, DC.

Allard, Wayne, April 26, 2007, Statement in *Hearing Before the
     [Senate] Subcommittee on National Parks of the Committee
     on Energy and Natural Resources in Miscellaneous National
     Parks Bills*, Senate Hearing 110-88, p. 5. *
"America's Trails," 1976, in *Outdoor Recreation Action*, a BOR
     publication, Report No. 42, Winter, 1976, pp. 3-4. *
American Hiking Society and Heritage Conservation
     Recreation Service, June, 1980, press packet for 1980
     Transcontinental Hike Route, with related articles. *
American Hiking Society and Rails-to-Trails Conservancy,
     May, 1996, *Trails and Trailways Into the 21st Century: The
     trails policy report of Trails for All Americans '94*, 50 pp. *
AHS, Aug., 2003, *National Trails Day 2003 Final Report.* *
_____, no date, "Senate Omnibus Public Land
     Management Act Facts." *
American Trails, etc., 1992, Proceedings – *11th National Trails
     Symposium, Sept. 19-22, Missoula, Montana.* *
_____, etc., 1994, *Proceedings [for] 12th National Trails
     Symposium, "Connecting our Communities," September 28-
     October 1, 1994, Anchorage, Alaska*, 237 pp. *
American Trails Network, 1986, *An Action Plan for Creating an Interconnected
     Network of Trails Across America: Report on a Conference Held Oct.,
     1986, at Rensselaerville Institute*, Rensselaerville, NY. *

Anderson, Larry, 2002, *Benton MacKaye: Conservationist, Planner, and Creator of the Appalachian Trail*, Baltimore and London: Johns Hopkins Press, 452 pp.

Andrus, Cecil, 1977, to Walter F. Mondale, President of the Senate, May 26, 1977. *

"Appalachian Trailway Agreement" in *Appalachian Trailway News*, Vol. 1, No. 1, January, 1939.

Aspinall, Wayne N., July 16, 1968, in *Congressional Record*, p. H 6696. *

Benton MacKaye profile in ATC, 2000, *Appalachian Trailway News, Special 75th Anniversary Issue*, p. 5.

Bureau of Land Management, 2006, *National Scenic and Historic Trail Strategy and Work Plan.*

BLM, FHWA, NEA, NPS, and USDA-FS, 2006, *National Historic and Scenic Trails: Accomplishments 2001-2005, 28 pp.* *

Bureau of Outdoor Recreation Correspondence Files, RG 368, Box 13, National Archives II, Greenbelt, MD.

Campbell, Robert, NPS, 11/17/17 e-mail to author.

Cantwell, Robert, as quoted in Henry L. Diamond, 1976, "From Rails to Trails," in *Outdoor Recreation Action*, Report No. 42, Winter,   1976, p.p. 9-10. *

Cardinet, George, 1971, in *Proceedings, National Symposium on Trails, Washington*, D.C., June 2-6, 1971, pp. 19-20. *

_____ in NPS and OCTA, 1993, *Connection – '93: The Third National Conference on National Scenic and National Historic Trails, Proceedings*, quote p. 45. *

Carter, President Jimmy, May 23, 1977, *The Environmental Message to Congress*, text in courtesy The American Presidency Project. *

Circle of Tribal Advisors and Lewis & Clark Bicentennial, no date, *Enough Good People: Reflections on Tribal Involvement and Inter-Cultural Collaboration 2003-2006*, Grand Junction: Colorado Printing Company, 148 pp., illustrated.

Clinton, President William J., Jan. 18, 2001, *Executive Order 13195: Trails for America in the 21st Century.* *

Cohen, Bonnie, April 11, 1995, in *Pathways Across America*, Summer, 1995, Vol. 7, No. 3, p. 8. *

Conoboy, John, Aug., 2, 1999, e-mail to meeting participants, "Thanks and flip chart notes." *

"Contributions Sustaining the National Scenic and Historic Trails Made by Partner Trail Organizations" in *Pathways Across America*, Spring/Summer, 2002, Vol. 15, No. 2, p. 9. *

Conway, Grant, 1967, for the National Parks Association, *Hearing Before the Subcommittee on National Parks and Recreation . . . on HR 4865 and Related Bills to Establish a Nationwide System of Trails*, held March 6-7, 1967, Wash., DC: GPO, p. 90.

Crafts, Edward C., May 30, 1962 remarks, "Birth of a Bureau." *

_____, June 21, 1962, "Birth of a Bureau," remarks made at the 40th annual convention and conservation congress at the Izaak Walton League of America, Portland, OR.

Dahl, Mike, Aug. 20, 2001, e-mail to ovta-list@ovta.org. *

Davey, Stuart P., June 3, 1971, "The National Scenic Trail Study Program, Status and Problems" in *Proceedings, National Symposium on Trails*, Washington, D.C., p. 16, June 2-4, 1971. *

Delaporte, Chris T., Sept. 21, 1979 memo to All State Liaison Officers, 2 pp. *

Douwes, Christopher, 9/24/2017, e-mail to author.

Dreskell, W.W., 1966, "Bureau of Outdoor Recreation, P.L. 88-29; and Land and Water Conservation Fund Act of 1965, P.L. 88-578."

"Eager Mrs. Johnson Feels Free as a Bird Outdoors," in *The Washington Post, Times Herald, April 16, 1967*, p. H12. (Accessed online through ProQuest Historical Newspapers.)

Eastman, Robert L., 1975, BOR Division of Resource Area Studies, "The National Trails System," in *Proceedings of the Third National Trails Symposium, 1975*, pp. 201-2. *

Eissler, Frederick, 1966, "The National Trails System Proposal" in *Sierra Club Bulletin*, June, 1966, Vol. 51., No. 6, pp. 16-17.

Elkinton, Steve, "At Last, a Full House: Federal Trail
    Administrators Get Together" in *Pathways Across
    America*, Summer, 1995, Vol. 7, No. 3, p. 8. *

_____, 2000, "Challenge Cost-Share Program:
    Summary of Issues and Observations." *

_____, 2000, "Benefits of Challenge Cost-Share Growing" in *Pathways
    Across America*, Winter, 2000, Vol. 13, No. 1, pp. 5 and 8. *

_____, Jan. 25, 2001, memo to National Park Service NST
    and NHT administrators, *Monthly Message No. 8.* *

_____, May 21, 2001, memo to NPS NST and NHT
    administrators, *Monthly Message, May 25, 2001,*
    and *Monthly Bulletin* – June, 2003. *

_____, with Helen Scully, Jim Miller, Jamie Schwartz,
    Deb Salt, and Gary Werner, 2002, "What Have We
    Accomplished in 10 Years?" in *Pathways Across America*,
    Spring/Summer 2002, Vol. 15., No. 2, pp. 7-10. *

_____, 2008, *The National Trails System – A Grand Experiment*,
    Wash., DC: GPO for National Park Service, 50 pp.

_____, 2010, *NPS Challenge Cost-Share Projects – 2004 to 2008*, 7 pp. *

_____, 2012, "5-Year Trends, a Federal Perspective," in
    Pathways Across America, Summer, 2012, p. 10.

_____, 2014, memo to Participants, Long-Distance Trails
    Meeting, Tucson, AZ, Jan. 26-28, 2014. *

_____, no date, "Challenge Cost-Share Aids 130
    Lewis and Clark Projects." *

Evans, Craig, 1980, "National Trails – the Unexplored Potential" in
    National Parks and Conservation Magazine, October 1980, p. 7. *

Federal Interagency Council on Trails, March, 2002,
    Annual Report for CY 2001 . . . . *

_____, Feb. 26, 2004, *YEAR 3 REPORT on Interagency Collaboration in the
    Administration and Management of National Scenic and Historic Trails.* *

_____, January, 2008, *National Trails System Annual
    Report for FY 2007*, 15 pp. *

_____, Nov., 2008, *The National Trails System at 40*, 22 pp. *

_____, 2010, *National Trails System Annual Report for FY 2009*, 28 pp. *

_____, Feb., 2013, *National Trails System Annual Report for FY 2012.* *

_____, Feb., 2014, *National Trails System Annual Report for FY 2013.* *

     Federal Register, Sept. 12, 1969, Vol. 34, No. 175, p. 14337. *

_____, April 19, 1979, Vol. 44, No. 77, p. 23384. *

_____, April 14, 1999, Vol. 64, No. 71, p. 18444. *

_____, March 28, 2000, Vol. 65, No. 60, pp. 16412-16418. *

"First Connecting Trails Designated" in *Pathways*
     Across America, Summer, 1990, p. 6. *

Fitzwilliams, Jeanette,1982, letter to Mary Lou Grier, Aug. 11,
     1982, attached to U.S. Senate Committee of Energy
     and Natural Resources, Aug. 4, 1982, *Hearing on*
     Amendments to the National Trails System Act, etc. *

Franzwa, Gregory M., OCTA, letter to William Penn
     Mott, NPS Director, July 15, 1985,. *

Friends of Acadia, etc., *Preserving Historic Trails: Conference*
     Proceedings, Oct. 17-19, 2000, 114 pp. *

Garvey, Ed Garvey, 1976, in U.S. House of Representatives, *Oversight*
     Hearings Before the Subcommittee on National Parks and Recreation
     . . . on the National Trails System Act of 1968, etc., March 11-12,
     1976, Wash., DC: GPO, Serial No. 94-50, p. 64. *

Gilbert, Thomas L., Feb. 4, 1992, Memo to Regional
     Director, Midwest Region, 5 pp. *

GPO, 1967, *Hearing Before the* [House] *Subcommittee on National Parks*
     and Recreation . . . on HR 4865 and Related Bills to Establish a
     Nationwide System of Trails, March 6-7, 1967, Serial No. 90-4. *

GPO, 1967, *Hearings Before the [Senate] Committee on Interior and*
     Insular Affairs . . . on S. 827, A Bill to Establish a Nationwide
     System of Trails and for Other Purposes, Mar. 15-16, 1967. *

_____, 1979, *Message from the President of the United States Transmitting*
     a Review of His Administration's Programs for the Protection of
     the Environment, House Document 96-174, p. 25. *

_____, March 28, 1983, Public Law 98-11 (97 Stat. 42), *An*
     Act to Amend the National Trails System Act, etc. *

"GPS Revolutionizes Trail Mapping" in *Pathways Across*
     America, Summer, 1996, Vol. 9, No. 3, p. 3. *

Heritage Conservation Recreation Service, Northwest Region,
    Dec., 1979, *Trails System Planning, Phase I Report.* *

Henley, Susan A., for AHS, July 15, 1992, letter
    to William T. Spitzer, NPS. *

Herbst, Bob, May 28, 1977, "The Appalachian Trail – A
    Model for a National Trails System," *Remarks of the
    Hon. Robert L. Herbst* . . . at the Appalachian Trail
    Conference, Shepherdstown, West Virginia. *

Horn, William P., 1987, letter to Hon. J. Bennett Johnson,
    in U.S. Senate Report 100-39, *Santa Fe National
    Historic Trail*, April 10, 1987, p. 5. *

Jackson, Donald Dale, 1988, "The Long Way 'Round: The National
    Scenic Trails System and how it grew. And how it didn't"
    in *Wilderness* Magazine, Summer, 1988, pp. 19-20. *

Jackson, Henry M., March 25, 1970, letter to Walter J. Hickel. *

Johnson, President Lyndon B., Feb. 8, 1965, *Special Message to
    Congress on Conservation and Restoration of Natural Beauty.* *

_____, Jan. 30, 1967, *Special Message to the Congress: Protecting Our
    Natural Heritage*, courtesy the American Presidency Project. *

Karotko, Robert, for William T. Spitzer, Aug. 19, 1986,
    memo to NPS Director with attachments.

_____, May 8, 2008, e-mail message to Steve Elkinton.

Kennedy, President John F., 1963, "Remarks Upon Signing the Outdoor
    Recreation Bill" on The American Presidency website.

King, Brian B., "Trail Years: A History of the Appalachian Trail
    Conference," in *Appalachian Trailway News*, July 2000, pp. 3-7.

Larson, Thomas D., in American Trails, etc., 1992,
    Proceedings – *11th National Trails Symposium, Sept.
    19-22, Missoula, Montana*, pp. pp. 8-16. *

Latschar, Dr. John A., Jan. 10, 1984, letter to Gregory M. Franzwa,
    Oregon-California Trails Association and attached *Proposal for
    the Establishment of Western Project Office, National Historic Trails,
    National Park Service*, and related correspondence in NTSAHA. *

Levin, Carl, Oct. 7, 1994, in *Congressional Record – Senate*, p. S 14860. *

Lewis, Wallace G., 2002, "Following in Their Footsteps: Creating the Lewis and Clark National Historic Trail," in *Columbia, the Magazine of Northwest History*, Vol. 16, No. 2.

Lillard, David, June, 1993, *National Trails Day 1993 Program Report*. *

Limarzi, Tullia, 1995, "What Does Your Trail Want from Congress?" in *Pathways Across America*, Spring, 1995, Vol. 7, No. 2. *

"Long-Distance Lobbyists Advocate Trails Funding" in *Pathways Across America*, Summer, 1993, p. 10. *

Luce, Charles F., Feb. 1, 1967, letter with attachments to Hubert Humphrey, President of the U.S. Senate, and *Congressional Record*, Feb. 3, 1967, p. S 1426. *

Lukei, Reese, Oct. 17, 2017, personal communication with the author.

Marshall, Ross, "Groups Craft Vision for NHTs" in *Pathways Across America*, Fall-Winter 1998-1999, Vol. 11, No. 4 and Vol. 12 No. 1., p. 6. *

Memorandum of Understanding for the Administration and Management of National Historic and National Scenic Trails Among [the five listed agencies], January, 2001. *

"Millers 'Write the Book' on Trails" in *Pathways Across America*, Spring, 1996, Vol. 9, No. 2, p. 11. *

Moore, Roger L., Vicki Lafarge, and Charles L. Tracy, 1992, *Organizing Outdoor Volunteers*, Boston: Appalachian Mountain Club.

_____ and Kelly Barthlow, 1998, *The Economic Impacts and Uses of Long-Distance Trails*, NPS. *

Mott, William Penn, 1986, "National Trails – Their Value and Management Within the National Park Service," in *International Congress on Trail and River Recreation Proceedings*, May 31- June 4, 1986, Vancouver, BC, p. 102. *

_____, March, 1987, memo to NPS regional directors, *National Park Service Administration of National Scenic and National Historic Trails*. *

Murray, Stanley A., Sept. 16, 1965, testimony in *Hearing Before the [Senate] Subcommittee on Parks and Recreation . . . on S. 622*, GPO: Wash., DC, pp. 25-27 and U.S. Senate, 1965, Senate reports on S 622 and S 2590.

National Conference on National Scenic and National Historic Trails – A Summary, no date, typescript MS in NTSAHA. *

National Park Service Recreation Grants Division, August, 1985, *Rails- to-Trails Grant Program, an evaluation of assistance provided under Public Law 94-210 to assist in the conservation of abandoned railroad rights of way to park and recreation use*, 23 pp. *

NPS, 1990, *Trails for All Americans*. *

_____, Jan., 1991, *Report on America's National Scenic, National Historic, and National Recreation Trails – 1989-1990*, 25 pp., Wash., DC: NPS. *

_____, Sept. 30, 1991, "Discussion Paper: *Should National Scenic and National Historic Trails Administered by the National Park Service Be Considered "Units" of the National Park System?* *

NPS Long Distance Trails Program, *Long Distance Trails Managers Meeting, Tucson, Arizona, January 26 28, 1993, Meeting Report*. *

NPS and OCTA, 1993, *Connection – '93: The Third National Conference on National Scenic and National Historic Trails, Proceedings*, quote p. 16-18. *

NPS, 1997, "CRM and the National Trails System" issue of *Cultural Resource Management*, Vol. 20, No. 1, 1997, Wash., DC: NPS. *

NPS Oral History interviews, 2007, National Trails System 40th Anniversary Oral History Project: John Conoboy, p. 23; Steve Elkinton, pp. 7-8, 11, 13-15; Tom Gilbert, pp. 5-6, 11-12, 19, 27-29; Susan "Butch" Henley, pp. 7, 10, 19; Jere Krakow, p. 13-14; Brian O'Neill, pp. 3, 5-8, 17; Cleve Pinnix, pp. 3-8, 10-14, 18-20; Leo Rasmussen, pp. 4-5;Nat Reed, pp. 2-8, 10; Chuck Rinaldi, pp. 2-4,11-13; Jim Snow, pp. 3, 6-7, 18-19; and Gary Werner, pp. 5, 11, 20, 27-28.

NPS National Trails System Program, *Monthly Bulletins* for May, 2003; April, 2004; May, 2006; July, 2007; June, August, October, and November, 2008; February, March, 2009 *

NPS, January 2011, *Connect Trails to Parks: A Three Year Program Report*, 31 pp. *

NPS, Office of Policy, May 28, 2013, memo from Chief to NPS National Leadership Council, *Director's Order #45: National Trails System*. *

"NPS Announces Cost-Share Awards for Trails" in
  Pathways Across America, Spring, 1994. *

"National Trails" in The *Washington Post*, April 8, 1966, p. A6.
  (Accessed through ProQuest Newspapers: *Washington Post*.)

National Trails Council, *Trail Tracks*, Vol. XII, No. 3, Sept., 1983, p. 6. *

National Trails System Act, 16 U.S.C. 1241-1251, various sections.

Nelson, Gaylord, Sept. 16, 1965, in *Hearing Before the [Senate]*
  Subcommittee on Parks and Recreation . . . on S. 622 . . . . , p. 6. *

_____, 1969, "Trails Across America" in *National Wildlife*
  magazine, Vol. 4, June-July, 1969, pp. 21-27. *

Nevel, Bonnie, March, 1989, *Closing the Gaps*, 54 pp.,
  Wash., DC: GPO. * *Ninth National Trails Symposium*
  Proceedings, Sept. 11-14, 1988, p. 46. *

Nofield, Stefan, 2016, NPS memo, "NPS Challenge
  Cost-Share Program: Update."

Noonan, Patrick F., May 16, 2006, testimony in *Hearing Before*
  the [Senate] *Committee of National Parks of the Committee*
  on Energy and Natural Resources [on eight bills], Senate
  Hearing pp. 109-547, Wash., DC: GOP, pp. 51-57. *

Ogden, Daniel M., Jr., Sept., 2008, "Development of the
  National Trails System Act" in *Pacific Crest Trail*
  Communicator, Vol. 20, No. 4, pp. 14-15.

O'Neill, Brian, memo for John D. Cherry, June 25, 1980, *National*
  Trails Assessment, Pacific Southwest Region, Phase II. *

"Outdoor Developed Areas Accessibility Guidelines: Access Board
  Issues ABA Final Guides for Outdoor Developed Areas,
  including Pedestrian Trails, on Federal Lands," in *Pathways*
  Across America, Autumn/Winter 2013-2014, p. 7-8.

Partnership for the National Trails System, 2001, "Strong Partnerships
  Make Great National Trails," The 7th Conference on National
  Historic and National Scenic Trails, Casper, Wyoming,
  August 17-21, 2001, *Conference Program and Information.* *

_____ and others, Oct. 17-21, 2002, "Telling Our Trail Stories – Educating the World About the National Trails System," *Conference Program and Information* booklet. *

_____, Sept. 15, 2008, "News Release: Partnership for the National Trails System Receives National Honor for Outstanding Achievement in Greenways Preservation." *

_____, 2009, *12th Conference on National Scenic and Historic Trails: Gearing Up for the Decade for the National Trails: Outreach, Protection, and Capacity,* registration booklet. *

_____, 2013, *14th Conference on National Scenic and Historic Trails – National Trails: Weaving the Tapestry of America's Cultures, Histories and Landscapes,* [registration booklet], 18 pp. *

Pathways Across America, Spring, 2000; Fall, 2009; Winter 2009-10, Summer, 2010; Autumn, 2010; Winter 2010-2011; Spring 2012; Autumn, 2014; Winter 2014-15; Spring, 2015; Spring, 2016; Winter 2015-16; Summer, 2016; Winter 2016-17; Summer, 2016; and Summer, 2017. *

Pritchard, Paul, 1976, testimony in U.S. House of Representatives, *Oversight Hearings Before the Subcommittee on National Parks and Recreation . . . on the National Trails System Act of 1968,* etc., March 11-12, 1976, Wash., DC: GPO, Serial No. 94-50, p, 102. *

Proceedings, National Symposium on Trails, Washington, D.C., June 2-6, 1971. *

Proceedings: the Second National Symposium on Trails, Colorado Springs, CO, June 14-17, 1973, 181+ pp. *

Proudman, Bob, 1984, "The AT: 30 Years of Making NTSA Effective" in *Pathways Across America,* Spring 1998, Vol. 11., No. 2, p. 8. *

_____, Oct. 20, 1997, letter to Lyle Laverty, Director of Recreation, Forest Service. *

Public Law 94-527, 1976, An Act to amend the National Trails System, etc. *

Public Law 104-333, 1996, Sec. 814 (D) (e). *

"Rail-Trail Case Studies" in *Pathways Across America,* Fall, 1990, p. 5. *

Ridenour, James M., in Jan., 1991, in *Report on America's National Scenic, National Historic, and National Recreation Trails – 1989-1990,* p. 18, Wash., DC: NPS. *

Rockefeller, Laurence S., Chairman, 1962, *Outdoor Recreation for America: A report to the President and Congress by the Outdoor Recreation Resources Review Commission, Washington, DC.*

Salt, Deb, "BLM's New National Landscape Conservation System" in *Pathways Across America*, Fall, 2000, Vol. 13, No. 4, pp. 6-7. *

Scherer, Glenn, 2002, *America's National Trails: Journeys Across Land and Time*, Guilford, CT: Falcon Press, pp. 62-65.

Scott, Doug, 1991, *Keynote Address, Second National Conference on National Scenic and National Historic Trails*, Nov. 14, 1991.

_____, 2001, "A Wilderness Forever" in *Campaign for America's Wilderness*.

Sebelius, Keith, 1980, *Congressional Record*, Sept. 22, 1980, p. 26465.

Siehl, George, Jan., 1989, *Trails Programs in Federal Agencies: A Data Compilation*, Wash., DC: Congressional Research Service of the Library of Congress, 81 pp. *

Simmons, Marc, 2006, "SFTA – The Early Years" and Jackson, Hal, 2006, "SFTA – The Mature Years" essays on SFTA website under "History."

Skubitz, Joe, March 6, 1967, in GPO, *Hearing Before the Subcommittee on National Parks and Recreation . . . on HR 4865 and Related Bills to Establish a Nationwide System of Trails*, March 6-7, 1967, Serial No. 09-4, p. 43.

Slater, Rodney, Secretary of the U.S, Dept. of Transportation, as quoted in Kathleen Cordes and Jane Lammers, 2002, *America's Millennium Trails: Pathways for the 21st Century*, American Association for Leisure and Recreation, p. 1.

Smith, Spencer M., 1967, for the Citizens Committee on Natural Resources, GPO, *Hearings Before the [Senate] Committee on Interior and Insular Affairs . . . on S. 827, A Bill to Establish a Nationwide System of Trails and for Other Purposes*, March 15 and 16, 1967, p. 151. *

Stanton, Robert, NPS Director, Sept. 14, 1999, letter to Participants [at the] Sixth National Conference on National Scenic and Historic Trails, Zephyr Point, Nevada. *

Stevens, Lawrence N., April 2, 1965, in memo to Directors of NPS and BLM. *

Spitzer, William T., Jan. 14, 1988, letter to Peggy
Robinson, American Trails Network. *

Threlkeld, Kay, and Adam Sobek, Nov., 2005, *Historic Resource
Database for the National Historic Trails: GPS Level Data
Instructions, Features and Attributes*, 80 pp., *
"Trail Notes" in *Pathway Across America*, Spring,
1998, Vol. 11, No. 2, p. 11.
Tynon, Joanne F., Deborah J. Chavez, and James A.
Harding, 1997, *National Recreation Trails: A
Comprehensive Nationwide Survey*, July, 1997. *

"Udall to Press 4 Outdoor Trails," Nov. 18, 1966, *New York Times*,
p. 27, (Courtesy ProQuest Historic Newspapers). *
Udall, Stewart L., 1967, in GPO, *Hearing Before the Subcommittee
on National Parks and Recreation . . . on HR 4865 and
Related Bills to Establish a Nationwide System of Trails*,
March 6-7, 1967, Serial No. 09-4, p. 23. *
_____ April 13, 1967, *Supplemental Statement by Secretary of the
Interior Stewart L. Udall on Condemnation in Reference to S.
827 and S. 1092, Bills to Establish a Nationwide System of
Trails and a Nationwide System of Scenic Rivers, Before the
Senate Interior and Insular Affairs Committee, 4-13-67*. *
_____ letter to Alabama Governor Albert P. Brewer, Nov. 15, 1968. *
_____, Dec. 31, 2007, "Where Trails Lead: Our
Heritage," in *Albuquerque Journal*.
USDA and U.S. DOI, 1969, Agreement for the development and
operation of the National Trails System, Federal Interagency
Council on Trails, 1969-2000 file, and Federal Regional
Working Groups on Trails Criteria, March 1974. *
U.S. Dept. of the Interior press release, April 2, 1962, "Udall Establishes
Bureau of Outdoor Recreation in Interior Department." *
U.S. Dept. of the Interior, March 31, 1966, cover letter,
draft legislation, and press release. *
_____, Bureau of Outdoor Recreation, Dec. 1966, *Trails for America*. *

_____ and others, 1977, *Expanding America's Trail System, An Investment in Energy-wise Recreation, Fourth National Trails Symposium, Sept. 7-10, Lake Junaluska, NC*, pp. 83-111.

_____, NPS, 1986, *National Trails Assessment*, 155 pp., quote on p. 23. *

_____, BOR, undated, *Establishing Trails on Right-of-Way: Principally Railroad Abandonments*, 54 pp., Wash., DC: GPO. *

U.S. House of Representatives, Sept. 12, 1968, 90th Congress, 2nd Session, *Conference Report: Nationwide System of Trails*, Report 1891.) *

_____, 1976, *Oversight Hearings Before the Subcommittee on National Parks and Recreation . . . on the National Trails System Act of 1968*, etc., March 11-12, 1976, Wash., DC: GPO, Serial No. 94-50, pp. 1 and 4-9. *

_____, Committee Report, 1980, *National Trails System Act Amendments of 1980* [to accompany H.R. 8087]. *

_____, Sept. 10, 1980, Report 96-1314, *Establishing the Ice Age National Scenic Trail and for Other Purposes*. *

_____, June 10, 1987, H.R. 2641, *To amend the National Trails System act to provide for State and local governments for the improved management of certain Federal lands and for other purposes*. *

_____, July 2, 2000, 106th Congress, 2nd Session, H.R. 5014, "To amend the National Trails System Act to update the feasibility and suitability studies of four national historic trails and provide for possible additions to such trails." *

U.S. Senate, bill S. 3316, April 5, 1975, *A Bill to establish National Historic Trails as a new category of trails within the National Trails System*. *

_____, 1978, Publication 95-126, *Hearing Before the Subcommittee for Parks and Recreation . . .* , May 1, 1978. *

_____ Committee of Energy and Natural Resources, Aug. 4, 1982, *Hearing on Amendments to the National Trails System Act*, etc. *

_____, January 31, 1983, *National Trails System Act Amendments*, 98th Congress, 1st Session, Report 98-1. *

U. S. Supreme Court, 1990, *Presault et ux. v. Interstate Commerce Commission et al.*, decided Feb. 21, 1990. *

U. S. Surface Transportation Board, July 8, 2009, Hearings on 25 Years of Rail Banking, Ex Parte No. 690, accessed through STB website.

Walters, William C., Jan. 18, 1990, memo to NPS Directorate, etc.,
    Meeting Report: Long-Distance Trails Policy Meeting, Nov. 8-9, 1989. *
"Washington Scene" in *Parks & Recreation*, April, 1975, p. 16. *
Watson, Bill and Jeanne, 1998, "The New CMP Most Complex Ever" in
    Pathways Across America, Spring, 1998, Vol. 11, No. 2, pp. 3-4. *
Watt, James G., 1973, memo to Legislative Counsel, Office
    of the [Interior] Secretary, Dec. 4, 1973. *
_____, 1981, in *Sixth National Trails Symposium,* June
    28-July 1, 1981, Davis, CA, workbook. *
Websites for:
        2017 National Trails System MOU
        Amigos de Anza
        Bureau of Land Management, "National Scenic
            and Historic Trails Strategy and Work Plan"
        Cherokee Heritage Center
        El Camino Real International Heritage Center
        Florida Trail Association
        Historical website: https://clinton2.nara.gov/
            Initiatives/Millennium/trails.html.
        Ice Age Trail Alliance
        Interagency Visitor Use Management Council
        Izaak Walton League of America
        Lewis and Clark Trail Heritage Foundation, "Our History"
        NPS website "Captain John Smith National Historic Trail"
        NPS website "El Camino Real de los
            Tejas National Historic Trail"
        NPS website, "El Camino Real de Tierra
            Adentro National Historic Trail"
        NPS website "Land and Water Conservation Fund"
        NPS website "Lewis and Clark National Historic Trail"
        NPS website "National Trails System,"
            search for "2017-2027 MOU"
        NPS website "North Country National Scenic Trail"
        NPS website "Oregon National Historic Trail"
        NPS website "Selma to Montgomery National Historic Trail"
        NPS Publications, "2006 National Trails System MOU"

       National Pony Express Association

       National Trails Training Partnership

       National Water Trails System

       Oregon-California Trails Association, "Our Beginnings"

       Pacific Crest Trail Association, "History" tab

       PNTS, "Decade for the National Trails Goals and Objectives."

       Rails-to-Trails Conservancy, "railbanking" tab

       Santa Fe Trail Association

       Trail of Tears Association

       Trail of Tears National Historic Trail

Welch, David, "The Importance of Setting," in *Pathways Across America*, Winter 2009-10. *

Werner, Gary, 1996, "Which Way for the National Trails System? A Call to Action," in *Pathways Across America*, Winter, 1996, pp. 1 and 6. *

_____, July 26, 2005, Statement . . . on Implementation of the National Trails System Act, 17 pp. *

_____, 2011-2, "Our Heritage and Challenge of Nature Cultural Landscape Stewardship" in *Pathways Across America*, Spring 2011, p. 14, also *Pathways* Winter 2011-12, p. 5. *

_____, editorial in *Pathways Across America*, Summer, 2012, p. 3, also CLP report on p. 8.

_____, 2013, "Three Big Ideas Emerge in 2012 and Spawn Transforming Actions,"

_____, 2013, "The National Trails System – A Culture of Citizen Stewardship," in *Pathways Across America*, Autumn/Winter, 2013-2014, p. 13.

_____, 2014, "The National Trails System – A Culture of Citizen Stewardship," in *Pathways Across America*, Autumn/Winter 2013-2014, p. 13. *

_____, 2016-7, "25 Years of the National Trails Community Working Together," Parts 1, 2, and 3 in *Pathways Across America*, Autumn-Winter, 2016, pp. 3-5, Spring, 2017, pp. 5-6, and Summer, 2017, pp. 3-4, also *Pathways Across America*, Spring, 2017, p. 6. *

Wikipedia entries for "Arizona Trail," "Benton MacKay," "Earth Day" "Environmental Protection Act of 1970." "Gaylord

Nelson and Earth Day," "Historic Preservation Act of
1966," "Howard R. Driggs," "Madonna of the Trail,"
"Ezra Meeker," "National Heritage Area," "National Scenic
Byways," "National Wild and Scenic Rivers System," "New
England National Scenic Trail," "Reuben Gold Thwaites,"
"Stewart Udall," "Olin D. Wheeler," "Werowocomoco,"
"Wild and Scenic Rivers," and "Wilderness Act of 1964."
Winters, Richard L., memo to Director, BOR, March 12, 1975. *
Wolph, William R., to BOR Director Ed Crafts, Aug. 2, 1968,
Memorandum on Delegation of Authority to BOR on Trails. *
"World Watches Story of a Border-to-Border Trail" in
Pathways Across America, Summer, 1993, p. 9. *
Zaslowsky and Dyan, 1986, *These American Lands: Parks, Wilderness,
and the Public Lands*, New York: H. Holt, p. 313

STEVE ELKINTON grew up in the Philadelphia suburbs and graduated from Kalamazoo College in 1969. After a few years wandering the U.S. (where he had a formative experience along the Pacific Crest Trail) and Europe, he settled down to study landscape architecture, obtaining a degree from the University of Pennsylvania in 1976. In 1978 he joined the National Park Service carrying out planning and design projects in the greater Washington, D.C. area

and the Cuyahoga Valley National Recreation area (now National Park) in Ohio. Starting in 1989 until he retired 25 years later, Steve served as program leader for National Trails System activities within NPS preparing legislative testimony, developing policy, coordinating with field staff, refining budgets and grants, and strengthening interagency cooperation. Steve now serves on the board of the Partnership for the National Trails System and played a leadership role in the Trails System's 50th anniversary in 2018.

INDEX